vegetarian lunches
for two

Also by Julia Barnard

Cooking

Vegetarian Tapas: 150 quick and delicious snacks and bites for sharing

Vegan Tapas: 150 quick and delicious snacks and bites for sharing

Wellbeing

Promoting Happiness: a workbook to help you appreciate and get the most out of your life

Make the Change: over 250 tips for your wellbeing and happiness

50 Ways to Increase Your Happiness

How to be Happy: a collection of 60 happiness writings

Online Counselling: a guide for therapists

vegetarian lunches

for two

all your lunch box and weekend meals planned for a year

Julia Barnard

MTC
BOOKS

MTC Books
PO Box 356
McLaren Vale
SA 5171
Australia
books@makethechange.com.au

National Library of Australia Cataloguing-in-Publication entry:
Creator: Barnard, Julia, author.
Title: Vegetarian lunches for two : all your lunch box and weekend
                meals planned for a year / Julia Barnard.
ISBN: 9780980759082 (paperback)
Notes: Includes index.
Subjects: Vegetarian cooking.
                Cooking for two.
                Lunchbox cooking.
Dewey Number: 641.5636

ISBN 978-0-9807590-8-2

Cover design by Pandelaide

http://veggielunches.com

Contents

Introduction 1

Spring lunches 5

Summer lunches 59

Autumn lunches 113

Winter lunches 167

Recipes 221

Index 233

Introduction

Vegetarian Lunches for Two was conceived to meet the desire for a more exciting lunch. My lunches have always disappointed me - especially during the working week. Even though I work from home, I would get to lunchtime and the last thing I wanted to think about was what to have for lunch. Inevitably it would be a sandwich of some sort and probably the not-so-exciting combination of cheese and tomato. What I needed was a go-to guide that would inspire me every week with easy to prepare, varied lunches, made in advance. So I decided to write my own.

I have created 52 menus – one for every week of the year. The book is broken down into the four seasons, each 13 weeks long. As such, I try to use seasonal produce, so you will have different things to look forward to at different times of the year. For you astute people, you will notice that there are just 364 lunches, yet a year is 365 days (not forgetting leap year). On the missing day, I give you permission to have take away!

Feel free to follow the book as the year goes on or dip in and select a week of your choosing. Ideally you would follow a week at a time as many lunches are made using ingredients from earlier in the week. Don't be afraid to choose your own preferred fruits, nuts, grains, beans, breads and vegetables. When choosing nuts, look for the raw unsalted variety.

You will notice I have included some recipes at the back of the book. These are optional but make delicious alternatives to shop-bought. They include mainly baked goodies including scones, muffins and damper. If you have the time, do make them. Do remember to add the ingredients to your shopping list. Most recipes can be frozen, which will save you time later on.

Some principles behind Vegetarian Lunches for Two

Preparation in advance
All lunches are prepared the day before, apart from weekend lunches. This way you can get up in the morning and not worry about having to make your lunch. In the 'daily tasks' section you will see that the week begins on a Sunday, with you preparing your lunch for the next day. Simply follow the instructions for that day. Prepared lunches should go into the fridge until you need them.

The shopping list
The shopping list specifies what you need for the whole week. Some weeks it may seem a long list. However, you will find your pantry soon builds up as you gather certain ingredients. Where quantities are important I have specified in the shopping list. Else all you need to do is check you have the ingredient in your pantry. Sometimes I may refer to 'handfuls'– generally for the dried fruit and nuts. You can eyeball your stores to check you have enough of that ingredient. You don't need to overthink what a handful means. I figure the bigger the hand, the bigger the appetite, the bigger the handful! The same principle applies to dollops and sprinkles!

Suitable for lunch boxes
All weekday lunches are lunch box friendly. I suggest you buy a number of containers – medium-sized ones to fit things like salads and smaller ones to store dried fruit, nuts and dips. All lunches can be eaten straight out of your lunch box. There is no need to heat anything up – unless you want to. Pop the container into the microwave for a minute or so, making sure your container is microwave-safe. Remember to have knives, forks and spoons handy. It may be worth buying a cheap set for work so if anything gets lost you still have a full set of cutlery. There are also a few smoothie and soup recipes. I suggest you use 500ml thermos flasks to keep the contents cool or warm.

They will save you

Not only will you save money preparing your own lunch each day, but you will also save time. No more wandering the streets in search for a sandwich at lunchtime. Just grab your lunch box, sit back and relax. You don't have to spend any time thinking about what to have for lunch, as I've done that for you. Even better, you know exactly what's in it as you made it yourself.

They will fill you up

It's important to me that I have a lunch that fills me up. I need a lunch that will take me through the afternoon and give me enough energy for a workout. As such, I try to follow the principles of a low GI diet, but really it is about knowing what will fill me up and what will leave me with an energy dip. My lunches are balanced and full of variety and nutrition.

Maximising ingredients

In a given week, I try not to let any ingredients go to waste. Frequently you will see I use half a can of something or half the amount of a vegetable and use the rest later on during the week. Sometimes different combinations of ingredients are prepared one day and are then turned into two different lunches.

Putting the freezer to good use

In recent years I've been using the freezer more and more. I love being able to get something out of the freezer when I'm too tired to cook. I've also come to realise how many things freeze well. As such, I have made use of the freezer here. You can freeze bread, rolls, tortillas, pitas as well as the slices, muffins and other goodies we will be cooking up. Get hold of freezer bags as well as containers that are suitable for freezing.

Relaxed weekend lunches

For the weekend, I tend to go for a more relaxed lunch option. Since these lunches are not prepared a day in advance, some of the lunches are also served warm. You will find some indulgent lunches here, but still plenty of variety. Think toasted sandwiches, hot dogs, baked Brie, delicious baguettes, bagels and much more.

You will notice I include a fruit option for weekdays, but generally not the weekend. You can include fruit if you like and add it to your shopping list, but often I find there is fruit still available to nibble on.

Serves two

Vegetarian Lunches has been designed for two people. However the menus can be easily halved if you are cooking just for yourself or doubled if you are cooking for more people. If it is just yourself, it means you will probably make even more use of the freezer.

Vegan lunches

A number of the lunches are vegan. These ones I have marked with a V. However, many lunches can be easily made vegan using substitutions. You can substitute cheese, butter and milk with vegan varieties and honey with agave syrup (although you may not need to use as much). Winter Week 7 is entirely vegan and includes a vegan quiche.

Ingredients

I hope you will be familiar with the ingredients listed. However, there are some whose names vary around the world and I have listed them here.

Canola oil = rapeseed oil
Capsicum = bell pepper
Coriander = cilantro
Plain flour = all-purpose flour
Polenta = cornmeal
Rocket = arugula
Savoury yeast flakes = nutritional yeast flakes
Self-raising flour = self-rising flour
Snow peas = mangetout
Spring onions = green onions, salad onions, scallions, the long skinny one
Zucchini = courgette

Canned goods

Lots of cans of beans, fruit and vegetables are used. In many cases, I only use half of the can and use the remaining contents later in the week. Make sure you remove the contents from the can and place in a container before refrigerating.

Cheese and Eggs

Not all cheeses are suitable for vegetarians. Make sure the cheese you use does not contain animal rennet. This is a particular problem when using Parmesan. Genuine Parmigiano-Reggiano uses animal rennet. In Australia you will find cheese labelled 'Parmesan cheese' that is vegetarian friendly, but this is not the case in other parts of the world. In the UK, look out for vegetarian hard cheese. Since Parmesan-style cheese is used mainly as a flavour boost you can always substitute it with savoury yeast flakes.

Large free range eggs are used throughout. Make sure to seek out genuine free range eggs. Not all eggs labelled 'free range' are genuine free range.

Milk and Butter

Do use your preferred type of milk. Also, feel free to use margarine or your favourite spread. Just make sure it is suitable for the purpose it is used in the instructions.

Pastry

The pastry sheets used in the recipes are roughly 24cm (9½in) squares. To thaw the pastry, remove the amount of sheets you need from the freezer and stand for 10 minutes.

Tofu

Some recipes require you to drain the tofu beforehand. To do this, remove the tofu from the pack and wrap in several sheets of paper towel. Place between two heavy chopping boards. You can add additional weight on top if you like. Let it drain for 30 minutes. Discard the paper towel and use as per the recipe.

Read your labels!

Keep an eye out for animal fat and gelatine in your ingredients. In particular, cream, cream cheese, sour cream and yogurt. You can use light versions, so long as they are suitable.

Measures used

Recipes use cups, grams and millilitres. The following conventions were used:

1 cup = 250ml

1 tablespoon = 15ml

1 teaspoon = 5ml

Conversions

Grams to ounces	Millilitres to fluid ounces	Centimetres to inches
25g = 1 oz	60ml = 2 fl oz	1.5cm = ½in
50g = 1¾ oz	80ml = 2½ fl oz	2cm = ¾in
75g = 2¾ oz	100ml = 3½ fl oz	2.5cm = 1in
100g = 3½ oz	125ml = 4 fl oz	4cm = 1½in
125g = 4 oz	160ml = 5 fl oz	5cm = 2in
150g = 5 oz	180ml = 6 fl oz	6cm = 2½in
200g = 7 oz	200ml = 7 fl oz	8cm = 3in
250g = 8 oz	250ml = 8 fl oz	10cm = 4in
500g = 16 oz	500ml = 16 fl oz	20cm = 8in
1kg = 32 oz	1 litre = 32 fl oz	30cm = 12in

Oven temperatures for fan ovens

If you have a fan oven you can reduce temperatures by 10-20°C/20-50°F. Consult your oven manual for precise instructions.

I hope you find plenty to inspire you and that your lunch boxes are transformed. Happy eating!

Best wishes

Julia

almonds apple asparagus
avocado baguette banana basil bean
blue cheese broccoli capsicum
cheese
carrot chargrilled capsicum
cherry tomatoes chickpeas corn couscous
cranberry cream cheese crispbread dates dip

spring

lentil mango mushroom nutmeg olives
onion orange papaya pasta
peach slices pears pecans pineapple pita popcorn
potato roasted vegetables rocket roll
salad sandwich slice spinach
sultanas sun-dried tomatoes tofu

Spring Week 1

This week begins by making up a batch of roasted vegetables on Sunday. The vegetables will then be used to create four different lunches. Later in the week you will make a simple homemade hummus to be enjoyed with crispbread and a tasty baguette.

Monday
Roasted Vegetable Pasta Salad / Cumquats or Orange

Tuesday
Roasted Vegetable Turnovers / Banana

Wednesday
Roasted Vegetable and Bean Wrap / Peach Slices

Thursday
Roasted Vegetable Frittata / Peach Slices

Friday
Crispbread with Hummus V / Olives, Sun-Dried Tomatoes and Chargrilled Capsicum / Popcorn with Cashews and Dried Apricots

Saturday
Baguette with Hummus, Chargrilled Capsicum, Bocconcini and Tomato / Peach Mess

Sunday
Bruschetta with Basil, Tomato and Bocconcini

Don't be afraid to use canned fruit. Just make sure it is in fruit juice rather than syrup. Canned fruit contributes to your daily fruit allowance, as does dried fruit.

shopping list

Fruit and Vegetables
- ☐ 1 onion
- ☐ 1 red capsicum
- ☐ 1 fennel bulb
- ☐ 1 sweet potato
- ☐ 150g mushrooms
- ☐ 1 bunch basil
- ☐ 6 cumquats or 2 oranges
- ☐ 2 bananas
- ☐ 2 cloves garlic
- ☐ 2 tomatoes
- ☐ 1 lettuce

Fridge
- ☐ 180g halloumi cheese
- ☐ 4 eggs
- ☐ 220g bocconcini cheese
- ☐ 100ml light cream

Freezer
- ☐ 1 sheet puff pastry

Bakery
- ☐ 1 baguette

Pantry
- ☐ 100g dried pasta
- ☐ pine nuts
- ☐ 400g can butter beans
- ☐ 2 wholegrain flour tortillas
- ☐ Tabasco sauce
- ☐ large can peach slices
- ☐ 400g can chickpeas
- ☐ unhulled tahini
- ☐ lemon juice
- ☐ smoked paprika
- ☐ 6-8 crispbread
- ☐ black olives
- ☐ sun-dried tomatoes
- ☐ chargrilled capsicum
- ☐ popcorn kernels
- ☐ cashews
- ☐ dried apricots
- ☐ 2 meringues

Staples
- ☐ salt
- ☐ black pepper
- ☐ extra virgin olive oil
- ☐ canola oil

daily tasks

Sunday

Prepare the roasted vegetables. Chop the onion, capsicum, fennel and sweet potato into bite-size pieces. Add to a roasting tray and drizzle with canola oil. Roast for 30 minutes on 210°C/410°F/Gas Mark 7. Add the mushrooms (halved or quartered) and the halloumi (cut into bite-size pieces). Roast for another 20 minutes. Remove then leave to cool. Spoon a quarter of the vegetables into a bowl and put the rest into a container. Put the container in the fridge.

Make up 100g of pasta according to the instructions on the packet. To prevent it sticking, stir the pasta whilst the water comes back to the boil. Drain, then rinse the pasta in cold water. Add it to the bowl of roasted vegetables. Stir in a handful of chopped basil and a handful of toasted pine nuts. You can toast the pine nuts by putting them in a frying pan and toss over a low heat for a few minutes until they start to brown. Divide the pasta salad between 2 lunch boxes. Refrigerate until tomorrow.

Monday

Make the roasted vegetable turnovers. Thaw a sheet of puff pastry then cut it into 4 squares. Add a can of rinsed and drained butter beans to the roasted vegetables. Add a spoonful of the beans and vegetables onto each pastry square. Put the rest of the veg and bean mix back into the fridge. Fold the pastry in half to form a triangle, then press the edges with a fork to seal. Place on a baking tray and bake in a 220°C/425°F/Gas Mark 7 oven for 20 minutes until golden.

Leave to cool than place in your lunch boxes. Refrigerate until tomorrow.

Tuesday

Make the roasted vegetable and bean wraps. Take 2 wholegrain flour tortillas then spoon some of the roasted vegetable filling on each. Sprinkle with a small amount of Tabasco sauce if desired. Fold in the sides, then roll up. Cut in half then cover in plastic wrap. Refrigerate until tomorrow. The rest of the tortillas can be frozen.

Spoon some of the peach slices into 2 containers for tomorrow. Transfer the rest of the slices to a container. Store in the fridge.

Wednesday

Make a roasted vegetable frittata. Beat together 4 eggs and season. Heat a 24cm frying pan over a medium heat. Add the remaining roasted vegetable mix and stir to warm up slightly. Add the eggs, then turn the heat down. Let cook for 8-10 minutes.

Preheat the grill. Once the eggs are nearly set, place the pan under the grill to finish cooking the top. Slide the frittata off the pan then leave to cool. Slice into quarters and place 2 quarters into each lunch box. Refrigerate until tomorrow.

Divide some peach slices between 2 containers. You will have any remaining peaches at the weekend.

Thursday

Make the hummus to go with the crispbread. In a small food processor, blitz together a can of rinsed and drained chickpeas with 1 clove of crushed garlic and 2 tablespoons each of tahini, lemon juice, extra virgin olive oil and water. Add ¼ teaspoon of smoked paprika and season to taste. Divide between 3 containers (you will use one of the containers on Saturday) and refrigerate until needed.

Put 3-4 crispbread (depending on appetite) per person in a lunch box or cover in plastic wrap. Mix together 2 spoonfuls each of olives, sun-dried tomatoes and chargrilled capsicum. Divide between 2 containers. Refrigerate.

Pop a small handful of popcorn. Mix it with 2 handfuls each of cashews and dried apricots. Divide between 2 containers.

Saturday

Prepare the baguettes. Use half the baguette to make 2 sandwiches. You will use the remaining baguette tomorrow for the bruschetta. Fill the sandwiches with the remaining hummus, some chargrilled capsicum slices, 1 sliced tomato, some sliced bocconcini cheese and lettuce. Season to taste.

Make the peach mess by dicing the peaches and dividing between 2 bowls. Break up a meringue into each bowl, then stir in a spoonful of light cream.

Sunday

To make the bruschetta, slice the baguette on an angle about 2.5cm thick. Toast the bread then rub a clove of garlic over it and brush with some extra virgin olive oil.

Top each with slices of tomato and bocconcini and some basil leaves. Drizzle with some more olive oil. Season with salt and some freshly ground black pepper.

Spring Week 2

We make good use of baby spinach this week. Spinach is a great source of iron. However, to further aid absorption have some Vitamin C at the same time. A glass of fresh orange juice would do the trick. This week you also get to try homemade bagels which are fun to make and delicious.

Monday
Kidney Bean Salad with Spinach, Broccoli, Carrot and More / Apple

Tuesday
Broccoli and Capsicum Slice / Dates and Pecans

Wednesday
Bean Wrap with Avocado, Spinach and Tomato V / Banana

Thursday
Cheese, Tomato and Spinach Sandwich with Aioli / Cranberries, Sultanas and Almonds

Friday
Cinnamon and Sultana Fruit Loaf with Cream Cheese / Hard Boiled Egg / Apple

Saturday
Bagels with Cream Cheese

Sunday
Cheese and Onion Scones

Always use genuine free range eggs. This is not that easy as many brands claim their eggs to be free range but are far from it. Do your research.

shopping list

Fruit and Vegetables
- ☐ 1 head broccoli
- ☐ 1 bag baby spinach
- ☐ 1 carrot
- ☐ 1 clove garlic
- ☐ 4 apples
- ☐ 1 red capsicum
- ☐ 1 bunch spring onions
- ☐ 2 tomatoes
- ☐ 1 avocado
- ☐ 2 bananas

Fridge
- ☐ 100g Gruyère cheese
- ☐ 6 eggs
- ☐ 125ml milk
- ☐ aioli
- ☐ 250g cream cheese

Bakery
- ☐ 4 slices wholegrain bread
- ☐ fruit loaf (or recipe)
- ☐ 2 bagels (or recipe)
- ☐ 4 savoury scones (or recipe)

Pantry
- ☐ 400g can kidney beans
- ☐ 420g can corn kernels
- ☐ red wine vinegar
- ☐ dried oregano
- ☐ 75g wholemeal self-raising flour
- ☐ 75g self-raising flour
- ☐ dates
- ☐ pecans
- ☐ lime juice
- ☐ Tabasco sauce or chilli powder
- ☐ 2 wholegrain flour tortillas
- ☐ dried cranberries
- ☐ sultanas
- ☐ almonds

Staples
- ☐ salt
- ☐ black pepper
- ☐ extra virgin olive oil

daily tasks

Sunday

Prepare the kidney bean salad. Halve your head of broccoli. Reserve one half for tomorrow and cut the rest into small florets. Place in a bowl with ½ a 400g can of rinsed and drained kidney beans and ½ a 420g can of rinsed and drained corn kernels (save the rest of the beans and corn in separate containers for later in the week). Add a good handful of baby spinach, 1 grated carrot and ½ cup (50g) of grated Gruyère cheese. Mix together.

For the dressing, mix in a small jar or bowl 2 tablespoons of extra virgin olive oil, 1 tablespoon of red wine vinegar, 1 teaspoon of dried oregano, 1 clove of crushed garlic and some seasoning. Pour the dressing over the salad. Divide between 2 lunch boxes and refrigerate until tomorrow.

Don't forget your apple.

Optional: You could make your fruit loaf today, slice, then freeze it until needed.

Monday

Make the broccoli and capsicum slice. Preheat the oven to 180°C/350°F/Gas Mark 4. Grease and line a 30 x 20cm baking tin. In a large bowl, whisk together 4 eggs and ½ cup (125ml) of milk. Beat in ½ cup (75g) of wholemeal self-raising flour and ½ cup (75g) of regular self-raising flour to make a batter.

Finely chop the broccoli, 1 red capsicum and ½ a bunch of spring onions. Add to the batter along with the remaining can of corn kernels. Season. Pour the mixture into the baking tin and bake for 30 minutes until golden brown and firm.

Leave to cool and remove from the tin. Slice into quarters, then halve each quarter. Place 2 slices into each lunch box then refrigerate. The rest can be frozen by wrapping each slice in plastic wrap then placing into a container or freezer bag, then popping them into the freezer.

Mix 2 handfuls of dates with 2 handfuls of pecans. Divide between 2 containers.

Tuesday

Prepare the bean wraps. Mash the remaining kidney beans in a bowl. Add a chopped tomato, a handful of spinach (keep some for tomorrow's sandwich) and a diced avocado. Stir in 1 tablespoon of lime juice and a couple of shakes of Tabasco sauce or some chilli powder. Divide the mixture between 2 flour tortillas, roll up and cut in half. Cover in plastic wrap then pop them into the fridge.

Don't forget your banana.

Wednesday

Make 2 sandwiches using 4 slices of wholegrain bread. On each sandwich add tomato slices, the remaining baby spinach, some sliced Gruyère cheese and some aioli. Season, cut in half, cover in plastic wrap then refrigerate.

Combine 2 handfuls of dried cranberries with 2 handfuls each of sultanas and almonds and divide between 2 containers.

Thursday

If you are making your own fruit loaf, follow the recipe on p.226. Slice thickly. Allow 2 slices per person for tomorrow's lunch. You can freeze the rest by slicing first then popping into freezer bags or containers. If you made the loaf earlier in the week, remove 2 slices per person, allow to thaw, than cover in plastic wrap.

If you have bought a loaf from the store, thickly slice the loaf – allow 2 slices per person for lunch. The rest you can freeze for a later date.

Divide 3-4 tablespoons of cream cheese between 2 containers. Don't forget a knife for spreading the cream cheese on your fruit loaf.

Hard boil 2 eggs. Place the eggs in a saucepan of cold water. Turn the heat to high and set the timer for 20 minutes. Rinse under cold water then allow to cool. Pop them into containers and refrigerate.

Don't forget your apple.

Saturday

Serve bagels with cream cheese. If you are making your own, you will find the recipe on p.222. You can freeze any remaining bagels or leftover dough, if desired.

Sunday

Prepare cheese and onion scones. If you are making your own scones, the recipe is on p.225. Any scones you do not eat can be frozen.

You can serve your scones with butter, margarine or some cream cheese mixed with chives.

Spring Week 3

It's a bit of a varied week this week. Lots of fresh vegetables in both the tofu salad and the lentil and rice salad, then we have a tasty quesadilla. Enjoy your favourite vegetarian sausages this week in a pita with fried onions and in a salad with a tasty cheese and herb damper.

Monday
Tofu Salad with a Sweet and Sour Dressing V / Banana

Tuesday
Lentil and Rice Salad with Broccoli, Carrot and Pine Nuts V / Pineapple with Nutmeg

Wednesday
Mushroom and Onion Quesadilla / Almonds and Dried Apricots

Thursday
Sausage and Onion Pita V / Banana

Friday
Lentil Spread with Crispbread / Banderillas / Apple

Saturday
Cheese and Herb Damper / Sausage, Apple and Tomato Salad

Sunday
Baked Mushroom and Tomato Slice

It is important to cool rice as quickly as possible if you are not eating it straightaway. The easiest way to do this is to rinse it under cold water once it is cooked.

shopping list

Fruit and Vegetables
- [ ] 2 carrots
- [ ] 1 head broccoli
- [ ] 50g bean sprouts
- [ ] 3 cloves garlic
- [ ] ginger
- [ ] 4 bananas
- [ ] 3 onions
- [ ] 275g mushrooms
- [ ] 3 tomatoes
- [ ] 3 apples
- [ ] 1 lettuce
- [ ] 125g cherry tomatoes

Fridge
- [ ] 200g marinated tofu
- [ ] 100g Cheddar cheese
- [ ] 6 vegetarian sausages
- [ ] 250g cream cheese
- [ ] 4 eggs
- [ ] 125ml milk

Bakery
- [ ] 2 pita breads
- [ ] 1 damper (or recipe)

Pantry
- [ ] 440g can pineapple chunks in juice
- [ ] soy sauce
- [ ] tomato paste
- [ ] 100g brown rice
- [ ] 400g can lentils
- [ ] pine nuts
- [ ] dried mint flakes
- [ ] balsamic vinegar
- [ ] whole nutmeg
- [ ] brown sugar
- [ ] chilli powder
- [ ] 4 wholegrain flour tortillas
- [ ] almonds
- [ ] dried apricots
- [ ] American mustard
- [ ] red wine vinegar
- [ ] sun-dried tomatoes
- [ ] dried oregano
- [ ] 6-8 crispbread
- [ ] gherkins
- [ ] green olives
- [ ] cocktail onions
- [ ] apple cider vinegar
- [ ] Dijon mustard
- [ ] honey
- [ ] 75g self-raising flour
- [ ] 75g wholemeal self-raising flour

Staples
- [ ] salt
- [ ] black pepper
- [ ] olive oil
- [ ] extra virgin olive oil
- [ ] olive oil spray

daily tasks

Sunday

Prepare the tofu salad. Cut the tofu into bite-size pieces and place in a bowl. To the bowl, add a diced carrot, ½ a head of broccoli, chopped (you will use the rest tomorrow), the bean sprouts and ½ a can of pineapple chunks (keep the juice for the dressing). Put the rest of the chunks in a container in the fridge.

Make the dressing by mixing together 3 tablespoons of the reserved pineapple juice, 1 tablespoon of soy sauce, 1 tablespoon of olive oil, ½ tablespoon of tomato paste, a clove of crushed garlic, and 1 teaspoon of grated ginger. You can pop the remaining ginger in the freezer for later use. Pour the dressing over the salad than divide the salad between 2 lunch boxes. Refrigerate until tomorrow.

Monday

Make the lentil and rice salad. Cook ½ cup (100g) of brown rice, according to packet instructions. Tip the rice into a sieve and rinse in cold water, to cool. Place the rice into a bowl. Add ½ a can of rinsed and drained lentils (keep the rest in a container in the fridge for later in the week), a handful of toasted pine nuts, the remaining broccoli (chopped), 1 grated carrot and 1 teaspoon of dried mint flakes (or 1 tablespoon of chopped fresh mint leaves is you have them).

Mix together 2 tablespoons of extra virgin olive oil, ½ tablespoon of balsamic vinegar and some seasoning. Pour the dressing over the salad, divide the salad between 2 containers then store in the fridge.

Grate some nutmeg over the remaining pineapple chunks and finish with a sprinkle of brown sugar. Divide between 2 containers then pop them into the fridge.

Tuesday

Make the quesadillas. Heat 1 tablespoon of olive oil in a frying pan over a medium heat. Add 1 sliced onion and fry for 5 minutes. Add 100g of sliced mushrooms and fry for a further 4 minutes until the mushrooms are soft. Add some chilli powder, to

taste. Remove from the heat. Dice a tomato and stir it into the mushroom and onion mixture. Season.

Divide the mixture between 2 flour tortillas, spreading it evenly over each. Sprinkle ½ cup (50g) of grated Cheddar cheese over the mushroom mixture. Top each with another tortilla, pressing down firmly. Cut each into quarters. Heat a frying pan or griddle pan and spray with olive oil. Add 4 triangles to the pan, heat for 1 minute, then turn and heat for another minute. Transfer to a plate and leave to cool before placing into 2 lunch boxes. Refrigerate until needed.

Mix 2 handfuls of almonds with 2 handfuls of dried apricots. Divide between 2 containers.

Wednesday

To make your sausage and onion pitas, heat 1 tablespoon of olive oil in a frying pan over a medium heat. Add a sliced onion and fry for a few minutes. Add 3 vegetarian sausages then continue cooking, turning the sausages regularly until they are heated through. Leave the sausages and onions to cool. Slice the sausages into bite-size pieces.

Split open 2 pita breads then divide the onion and sausages between them. Add a diced tomato and some American mustard. Cover in plastic wrap then pop them into the fridge for tomorrow.

Thursday

Blitz up a quick lentil spread. In a food processor, mix together ½ a can of lentils, ½ tablespoon of red wine vinegar, 3 sun-dried tomatoes, a crushed garlic clove, 1 tablespoon of cream cheese, and ½ teaspoon of dried oregano. Divide between 2 containers, then pop them into the fridge. Allow 3-4 crispbread per person, to serve with the spread.

Make banderillas by popping a piece of gherkin, a green olive and a cocktail onion on a cocktail stick. Make 3-4 per person. Add to your lunch boxes.

Saturday

Make your cheese and herb damper as per the recipe on p.223 (unless you have bought from the store). Serve with cream cheese, butter or margarine.

Make the accompanying salad by ripping up a good handful of lettuce and adding to a bowl with some cherry tomatoes, a chopped apple and 3 cooked and diced vegetarian sausages.

For the dressing, mix together 2 tablespoons extra virgin olive oil, 1 tablespoon apple cider vinegar, 1 teaspoon Dijon mustard, 1 teaspoon of honey and some seasoning. Pour the dressing over the salad.

Sunday

Make the baked mushroom and tomato slice. Preheat the oven to 180°C/350°F/Gas Mark 4. Grease and line a 30 x 20cm baking tin. Heat 1 tablespoon of olive oil in a frying pan over a medium heat. Add 1 sliced onion and fry for 4 minutes. Add 175g of sliced mushrooms and 1 clove of crushed garlic and fry for a further 5 minutes until the mushrooms are soft.

Meanwhile, chop 1 tomato and grate ½ cup (50g) of Cheddar cheese. In a large bowl, whisk together 4 eggs and ½ cup (125ml) of milk. Beat in ½ cup (75g) of self-raising flour and ½ cup (75g) of wholemeal self-raising flour to make a batter. Stir in the onions, mushrooms, tomato and cheese. Pour the mixture into the baking tin and bake for 30 minutes until golden and firm to the touch. Leave to cool. Remove from the tin and slice into 8 pieces.

Any leftovers can be frozen by popping the slices in freezer bags, containers or plastic wrap, then into the freezer.

Spring Week 4

This is one of those weeks where you do most of the prep on one day and it will last you two days – with just a slight modification. So the pasta salad becomes a frittata and the bean salad will become a couscous salad.

Monday
Pasta Salad with Goat's Cheese, Artichoke Hearts, Red Onion, Peas and Rocket / Grapefruit

Tuesday
Pasta Frittata / Apple

Wednesday
Cannellini Bean Salad with Capsicum, Olives, Tomatoes and Spring Onions V / Dates and Pecans

Thursday
Bean Salad with Couscous V / Fruit Salad

Friday
Spinach, Corn and Goat's Cheese Turnovers / Orange

Saturday
Baguette with Smoked Cheese and Sun-Dried Tomatoes

Sunday
English Muffin with Fried Egg, Vegetarian Bacon and Tomato Ketchup

You can make couscous with vegetable stock rather than water. You can also add your choice of dried herbs to it before adding the liquid, for additional flavour.

shopping list

Fruit and Vegetables
- [ ] 1 red onion
- [ ] 1 small bag rocket
- [ ] 1 grapefruit
- [ ] 2 apples
- [ ] 1 red capsicum
- [ ] 2 tomatoes
- [ ] 1 bunch spring onions
- [ ] 1 bunch parsley
- [ ] 1 small bag baby spinach
- [ ] 1 small bag mixed lettuce
- [ ] 2 oranges

Fridge
- [ ] 120g goat's cheese
- [ ] 6 eggs
- [ ] 30g Parmesan-style cheese
- [ ] 75g smoked cheese
- [ ] aioli
- [ ] 2 slices vegetarian bacon

Freezer
- [ ] ½ cup (60g) frozen peas
- [ ] 1 sheet puff pastry

Bakery
- [ ] 1 baguette
- [ ] 2 English muffins

Pantry
- [ ] 200g dried pasta
- [ ] 275g marinated artichoke hearts
- [ ] 400g can cannellini beans
- [ ] 80g green olives
- [ ] lemon juice
- [ ] pecans
- [ ] dates
- [ ] 100g couscous
- [ ] 400g can fruit salad in juice
- [ ] 125g can creamed corn
- [ ] whole nutmeg
- [ ] sun-dried tomatoes
- [ ] tomato ketchup

Staples
- [ ] salt
- [ ] black pepper
- [ ] olive oil
- [ ] extra virgin olive oil

daily tasks

Sunday

Prepare the pasta salad. Cook 200g of dried pasta according to package instructions. Two minutes before the cooking time is up, add ½ cup (60g) of frozen peas. Once cooked, drain then rinse under cold water. Place in a bowl.

Meanwhile, heat 1 tablespoon of olive oil in a frying pan. Add a sliced red onion and cook for 4-5 minutes until soft. Add the onions to the peas and pasta. Finally, stir in a good handful of rocket, 275g jar of drained and quartered artichoke hearts and 60g of crumbled goat's cheese. Season to taste. Put half in a container for another day and divide the rest between 2 lunch boxes for tomorrow's lunch. Pop everything in the fridge.

Halve your grapefruit, sprinkle with sugar if desired, than wrap each half in plastic wrap. Refrigerate until tomorrow.

Monday

Make a pasta frittata. Beat 4 eggs together and add some seasoning. Heat a medium frying pan over a medium heat. Add the pasta salad to the pan and heat through. Add the eggs, turn the heat down and cook for 8-10 minutes. Meanwhile, preheat the grill. Once the frittata is nearly set, add some grated Parmesan-style cheese and pop the pan under the grill to finish off the top. This will only take a couple of minutes. Remove the frittata from the pan and leave to cool. Slice into 4 then divide between your 2 lunch boxes. Refrigerate.

Tuesday

You will make a bean salad that will last 2 days. Rinse and drain a can of cannellini beans. Place in a bowl along with a chopped red capsicum, 2 chopped tomatoes (seeds removed, if you prefer), ½ cup (80g) of green olives, ½ a bunch of chopped spring onions and 1 tablespoon of chopped parsley. Stir in 1 tablespoon of extra virgin olive oil and ½ tablespoon of lemon juice. Season to taste. Divide half of the salad between your 2 lunch boxes and put the rest in another container. Pop everything into the fridge.

Mix 2 handfuls of pecans with 2 handfuls of dates. Divide between 2 containers.

Wednesday

To make the couscous to go with the remaining bean salad, place ½ cup (100g) of couscous in a bowl. Stir in ½ cup (125ml) of boiling water and leave to stand for 3 minutes. Fluff it up with a fork then stir in the remaining bean salad. Divide between your 2 lunch boxes and you're done! Pop them into the fridge.

Drain the can of fruit salad then divide between 2 containers. Keep in the fridge until tomorrow.

Thursday

Make spinach, corn and goat's cheese turnovers. Thaw a sheet of puff pastry. Whilst the pastry is thawing, put together the filling. Mix a 125g can of creamed corn with the remaining ½ bunch of spring onions, chopped. Add 60g of crumbled goat's cheese and ½ cup (25g) of baby spinach, coarsely chopped. Season with a grating of nutmeg and salt and pepper.

Cut the pastry into 4 squares and add a spoonful of filling to each square. Fold the pastry in half to form a triangle, then press the edges with a fork to seal. Place on a baking tray and bake in a 220°C/425°F/Gas Mark 7 oven for 20 minutes until golden. Leave to cool than place in your lunch boxes. Refrigerate until tomorrow.

Saturday

Make 2 sandwiches from your baguette. Add slices of smoked cheese, some sun-dried tomatoes and a handful of lettuce. Finish with a dollop of aioli. If you have any leftover baguette, you can use it for tomorrow's lunch.

Sunday

Egg and vegetarian bacon muffins for Sunday lunch!

Heat some olive oil in a large frying pan. Add your eggs, cooking them to your liking. Add 2 slices of vegetarian bacon, turning once to cook. Toast 2 English muffins (or slices of leftover baguette). Top with the eggs, vegetarian bacon and a dollop of tomato ketchup.

Spring Week 5

Another week of fill-you-up but good for you options. The pizza tart is full of vegetables, however I've included a cannellini bean base for extra nourishment. The beans are also used on Wednesday to make a dip. Sunday's tostada would make a great brunch.

Monday
Pizza Tart / Dried Mango

Tuesday
Egg Salad Roll / Banana

Wednesday
Cannellini Dip and Goodies to Dip with / Dried Cranberries and Almonds

Thursday
Tofu, Capsicum and Tomato Wrap with Sweet Chilli Sauce V / Pecans and Dates with Yogurt and Maple Syrup

Friday
Broccoli and Capsicum Slice / Orange

Saturday
Burger with Fried Onions, Pickles, Mustard, Sauce, Cheese and Lettuce

Sunday
Baked Bean, Onion, Capsicum and Goat's Cheese Tostada

To prepare an avocado, cut in half, around the stone. Easily remove the stone by bashing it with the blade of your knife. Give the knife a tug and the stone will come out. Use a spoon to scoop out the flesh, then use as needed.

shopping list

Fruit and Vegetables
- [ ] 3 onions
- [ ] 75g mushrooms
- [ ] 1 clove garlic
- [ ] 2 red capsicums
- [ ] 1 bunch basil
- [ ] 2 tomatoes
- [ ] 2 carrots
- [ ] 1 avocado
- [ ] 2 bananas
- [ ] 100g cherry tomatoes
- [ ] 1 small bag lettuce
- [ ] 2 oranges

Fridge
- [ ] 50g mozzarella cheese
- [ ] 2 eggs
- [ ] 200g natural yogurt
- [ ] 200g marinated tofu
- [ ] 2 vegetarian burgers
- [ ] 2 cheese slices
- [ ] 60g goat's cheese

Freezer
- [ ] 1 sheet puff pastry
- [ ] 4 slices broccoli and capsicum slice

Bakery
- [ ] 2 wholegrain rolls
- [ ] 2 burger buns

Pantry
- [ ] dried oregano
- [ ] 400g can cannellini beans
- [ ] dried mango
- [ ] smoked paprika
- [ ] grissini (breadsticks)
- [ ] unhulled tahini
- [ ] lemon juice
- [ ] dried mint flakes
- [ ] ground cumin
- [ ] dried cranberries
- [ ] almonds
- [ ] 4 wholegrain flour tortillas
- [ ] sweet chilli sauce
- [ ] pecans
- [ ] dates
- [ ] maple syrup
- [ ] gherkins
- [ ] mustard
- [ ] tomato ketchup
- [ ] 400g can baked beans
- [ ] chilli powder
- [ ] chargrilled capsicum

Staples
- [ ] salt
- [ ] black pepper
- [ ] olive oil
- [ ] extra virgin olive oil

daily tasks

Sunday

Make the pizza tarts. Thaw a sheet of puff pastry and place it on a baking tray. Whilst thawing, heat 1 tablespoon of olive oil in a frying pan on medium heat. Add a sliced onion and cook for a few minutes. Next, add 75g of sliced mushrooms and a clove of crushed garlic and fry for another 5 minutes until the mushrooms are soft. Remove from the heat. Dice a red capsicum and stir it into the mushroom mixture with 1 teaspoon of dried oregano and 1 tablespoon of chopped fresh basil.

Mash ½ a can of rinsed and drained cannellini beans (keep the rest in a container for later in the week) and spread over the pastry sheet. Top with the mushroom mixture, a sliced tomato and ½ cup (50g) of grated mozzarella cheese. Season with salt and black pepper. Bake in a preheated oven at 200°C/400°F/Gas Mark 6 for 30 minutes until the pastry is golden. Leave to cool, then slice into quarters with a sharp knife. Put 2 pieces into each lunch box, then refrigerate until tomorrow.

Monday

Make egg and avocado rolls. Hard boil 2 eggs. Cool and peel. Mash the eggs with ½ teaspoon of smoked paprika, 1 grated carrot, 1 mashed avocado and 1 tablespoon of natural yogurt. Season to taste. Divide between 2 large wholegrain rolls. Cover in plastic wrap or place in 2 lunch boxes, then refrigerate.

Tuesday

Prepare your snacks for dipping. Slice 100g of marinated tofu into dipping-sized strips. Slice a carrot and ½ a red capsicum into strips. Place between 2 containers with a handful of cherry tomatoes and some grissini.

To make the dip, blitz the following in a food processor: the remaining ½ can of cannellini beans, 1 tablespoon of natural yogurt, ½ tablespoon of tahini, 1 teaspoon of lemon juice and ½ teaspoon each of dried mint flakes and ground cumin. Divide between 2 containers. Pop everything into the fridge.

Mix together a handful of dried cranberries with a handful of almonds per person. Divide between 2 containers.

Wednesday

Prepare the tofu salad wraps. Slice the remaining tofu, then dice the remaining capsicum and a tomato. Divide between 2 wholegrain flour tortillas, top with a handful of lettuce and drizzle with some sweet chilli sauce. Fold the sides in then roll up. Cut in half if desired, then cover in plastic wrap. Pop the wraps into the fridge.

In a small bowl mix together 2 handfuls of chopped pecans with 2 handfuls of chopped dates. Stir in 2 tablespoons of natural yogurt and ½ tablespoon of maple syrup. Divide between 2 containers and refrigerate until tomorrow.

Thursday

If you have any broccoli and capsicum slice in the freezer, thaw overnight in the fridge. It will be ready to eat for lunch tomorrow. If you do not have any leftovers, follow the recipe below (remember to add the ingredients to your shopping list):

Make the broccoli and capsicum slice. Preheat the oven to 180°C/350°F/Gas Mark 4. Grease and line a 30 x 20cm baking tin. In a large bowl, whisk together 4 eggs and ½ cup (125ml) of milk. Beat in ½ cup (75g) of wholemeal self-raising flour and ½ cup (75g) of regular self-raising flour.

Finely chop the broccoli, red capsicum and ½ a bunch of spring onions. Add to the batter along with ½ a 420g can of rinsed and drained corn kernels. Season. Pour the mixture into the baking tin and bake for 30 minutes until golden brown and firm.

Leave to cool and remove from the tin. Slice into quarters, then halve each quarter. Place 2 slices into each lunch box. The rest can be frozen by wrapping each slice in plastic wrap then into a container or freezer bag, then popping them into the freezer.

Saturday

Prepare your burgers. Cook your choice of burgers according to packet instructions. Whilst they are cooking, heat 1 tablespoon of olive oil in a frying pan over a medium heat. Add a sliced onion and fry for 5-6 minutes until starting to brown.

Split the burger buns then add the burger, onions, some sliced gherkins, a slice of cheese, your choice of mustard, some ketchup and lettuce. To Aussie the burger up you could add some or all of the following: pineapple ring, beetroot slices, fried egg.

Sunday

To make tostadas, pop 2 lightly oiled flour tortillas into a 180°C/350°F/Gas Mark 4 oven for 5 minutes to warm and crisp slightly. Place 1 on each plate.

Fry a sliced onion in 1 tablespoon of olive oil in a frying pan over a medium heat. Stir in a 400g can of baked beans, ½ teaspoon of smoked paprika, ¼ teaspoon of chilli powder (or to taste) and 3 tablespoons of chopped chargrilled capsicum. Cook for 2-3 minutes until heated through. Spoon the mixture over each tortilla and top with 60g of crumbled goat's cheese. Serve warm.

Spring Week 6

This week I thought I'd have a go at making some polenta for lunch. I normally serve it warm, but thought it could work well cold for your lunch box. It tasted just fine cold, although if you have access to a microwave feel free to warm it up.

Monday
Polenta Wedges with Feta and Parsley / Tofu, Capsicum, Asparagus and Spinach Salad V / Grapefruit

Tuesday
Papaya Salad with Brown Rice, Tofu, Bean Sprouts and Asparagus V / Dried Apricots

Wednesday
Polenta Fingers with Barbecue, Tomato or Sweet Chilli Sauce / Mix of Olives, Chargrilled Capsicum, Sun-Dried Tomatoes and Baby Spinach / Hard Boiled Egg / Papaya

Thursday
Bean and Potato Salad / Apple

Friday
Potato, Bean and Leek Pancakes with Sour Cream / Popcorn, Almonds and Dried Apricots

Saturday
Cheese and Onion Muffins

Sunday
Mexican Ponchos (aka Mexican jackets)

When fruit is dried, many nutrients become more concentrated. Eating dried apricots gives you a good dose of fibre, iron, potassium, Vitamin A and carotenoids (an antioxidant).

shopping list

Fruit and Vegetables
- ☐ 1 bunch parsley
- ☐ 1 red capsicum
- ☐ 1 bunch asparagus
- ☐ 1 bunch spring onions
- ☐ 1 small bag baby spinach
- ☐ 1 grapefruit
- ☐ 1 papaya
- ☐ 30g bean sprouts
- ☐ 2 apples
- ☐ 1 leek
- ☐ 1 bunch chives
- ☐ 2 potatoes for baking
- ☐ 1 avocado

Fridge
- ☐ butter
- ☐ 200g feta cheese
- ☐ 200g marinated tofu
- ☐ 4 eggs
- ☐ 180ml milk
- ☐ small tub sour cream
- ☐ 50g Cheddar cheese

Bakery
- ☐ 4 savoury muffins (or recipe)

Pantry
- ☐ vegetable stock
- ☐ 225g polenta (cornmeal)
- ☐ savoury yeast flakes
- ☐ lemon juice
- ☐ 100g brown rice
- ☐ pine nuts
- ☐ dried apricots
- ☐ barbecue, tomato or chilli sauce
- ☐ olives
- ☐ chargrilled capsicum
- ☐ sun-dried tomatoes
- ☐ 800g can potatoes
- ☐ 400g can butter beans
- ☐ white wine vinegar
- ☐ 75g wholemeal self-raising flour
- ☐ 75g self-raising flour
- ☐ popcorn kernels
- ☐ almonds
- ☐ 400g can refried beans
- ☐ 1 jar salsa
- ☐ sliced jalapeños (optional)

Staples
- ☐ salt
- ☐ black pepper
- ☐ olive oil
- ☐ extra virgin olive oil
- ☐ canola oil

daily tasks

Sunday

Prepare the polenta. Bring $3\frac{2}{3}$ cups (900ml) of vegetable stock to the boil in a medium saucepan. Once boiling, gradually add $1\frac{1}{2}$ cups (225g) of polenta, stirring constantly with a wooden spoon. Reduce the heat and continue stirring until the polenta has thickened and is coming away from the side of the saucepan.

Remove from the heat and stir in 1 tablespoon of butter, 1 tablespoon of savoury yeast flakes, 1 tablespoon of chopped parsley and 100g of diced feta cheese. Season. Tip the mixture into a 30 x 20cm oiled baking tin and spread the mixture evenly. Leave to cool then place in the fridge for a few hours to firm up.

Preheat the grill. Remove the polenta from the tin and slice in half. Wrap half in plastic wrap and pop it into the fridge for use later in the week. Slice the remaining into 6 squares and brush with olive oil. Place on a wire grill tray and grill for about 10 minutes on each side until golden and crisp. Leave to cool then place in your lunch boxes, then into the fridge.

To make the accompanying salad, slice 100g of marinated tofu, dice $\frac{1}{2}$ a red capsicum, $\frac{1}{2}$ a bunch of asparagus and $\frac{1}{2}$ a bunch of spring onions. Add a handful of baby spinach, coarsely chopped. Mix together.

Make a dressing that will last for two days. Mix together 2 tablespoons of chopped parsley with 2 tablespoons of extra virgin olive oil and 1 tablespoon of lemon juice. Pour half of the dressing over the salad and store the rest in the fridge for tomorrow. Divide the salad between 2 containers and pop them into the fridge.

Halve a grapefruit, sprinkle with sugar if desired then cover each half in plastic wrap. Refrigerate.

Monday

Prepare the papaya salad. Cook $\frac{1}{2}$ cup (100g) of brown rice according to packet instructions. Once cooked, rinse under cold water to cool. Place in a bowl. Meanwhile, slice the papaya in half and wrap one of the halves in plastic wrap and keep in the fridge. With the other half, scoop out the seeds, then use a spoon to remove the flesh from the skin. Dice into bite-size pieces and add to the rice. Add the remaining asparagus and tofu (both diced), the bean sprouts and 2 tablespoons of toasted pine nuts. Pour the dressing you made yesterday over the salad. Mix together than divide between 2 lunch boxes and refrigerate until needed.

Divide 2 handfuls of dried apricots between 2 containers.

Tuesday

Prepare the polenta fingers. Begin by preheating the grill. Slice the remaining polenta into 8 fingers. Brush with olive oil and place on a wire grill tray. Grill for about 6 minutes on each side until golden and crisp. Leave to cool then place in your lunch boxes. In 2 small containers add your choice of dip. Tomato ketchup, barbecue sauce and sweet chilli sauce are good options.

Mix together a spoonful of olives with a spoonful of chargrilled capsicum, a spoonful of sun-dried tomatoes and the remaining baby spinach. Divide between 2 containers. Whilst you are doing all of the above, hard boil 2 eggs. My way is to pop eggs in a saucepan of cold water and cook over a high heat for 20 minutes. Rinse under cold water, leave to cool then add to your lunch boxes.

Dice up the remaining papaya and divide between 2 containers.

Refrigerate everything until tomorrow.

Wednesday

Make the potato salad. In a bowl place ½ a can of drained potatoes (diced if necessary) and ½ a can of rinsed and drained butter beans. Store the remaining potatoes and beans in a container in the fridge. Add the remaining capsicum (diced) and the remaining spring onions (chopped). Finally, dice 100g of feta cheese and add it to the salad. Make a dressing by whisking together 1 tablespoon of extra virgin olive oil with ½ tablespoon of white wine vinegar and 1 tablespoon of chopped parsley. Pour the dressing over the salad and stir in. Season to taste. Divide the salad between your lunch boxes, then refrigerate until needed.

Thursday

Make the potato, bean and leek pancakes. Heat 1 tablespoon of olive oil in a frying pan over a medium heat. Add a chopped leek and fry for about 6 minutes until soft. Remove from the heat.

Make the batter by combining ½ cup (75g) of wholemeal self-raising flour with ½ cup (75g) of self-raising flour and a pinch of salt. Beat together 2 eggs with ¾ cup (180ml) of milk and stir into the flour, mixing well to form a batter. Add the leek, remaining butter beans, remaining potatoes (diced) and 1 tablespoon of chopped chives.

Heat 2 tablespoons of canola oil in a large frying pan. Add heaped spoonfuls of the batter mix to the pan, flattening down to form pancakes. Cook for 3-4 minutes, turn and cook for another 3 minutes until golden. Drain on paper towel and leave to cool.

Put 3 into each lunch box. You can freeze the rest by placing baking paper between each pancake then pop them into a container then into the freezer. If you like, you can put some sour cream into a pot to serve with your pancakes. Refrigerate the pancakes and sour cream.

Pop a small handful of popcorn kernels then mix with some almonds and dried apricots and divide between 2 containers.

Saturday

Make cheese and onion muffins according to the recipe (p.224), or buy your favourite savoury muffins from the bakers.

Sunday

Bake jacket potatoes. Prick 2 large potatoes and microwave for 8-10 minutes until they start to soften. Preheat the oven to 210°C/410°F/Gas Mark 7. Pop the potatoes into the oven and bake for 30 minutes until crisp. Heat a can of refried beans. Cut open the jacket potatoes then top with refried beans, salsa, a diced avocado, some grated Cheddar cheese and a spoonful of sour cream. Top with some jalapeños, if desired.

Spring Week 7

It's a cheesy week this week. Camembert, halloumi, Cheddar, mozzarella and smoked cheese all feature this week. This menu shows just how versatile cheese can be. Do feel free to substitute for your favourite cheeses.

Monday
Crepes with Camembert, Pine Nuts, Tomato and Rocket / Peach Slices

Tuesday
Pasta Salad with Halloumi, Cherry Tomatoes, Capsicum and Chickpeas / Banana

Wednesday
Wholemeal Roll Filled with Camembert, Rocket and Cranberry Sauce / Peach Slices

Thursday
Couscous with Halloumi, Cherry Tomatoes, Capsicum and Chickpeas / Dried Mango

Friday
Bean and Mushroom Wrap / Macadamias and Dried Cranberries

Saturday
Club Sandwich with Mozzarella and Smoked Cheese

Sunday
Sausage Rolls with Mozzarella

Cheese has many health benefits. It is a great source of calcium and protein. It also contains zinc (for tissue repair and growth), Vitamin B (helps body absorb calcium) and phosphorous (for strong bones).

shopping list

Fruit and Vegetables
- [ ] 2 tomatoes
- [ ] 1 small bag rocket
- [ ] 200g cherry tomatoes
- [ ] 1 red capsicum
- [ ] 1 bunch spring onions
- [ ] 2 bananas
- [ ] 100g mushrooms
- [ ] 1 lettuce

Fridge
- [ ] 1 egg
- [ ] 300ml milk
- [ ] 150g Camembert
- [ ] 180g halloumi cheese
- [ ] 50g Cheddar cheese
- [ ] 100g mozzarella cheese
- [ ] 50g smoked cheese
- [ ] 4 vegetarian sausages

Freezer
- [ ] 1 sheet puff pastry

Bakery
- [ ] 2 wholemeal rolls
- [ ] 6 slices bread

Pantry
- [ ] 75g plain flour
- [ ] 75g wholemeal plain flour
- [ ] sesame seeds
- [ ] pine nuts
- [ ] large can peach slices
- [ ] 100g dried pasta
- [ ] 400g can chickpeas
- [ ] dried mint flakes
- [ ] cranberry sauce
- [ ] 100g couscous
- [ ] dried mango
- [ ] 400g can kidney beans
- [ ] sun-dried tomatoes
- [ ] lime juice
- [ ] 2 flour tortillas
- [ ] macadamia nuts
- [ ] dried cranberries
- [ ] mustard
- [ ] tomato ketchup

Staples
- [ ] salt
- [ ] black pepper
- [ ] olive oil
- [ ] extra virgin olive oil
- [ ] olive oil spray

daily tasks

Sunday

Begin by making the crepes. Combine ½ cup (75g) of plain flour and ½ cup (75g) of wholemeal plain flour in a large bowl with a teaspoon of sesame seeds and a pinch of salt. Stir in a beaten egg. Gradually add 1¼ cups (300ml) of milk, beating to form a smooth batter. Pour into a jug.

Spray a medium non-stick frying pan with olive oil and heat over a medium heat. Add enough batter to thinly cover the pan. Cook for 2-3 minutes, turn then cook for another 2 minutes, until lightly browned. Transfer to a plate and leave to cool. Spray the pan again with olive oil before cooking the next crepe. Allow 2 per person. You can freeze the rest. Interleaf with baking paper then place in a freezer bag or container before popping them into the freezer.

Fill your crepes by placing 75g of sliced Camembert, 1 sliced tomato, some rocket and 2 tablespoons of toasted pine nuts on a quarter of the crepe. Fold in half, then half again to form a triangle. Cover in plastic wrap or place into 2 containers. Store in the fridge until tomorrow.

Divide ½ a can of peach slices between 2 containers. Put the rest in a container in the fridge for later in the week.

Monday

Prepare the pasta salad. Cook 100g of dried pasta according to packet instructions. Rinse under cold water, then drain. Whilst the pasta is cooking prepare your other ingredients.

Heat a frying pan over a medium heat and add 180g of sliced halloumi cheese. Once it is golden, turn to brown the other side. Remove from the pan, then cut into bite-size pieces. Place in a bowl and add 200g of cherry tomatoes (halved if you wish), a diced red capsicum and a 400g can of rinsed and drained chickpeas. Chop a bunch of spring onions (reserving 2 for later in the week) and add to the bowl. Stir in 1 teaspoon of dried mint flakes and 1 tablespoon of extra virgin olive oil.

Once your pasta is cooked, add half of the halloumi mixture to the pasta. Pop the remaining mixture in a container in the fridge for later in the week. Divide the pasta salad between your lunch boxes. Refrigerate until tomorrow.

Tuesday

Prepare your rolls. Slice 2 wholemeal rolls in half then fill with Camembert, some rocket and a dollop of cranberry sauce. Cover in plastic wrap then pop them into the fridge.

Divide the remaining peach slices between 2 containers.

Wednesday

Make the couscous salad. Place ½ cup (100g) of couscous in a bowl. Add ½ cup (125ml) of boiling water and leave to stand for 3 minutes. Fluff it up with a fork then stir in the remaining halloumi and vegetable mix you prepared on Monday. Divide between your 2 lunch boxes and store in the fridge.

Thursday

Make the bean and mushroom wraps. Blitz the following in a food processor: 400g can of rinsed and drained kidney beans, 100g mushrooms, coarsely chopped, 2 sun-dried tomatoes, 2 teaspoons of lime juice and some seasoning. Spread the mixture over 2 flour tortillas, then top with 2 chopped spring onions and ½ cup (50g) of grated Cheddar cheese. Roll each wrap up, cut in half then cover in plastic wrap. Refrigerate until tomorrow.

Mix 2 handfuls of macadamias with 2 handfuls of dried cranberries. Divide between 2 containers.

Saturday

Make your club sandwiches. Lightly toast 6 slices of your favourite bread. On 2 slices, add some mustard (your choice but I like Dijon or English), 50g of thinly sliced mozzarella cheese and a sliced tomato. Top each slice with another slice of bread then add 50g of sliced smoked cheese, some lettuce and some salt and a grind of black pepper. Top with the remaining slices of bread. Skewer each corner with a cocktail stick then cut into quarters. Allow 4 quarters per person.

Sunday

To make the sausage rolls, preheat the oven to 220°C/425°F/Gas Mark 7. Thaw a sheet of puff pastry then cut it into 12 rectangles. Slice 4 vegetarian sausages into 3 pieces and slice 50g of mozzarella cheese into 12 pieces. Place a piece of mozzarella cheese on the pastry, top with a sausage piece, then roll up the pastry. Place seam side down on a baking tray. Roll the rest in the same way. Bake in the oven for 20 minutes until golden brown and puffed. Serve warm with tomato ketchup, if desired.

Spring Week 8

This week's menu includes smoothies. They are a tasty way to get your fruit intake as well as extra calcium from the yogurt and milk used. You can make up the drink the day before then pop it into a flask and into the fridge. Look for a flask that is 500ml in volume and make sure it is insulated to keep the contents cool.

Monday
Roasted Beetroot with Couscous, Spinach, Goat's Cheese, Dates and Pecans / Cranberry Flapjacks

Tuesday
Egg and Butter Bean Salad with Asparagus, Olives, Tomatoes and Watercress / Pineapple Chunks with Mixed Spice or Nutmeg

Wednesday
Asparagus, Tomato and Bean Frittata / Cranberry Flapjacks

Thursday
Cheese, Coleslaw, Avocado and Watercress Sandwich / Pineapple Chunks with Yogurt

Friday
Mushroom, Spinach and Tomato Turnovers V / Banana, Honey and Vanilla Smoothie

Saturday
Toasted Turkish SOCA Rolls

Sunday
Cheese and Herb Damper Served with Butter and Coleslaw

When peeling hard boiled eggs, peel them onto some paper towel. This way you just need to gather up the paper towel when you're done and pop it in the bin. Thanks mum for this tip.

shopping list

Fruit and Vegetables
- [ ] 4 baby beetroot
- [ ] 1 bag baby spinach
- [ ] 200g cherry tomatoes
- [ ] 1 bunch asparagus
- [ ] 1 bunch watercress
- [ ] 1 avocado
- [ ] 100g mushrooms
- [ ] 1 clove garlic
- [ ] 1 tomato
- [ ] 1 banana
- [ ] 1 onion

Fridge
- [ ] 120g goat's cheese
- [ ] 100g unsalted butter
- [ ] 6 eggs
- [ ] 100g Cheddar cheese
- [ ] small tub coleslaw
- [ ] 200g natural yogurt
- [ ] 375ml milk
- [ ] aioli

Freezer
- [ ] 1 sheet puff pastry

Bakery
- [ ] 4 slices wholegrain bread
- [ ] 2 Turkish rolls
- [ ] damper (or recipe)

Pantry
- [ ] 100g couscous
- [ ] dates
- [ ] pecans
- [ ] lemon juice
- [ ] 65g light brown sugar
- [ ] 60ml golden syrup
- [ ] 300g rolled oats
- [ ] 60g dried cranberries
- [ ] green olives
- [ ] 400g can butter beans
- [ ] Dijon mustard
- [ ] 440g can pineapple chunks in juice
- [ ] mixed spice
- [ ] whole nutmeg
- [ ] honey
- [ ] vanilla extract

Staples
- [ ] salt
- [ ] black pepper
- [ ] olive oil
- [ ] extra virgin olive oil

daily tasks

Sunday

Prepare the beetroot couscous. Scrub 4 baby beetroot, cut off the roots and stalks and place on a baking tray. Drizzle with olive oil. Bake in an oven preheated to 200°C/400°F/Gas Mark 6 for about 40 minutes (depending on size), until tender. Leave to cool, then slice into quarters.

To make the couscous, place ½ cup (100g) of couscous in a bowl and add ½ cup (125ml) of boiling water or stock. Stand for 3 minutes, then fluff up with a fork. Stir in the beetroot, a handful of spinach, 60g of crumbled goat's cheese and a handful each of chopped dates and pecans. Finally, stir in 1 tablespoon of extra virgin olive oil and ½ tablespoon of lemon juice. Season to taste. Divide between 2 lunch boxes, then pop them into the fridge.

Next, make the cranberry flapjacks. Preheat the oven to 180°C/350°F/Gas Mark 4. In a large saucepan place 100g of unsalted butter or margarine, ⅓ cup (65g) of light brown sugar and ¼ cup (60ml) of golden syrup. Melt the mixture over a low heat, stirring to bring the ingredients together. Once melted remove from the heat. Stir in 1¾ cups (300g) of rolled oats, and ½ cup (60g) of dried cranberries. Tip into a lined 20 x 20cm baking tin and press down with the back of a spoon to spread evenly. Bake for 25 minutes until golden. Slice into 8 and leave to cool in the pan. Once cooled, allow 2 per person. Pop the rest into a container for later in the week.

Monday

Make the egg and bean salad. Hard boil 2 eggs. Once cooked, rinse under cold water and leave to cool. Peel the eggs, roughly chop and pop them in a bowl. To the chopped egg, add 100g halved cherry tomatoes, ½ bunch chopped asparagus, a handful of green olives and ½ a 400g can of rinsed and drained butter beans (put the rest in a container, in the fridge). Roughly chop a handful of watercress and stir this in.

Make the dressing by mixing together 1 tablespoon of extra virgin olive oil, ½ tablespoon of lemon juice, ½ teaspoon of Dijon mustard and some seasoning.

Stir the dressing into the salad. Divide the salad between 2 lunch boxes, then refrigerate until tomorrow.

Divide ½ a can of pineapple chunks between 2 containers then sprinkle with some mixed spice or grated nutmeg. Put the remaining pineapple into a container and pop everything into the fridge.

Tuesday

Prepare the frittata. In a bowl, beat together 4 eggs and season. Chop up the remaining asparagus and cut 100g of cherry tomatoes in half. Add to the eggs along with the remaining butter beans. Heat 1 tablespoon of olive oil in a 24cm frying pan over a medium heat. Add the egg mixture, top with 60g of goat's cheese then turn the heat down. Let cook for 8-10 minutes.

Preheat the grill. Once the eggs are nearly set, place the pan under the grill to finish cooking the top. Slide the frittata off the pan then leave to cool. Slice into quarters and place 2 quarters into each lunch box. Refrigerate until tomorrow.

Divide the remaining pieces of flapjack between 2 lunch boxes, or cover in plastic wrap.

Wednesday

Prepare the sandwiches using 4 slices of wholegrain bread. Divide the following between 2 sandwiches: 50g sliced Cheddar cheese, 1 sliced avocado, some chopped watercress and a good spoonful of coleslaw. Slice each sandwich in half then cover in plastic wrap and refrigerate until tomorrow.

Mix the remaining pineapple chunks with 3 tablespoons of natural yogurt. Add some grated nutmeg if you wish. Divide between 2 containers.

Thursday

Make the mushroom and spinach turnovers. Thaw a sheet of puff pastry then cut it into 4 squares. Whilst thawing, heat 1 tablespoon of olive oil in a frying pan over a medium heat. Add 100g of sliced mushrooms and a clove of crushed garlic. Cook for about 5 minutes, until soft. Remove from the heat. Stir in a handful of roughly chopped baby spinach and a chopped tomato, seeded. Grate some nutmeg into the mixture, then season to taste.

Add a spoonful of the mixture to each pastry square. Fold the pastry in half to form a triangle, then press the edges with a fork to seal. Place on a baking tray and bake in a 220°C/425°F/Gas Mark 7 oven for 20 minutes until golden. Leave to cool than place in your lunch boxes. Refrigerate until tomorrow.

Make 2 smoothies. In a blender add 1 banana, 1½ cups (375ml) of milk, the remaining tub of natural yogurt, 1 tablespoon of honey and ½ teaspoon of vanilla extract. Blend until smooth. Divide between 2 thermos flasks, then refrigerate until tomorrow.

Saturday

Make your Turkish rolls. Heat 1 tablespoon of olive oil in a frying pan over a medium heat. Add 1 peeled and sliced onion and fry for 5-6 minutes until soft. Remove from the heat. Preheat the grill. Split the Turkish rolls then top with 50g of sliced or grated Cheddar cheese. Pop under the grill and cook until the cheese has melted. Top with the onions, the remaining baby spinach and a dollop of aioli.

Sunday

You can buy ready-made damper, or make your own. You will find the recipe on p.223. You may even have some in the freezer. Thaw at room temperature for a couple of hours. You can then heat the damper up by covering in foil, placing on a baking tray then heating in a 180°C/350°F/Gas Mark 4 oven for about 20 minutes.

Serve the cheese and herb damper with butter and leftover coleslaw, if you like.

Spring Week 9

Lots of fresh ingredients in this week's menu, beginning with some cold rolls. I love the crunchy freshness of the cold rolls – you feel healthier with every bite. Also this week, another chance to tuck into some juicy, sweet papaya.

Monday
Cold Rolls with Sweet Chilli Sauce V / Walnuts, Almonds and Dried Apricots

Tuesday
Tofu Salad with a Ginger and Lime Dressing / Canned Pears

Wednesday
Pita Bread Stuffed with Omelette, Broccoli and Cherry Tomatoes / Papaya

Thursday
Sausage, Apple and Avocado Salad with Plenty More Goodies / Canned Pears

Friday
Crispbread with Kidney Bean Spread V / Sliced Carrot and Cherry Tomatoes / Papaya

Saturday
Cheese and Pickled Onion Toasted Sandwich

Sunday
Mushroom, Bean and Zucchini Chimichanga V

Nuts can quickly go rancid. Try to buy small quantities, unless you know you will soon be using them up. Once the packet is open store in a container in the fridge. You can also freeze nuts.

shopping list

Fruit and Vegetables
- [ ] 2 carrots
- [ ] 1 small bunch spring onions
- [ ] 30g bean sprouts
- [ ] 1 head broccoli
- [ ] ginger
- [ ] 1 clove garlic
- [ ] 1 lime
- [ ] 1 bunch coriander
- [ ] 200g cherry tomatoes
- [ ] 1 papaya
- [ ] 1 apple
- [ ] 1 avocado
- [ ] 1 small bag rocket
- [ ] 1 onion
- [ ] 1 zucchini
- [ ] 100g mushrooms
- [ ] 1 tomato

Fridge
- [ ] 200g marinated tofu
- [ ] 2 eggs
- [ ] 2 vegetarian sausages
- [ ] 50g smoked cheese
- [ ] 50g Cheddar cheese
- [ ] small tub sour cream (optional)

Bakery
- [ ] 2 pita breads
- [ ] 4 slices bread

Pantry
- [ ] 6 rice paper rounds
- [ ] sweet chilli sauce
- [ ] walnuts
- [ ] almonds
- [ ] dried apricots
- [ ] 100g brown rice
- [ ] 420g can corn kernels
- [ ] honey
- [ ] 825g can pears
- [ ] dried cranberries
- [ ] apple cider vinegar
- [ ] Dijon mustard
- [ ] 400g can kidney beans
- [ ] tomato ketchup
- [ ] savoury yeast flakes
- [ ] Tabasco sauce
- [ ] 8 crispbread
- [ ] pickled onions
- [ ] 2 jumbo flour tortillas or 4 regular
- [ ] chilli powder
- [ ] ground cumin
- [ ] ground coriander

Staples
- [ ] salt
- [ ] black pepper
- [ ] olive oil
- [ ] extra virgin olive oil
- [ ] canola oil

daily tasks

Sunday

Prepare the cold rolls. Slice 1 carrot thinly into matchstick-size pieces about 2cm long. Slice half the pack of marinated tofu the same way. Place in a bowl with a small bunch of chopped spring onions and the bean sprouts. Mix together.

Take 1 rice paper round and soak it in a dish of lukewarm water for 30 seconds, until soft. Drain on a tea towel, taking care not to fold it. Take a heaped tablespoon of the mixture and place it at the bottom of the rice paper, leaving a 1cm gap at the bottom and sides. Fold the bottom piece over the mixture then fold in the sides. Then roll the whole thing up to form your cold roll. Continue with the other ingredients to make 6 cold rolls, soaking each rice paper as you go.

Any remaining ingredients can be kept for tomorrow's salad. Place 3 cold rolls in each lunch box and refrigerate. In 2 small containers add some sweet chilli sauce for serving with.

Mix 2 handfuls each of walnuts, almonds and dried apricots together and divide between 2 containers.

Monday

Make the tofu salad. Cook ½ cup (100g) of brown rice, according to packet instructions. Tip the rice into a sieve and rinse in cold water, to cool. To the bowl of ingredients chopped up yesterday, add the remaining tofu, diced into cubes. Add ½ a 420g can of rinsed and drained corn kernels and ½ a head of broccoli florets, chopped into pieces. Keep the remaining corn kernels in a container in the fridge, along with the remaining broccoli. Stir in the cooled rice. Make the ginger and lime dressing. In a jar or bowl, mix together 1 teaspoon of grated ginger, 1 clove of crushed garlic, the juice of 1 lime, ½ tablespoon of honey, 1 tablespoon of chopped coriander and some salt and pepper. Pour the dressing over the salad and mix thoroughly to combine. Divide between 2 lunch boxes then refrigerate until tomorrow.

Divide ½ a can of pears between 2 containers and put the rest in another container for another day. Place everything in the fridge.

Tuesday

Make the omelette strips for the pitas. Heat 1 tablespoon of olive oil in a frying pan over a medium heat. Beat together 2 eggs, some seasoning and 1 tablespoon of chopped coriander. Pour into the frying pan and cook for 3 minutes. Carefully turn and cook for a further minute, until cooked. Transfer to a plate to cool. Once cooled, cut into strips.

Combine 100g of halved cherry tomatoes and the remaining broccoli, chopped into small pieces. Add the omelette strips. Split 2 pita breads and fill with the mixture. Finish with a dollop of sweet chilli sauce. Cover in plastic wrap and refrigerate until tomorrow.

Cut the papaya in half. Store half in the fridge for later in the week. With the remaining half, scoop out the seeds, then use a spoon to remove the flesh from the skin. Dice into bite-size pieces then divide between 2 containers. Refrigerate.

Wednesday

Put together your salad. Heat 1 tablespoon of olive oil in a frying pan over a medium heat. Add 2 vegetarian sausages and cook, turning often until they are golden on all sides and heated through. Remove from the heat, chop into small pieces and place in a bowl. Core an apple, chop into cubes and add to the bowl. Dice an avocado and add to the sausage and apple. Cube 50g of smoked cheese and add to the bowl along with a handful of dried cranberries and a handful of rocket. Add the remaining corn kernels.

Make the dressing. Mix 1 tablespoon of extra virgin olive oil with ½ tablespoon of apple cider vinegar, 1 teaspoon of honey and ½ teaspoon of Dijon mustard. Add some seasoning. Pour the dressing over the salad and mix well to coat the ingredients. Divide the salad between 2 lunch boxes, then pop them into the fridge until tomorrow.

Divide the remaining pears between 2 containers, then put them into the fridge.

Thursday

Blitz up a kidney bean spread. Rinse and drain a 400g can of kidney beans. Place half in a container and refrigerate and put the rest in a food processor. Add 1 tablespoon of tomato ketchup, 1 tablespoon of savoury yeast flakes, a dash of Tabasco sauce and some salt and pepper. Blitz until smooth. Divide between 2 containers.

Slice a carrot into sticks and divide between 2 containers along with some cherry tomatoes. Add some crispbread (about 4 per person). Pop them into the fridge with the kidney bean spread.

Remove the seeds from the remaining papaya, scoop out the flesh and chop into bite-size pieces. Divide between 2 containers then refrigerate until tomorrow.

Saturday

Make 2 cheese and pickled onion sandwiches. Preheat the grill. Slice 50g of Cheddar cheese and some pickled onions. Divide between 2 slices of bread, then top with another to make a sandwich! Place under a grill and cook until the bread is toasted. Turn the sandwich and toast the other side. Alternatively you can use a sandwich maker,

following manufacturer's instructions. Slice each sandwich in half, then serve.

Sunday

Make the chimichangas. Heat 1 tablespoon of olive oil in a large frying pan over a medium heat. Add a sliced onion and cook for 4 minutes until soft. Add a diced zucchini and 100g of sliced mushrooms, cooking for 3-4 minutes. Add ½ teaspoon each of chilli powder, ground cumin and ground coriander. Cook for a couple of minutes. Then add 1 diced tomato and the remaining kidney beans. Continue cooking for another 2 minutes. Season to taste. Remove from the heat.

Lay out 2 jumbo flour tortillas (or 4 regular-sized). Spoon the filling into the centre of each tortilla. Fold in the sides to form a parcel. Use cocktail sticks to hold the sides in place.

Heat 2 tablespoons of canola oil in a clean frying pan. Add the chimichangas and cook until golden on both sides, about 6 minutes in total. Drain on paper towel, remove the cocktail sticks, then serve with a side salad (you may have some leftover rocket and cherry tomatoes) and some sour cream if you like.

Spring Week 10

I thought it was time to start raiding the freezer for some of the foodstuffs we've been making in previous weeks. Also this week I've made a frittata then later on added it to a salad. I thought this was a change from the weeks when I've made a salad then used the leftover ingredients to make a frittata.

Monday
Bean, Potato and Onion Frittata / Pickled Onions and Gherkins / Dates and Macadamias

Tuesday
Frittata Salad with Olives, Capsicum, Baby Spinach and Sun-Dried Tomatoes / Orange

Wednesday
Pita Dippers with Tahini Dip, Carrot and Button Mushrooms V / Dark Chocolate

Thursday
Cheese and Onion Muffins with Cream Cheese / Mango Salad V / Popcorn

Friday
Baked Mushroom and Tomato Slice / Banana

Saturday
Baguette Slices with Blue Cheese Spread, Grapes and Muscatels

Sunday
Blue Cheese and Sun-Dried Tomato Quiche / Watercress and Lettuce Salad

Tahini is a sesame seed paste. You can get a hulled variety and an unhulled variety. The unhulled variety gives a richer sesame taste. Try both and see what you prefer. The tiny sesame seed is a good source of fibre, copper, magnesium and even calcium.

shopping list

Fruit and Vegetables
- ☐ 450g potatoes
- ☐ 1 onion
- ☐ 1 red capsicum
- ☐ 1 small bag baby spinach
- ☐ 2 oranges
- ☐ 1 clove garlic
- ☐ 1 carrot
- ☐ 100g button mushrooms
- ☐ 1 lettuce
- ☐ 1 small bunch watercress
- ☐ 1 small mango
- ☐ 2 bananas
- ☐ 1 small bunch grapes (or 1 pear)

Fridge
- ☐ 6 eggs
- ☐ 50g cream cheese
- ☐ tub blue cheese spread
- ☐ 100g blue cheese
- ☐ small tub double cream

Freezer
- ☐ 4 slices mushroom and tomato slice
- ☐ 1 sheet puff pastry

Bakery
- ☐ 2 pita breads
- ☐ 4 savoury muffins (or recipe / freezer)
- ☐ 1 baguette

Pantry
- ☐ 400g can butter beans
- ☐ smoked paprika
- ☐ pickled onions
- ☐ gherkins
- ☐ dates
- ☐ macadamias
- ☐ green olives
- ☐ sun-dried tomatoes
- ☐ cumin seeds
- ☐ ground coriander
- ☐ sesame seeds
- ☐ unhulled tahini
- ☐ lemon juice
- ☐ sugar
- ☐ ground cumin
- ☐ dried chilli flakes
- ☐ onion powder
- ☐ 2 x 50g bars dark chocolate
- ☐ pine nuts
- ☐ lime juice
- ☐ dried mint flakes
- ☐ popcorn kernels
- ☐ muscatels (or dried figs)
- ☐ dried rosemary

Staples
- ☐ salt
- ☐ black pepper
- ☐ olive oil
- ☐ extra virgin olive oil

daily tasks

Sunday

Make the bean, potato and onion frittata. Bring a large saucepan of lightly salted water to the boil. Peel then thinly slice 450g of potatoes. Cut each slice in half. Add the potatoes to the saucepan and once the water comes back up to the boil, parboil for 5 minutes. Drain.

Heat 1 tablespoon of olive oil in a 24cm frying pan over a medium heat. Fry a sliced onion for 3-4 minutes, until pale. Add the potatoes and stir to coat them in the oil. Turn the heat down to low. Put the lid on and continue cooking until the potatoes are tender, about 7-8 minutes. Stir occasionally. Add a 400g can of rinsed and drained butter beans.

Lightly whisk 4 eggs in a small bowl. Add ½ teaspoon of smoked paprika, a pinch of salt and a grind of black pepper. Ensure the potato, onion and bean mixture is fairly level in the pan and then add the eggs. Cook over a low heat for 8-10 minutes, until the eggs are nearly set. A few minutes before the end, preheat the grill.

Place the frying pan under the grill to cook the top of the frittata. This will only take about 2 minutes. Slide the frittata off the pan then leave to cool. Slice in half. Wrap half in plastic wrap and refrigerate. Cut the remaining piece in half then place in your lunch boxes. Refrigerate.

In a small container add some pickled onions and gherkins. You can pop them on cocktail sticks if you like.

Finally, mix 2 handfuls of dates with 2 handfuls of macadamias and divide between 2 containers.

Monday

Make your leftover frittata salad. Chop the remaining frittata half into bite-size pieces then place in a bowl. To the bowl add a chopped red capsicum, a handful of green olives, a handful of baby spinach and some chopped sun-dried tomatoes. Mix together, then divide between 2 lunch boxes. Pop them into the fridge.

Tuesday

Prepare the pita dippers. Preheat the oven to 200°C/400°F/Gas Mark 6. In a small bowl, mix together 1 teaspoon each of cumin seeds, ground coriander and sesame seeds. Add a pinch of salt and a grind of black pepper. Brush the pita breads with olive oil. Distribute the spice mix across the 2 pitas. Slice into 3cm strips. A pizza cutter works well for this. Place on a baking tray and bake in the oven for 10 minutes, until crisp. Leave to cool, then divide between 2 lunch boxes.

Make the tahini dip. In a bowl, mix together ½ cup (120g) of tahini, 1 clove of crushed garlic, 1 teaspoon of lemon juice, 1 teaspoon of sugar, 1 teaspoon of ground cumin and ½ teaspoon each of dried chilli flakes and onion powder. Gradually add ¼ cup (60ml) of water, stirring well to combine. Season to taste with salt and freshly ground black pepper. Divide between 2 containers.

Chop a carrot into sticks, divide between 2 lunch boxes along with 100g of button mushrooms. Place everything in the fridge until tomorrow.

Don't forget the chocolate bars!

Wednesday

Thaw 4 cheese and onion muffins at room temperature for a couple of hours, or overnight in the fridge. If you do not have any in the freezer, you can use store bought or follow the recipe on p.224. Cover in plastic wrap, or place in lunch boxes along with a dollop of cream cheese for serving with the muffins.

Make up the mango salad. Put a layer of shredded lettuce and watercress at the bottom of each lunch box. Peel the mango. Slice the flesh away from the stone, cut into chunks, and then divide evenly between the lunch boxes. Top with a handful of toasted pine nuts. Mix together 1 tablespoon of extra virgin olive oil with ½ tablespoon of lime juice and ½ teaspoon of dried mint flakes. Drizzle the dressing over the salad. Refrigerate until needed.

Pop a small handful of popcorn. You can add some spices if you wish. Divide between 2 containers.

Thursday

If you have any mushroom and tomato slice in the freezer, thaw overnight in the fridge. It will be ready to eat for lunch tomorrow. If you do not have any leftovers, follow the recipe below (remember to add the ingredients to your shopping list):

Preheat the oven to 180°C/350°F/Gas Mark 4. Grease and line a 30 x 20cm baking tin. Heat 1 tablespoon of olive oil in a frying pan over a medium heat. Add 1 sliced onion and fry for 4 minutes. Add 175g of sliced mushrooms and 1 clove of crushed garlic and fry for a further 5 minutes until the mushrooms are soft. Meanwhile, chop 1 tomato and grate ½ cup (50g) of Cheddar cheese.

In a large bowl, whisk together 4 eggs and ½ cup (125ml) of milk. Beat in ½ cup (75g) of self-raising flour and ½ cup (75g) of wholemeal self-raising flour to make a batter. Stir in the onions, mushrooms, tomato and cheese. Pour the mixture into the baking tin and bake for 30 minutes until golden and firm to the touch. Leave to cool. Remove from the tin and slice into 8 pieces. Place 2 slices into each lunch box. The rest can be frozen by wrapping each slice in plastic wrap then placing them into a container or freezer bag and then into the freezer.

Saturday

Prepare your bread and cheese platter. Thickly slice a baguette on an angle. Place on 2 large plates. To each plate add a small dish of blue cheese spread, a small bunch of grapes and a handful of muscatels. Enjoy a relaxing lunch.

If you cannot find blue cheese spread, choose your favourite cheese spread or make your own. You can stir in some blue cheese into some softened cream cheese. If you cannot find grapes, chop up a pear. Also, use dried figs if you cannot find muscatels.

Sunday

Make your cheese and tomato quiche. Preheat the oven to 200°C/400°F/Gas Mark 6. Thaw a sheet of puff pastry at room temperature. Line a 20cm tart tin with the pastry. Spread ¼ cup (60g) of chopped sun-dried tomatoes over the base. Add 100g of crumbled blue cheese and 1 teaspoon of dried rosemary, sprinkled evenly.

Beat together 3 tablespoons of double cream, 2 beaten eggs and some seasoning. Pour into the tart tin and bake for 40-45 minutes until golden and puffed. Leave to cool slightly, then slice and serve with a side salad using any remaining lettuce and watercress you may have.

You can freeze any remaining double cream in ice cube trays. Use in cooking, from frozen.

Spring Week 11

This week I have included tempeh in one of the lunches. If you are not a fan of tempeh, do use tofu instead. I have also popped fruit into a few lunches (rather than just as a serving on its own). Enjoy a fruity couscous salad, a tasty ploughman's lunch and end the week with orange and sultana scones.

Monday
Bean and Vegetable Loaf / Peach Slices

Tuesday
Borlotti Bean Wrap with Avocado, Corn and Tomato / Pear, Blue Cheese and Honey

Wednesday
Fruity Couscous Salad with Red Onion and Capsicum / Grapefruit

Thursday
Feta, Capsicum, Onion and Tomato Wrap / Peach Slices

Friday
Tempeh Sticks and Carrots with Barbecue Sauce V / Apple, Cheese and Crackers / Dried Cranberries and Almonds

Saturday
Ploughman's Lunch

Sunday
Orange and Sultana Scones with Orange Cream

As soon as you get fresh herbs home from the shops, give them a wash. Shake as much excess water from them as possible, then wrap in paper towel. Place in a plastic bag and store in the fridge. This way they are all prepared for when you need them and will stay fresh for much longer.

shopping list

Fruit and Vegetables
- [ ] 1 onion
- [ ] 1 clove garlic
- [ ] 1 small bag baby spinach
- [ ] 2 carrots
- [ ] 2 tomatoes
- [ ] 1 avocado
- [ ] 1 bunch coriander
- [ ] 1 pear
- [ ] 1 red capsicum
- [ ] 1 red onion
- [ ] 1 bunch mint
- [ ] 1 grapefruit
- [ ] 2 apples

Fridge
- [ ] 5 eggs
- [ ] 50g cream cheese
- [ ] 150g blue cheese
- [ ] 180g feta cheese
- [ ] 200g tempeh
- [ ] 150g Cheddar cheese
- [ ] butter or margarine

Bakery
- [ ] 1 baguette or crusty loaf
- [ ] 4 sweet scones (or recipe)

Pantry
- [ ] 420g can corn kernels
- [ ] 400g can borlotti beans
- [ ] 75g self-raising flour
- [ ] 75g wholemeal self raising flour
- [ ] large can peach slices
- [ ] 4 wholegrain flour tortillas
- [ ] lime juice
- [ ] honey
- [ ] 100g couscous
- [ ] dates
- [ ] dried apricots
- [ ] cashews
- [ ] lemon juice
- [ ] Dijon mustard
- [ ] barbecue sauce
- [ ] wholegrain crackers
- [ ] dried cranberries
- [ ] almonds
- [ ] pickled onions
- [ ] chutney

Staples
- [ ] salt
- [ ] black pepper
- [ ] olive oil
- [ ] extra virgin olive oil
- [ ] canola oil

daily tasks

Sunday

Make the bean and vegetable loaf. Begin by preparing the vegetables. Heat 1 tablespoon of olive oil in a frying pan over a medium heat. Add 1 chopped onion and a clove of crushed garlic. Cook for 5 minutes, until soft. Remove from the heat. Stir in a handful of chopped baby spinach and 1 grated carrot. Rinse and drain a 420g can of corn kernels and a 400g can of borlotti beans. Add half the amount from each can and reserve the rest for tomorrow. Season with black pepper.

Preheat the oven to 180°C/350°F/Gas Mark 4. In a large bowl, combine ½ cup (75g) of self-raising flour with ½ cup (75g) of wholemeal self-raising flour and a pinch of salt. Whisk together ⅓ cup (80ml) of canola oil with 5 eggs. Add the egg mixture to the flour, mixing well to make a batter. Finally, stir in the vegetables. Pour into a greased 23 x 13cm loaf tin and bake in the oven for 45 minutes, until golden and firm.

Leave to cool before removing from the tin. Slice into 6. Allow 1 slice per person for tomorrow's lunch. The rest can be placed in freezer bags and frozen for another day.

Divide ½ a can of peach slices between 2 containers. Store the remaining peach slices in a container for later in the week.

Place everything into the fridge until needed.

Monday

Make the bean wraps. Lay out 2 flour tortillas on your work surface. Spread 50g of cream cheese over the tortillas.

In a bowl combine the remaining borlotti beans with the corn kernels, mashing them slightly. Add a chopped tomato, a chopped avocado, 1 tablespoon of lime juice and 1 tablespoon of chopped coriander. Mix together, season to taste, then divide between the 2 tortillas. Roll up, cut in half then cover in plastic wrap. Refrigerate until tomorrow.

Core and dice a pear and divide it between 2 containers. Crumble 50g of blue cheese over the pear and finish with a drizzle of honey. Pop the containers into the fridge.

Tuesday

Make the fruity couscous salad. Place ½ cup (100g) of couscous in a bowl. Stir in ½ cup (125ml) of boiling water and leave to stand for 3 minutes. Fluff it up with a fork.

In a bowl mix together 90g of cubed feta cheese, ½ a red capsicum (diced), ½ a red onion (diced) and a handful each of dates and dried apricots (both chopped). Add a handful of toasted cashews and 2 tablespoons each of chopped coriander and mint. Finally, stir in the couscous. Store the remaining capsicum and red onion in the fridge.

Make the dressing by mixing together 2 tablespoons of extra virgin olive oil, 1 tablespoon of lemon juice, 1 teaspoon of Dijon mustard and some salt and pepper. Mix the dressing into the couscous salad. Divide between 2 containers, then refrigerate until tomorrow.

Slice a grapefruit in half, sprinkle some sugar on each half if desired, then cover each half in plastic wrap. Refrigerate.

Wednesday

Prepare the feta and vegetable wraps. In a bowl mix together 90g of cubed feta, ½ a chopped red onion and ½ a chopped red capsicum. Add a diced tomato and a tablespoon of chopped mint. Season with plenty of black pepper. Divide the mixture between 2 flour tortillas. Roll up, slice in half then cover in plastic wrap. Refrigerate.

Divide the remaining peach slices between 2 containers, then pop them into the fridge.

Thursday

Prepare your snacks for dipping. Slice 200g of tempeh into dipping-sized sticks. Heat 1 tablespoon of olive oil in a frying pan over a medium heat. Fry the tempeh on each side until golden, about 5 minutes in total. Remove from the pan and leave to cool. Divide between 2 containers. Slice 1 carrot into sticks and add to the containers. Spoon some barbecue sauce into containers for dipping the tempeh and carrots.

Prepare the cheese, crackers and apple. Slice 50g of Cheddar cheese and divide between 2 containers. Allow as many crackers as you need to eat with your cheese. Slice an apple and drizzle with lemon juice to stop the apple from going brown. Add to your containers. Pop everything into the fridge.

Mix together a handful of dried cranberries with a handful of almonds per person. Divide between 2 containers.

Saturday

Prepare a tasty ploughman's lunch. Cut some crusty bread or baguette into thick slices. Place on 2 plates. On each plate, add the following: 50g of blue cheese, 50g of Cheddar cheese, ½ an apple, some pickled onions, a dollop of chutney and a serving of butter or margarine. You can slice the cheeses and apple, or present them as a chunk, for you to eat as you wish.

Sunday

Prepare the orange and sultana scones. If you have bought shop-bought sweet scones, you may like to warm them up before serving. Else follow the recipe on p.231. Serve the scones with orange cream, as included in the recipe.

Spring Week 12

A variety of foods this week, starting with an oven-baked omelette – quick and easy. I've also used lentils this week – firstly in a pasta salad and then in some turnovers. The week ends with some Turkish bread. If you cannot find it, ciabatta or focaccia would work just as well.

Monday
Oven-Baked Omelette with Spinach, Capsicum and Basil / Orange

Tuesday
Wholegrain Roll Filled with Goat's Cheese, Basil, Chargrilled Capsicum and Tomato / Apple

Wednesday
Pasta Salad with Onion, Spinach, Lentils and Capsicum with a Sun-Dried Tomato Dressing
V / Dried Apricots and Almonds

Thursday
Goat's Cheese Turnovers with Onion, Spinach and Lentils / Banana

Friday
Potato, Bean and Leek Pancakes with Salsa and Sour Cream / Orange

Saturday
Potato Wedges with Salsa, Avocado and Sour Cream

Sunday
Roasted Olives and Halloumi with Cherry Tomatoes and Turkish Bread

Don't worry about using fresh lemons and limes when needed – bottled juice works just as well. It is worth checking on the bottle for the percentage of juice it contains, as there is quite a lot of variation. The higher the percentage, the better.

shopping list

Fruit and Vegetables
- [ ] 1 red capsicum
- [ ] 1 small bag baby spinach
- [ ] 1 bunch basil
- [ ] 4 oranges
- [ ] 5 tomatoes
- [ ] 2 apples
- [ ] 1 onion
- [ ] 2 bananas
- [ ] 1 green chilli
- [ ] 2 cloves garlic
- [ ] 1 bunch coriander
- [ ] 2 medium potatoes
- [ ] 1 avocado
- [ ] 100g cherry tomatoes

Fridge
- [ ] 4 eggs
- [ ] 160ml milk
- [ ] 120g goat's cheese
- [ ] small tub sour cream
- [ ] 180g halloumi cheese

Freezer
- [ ] 1 sheet puff pastry
- [ ] 4-6 potato, bean and leek pancakes

Bakery
- [ ] 2 wholegrain rolls
- [ ] 1 Turkish bread

Pantry
- [ ] onion powder
- [ ] chargrilled capsicum
- [ ] 100g dried pasta
- [ ] 400g can lentils
- [ ] sun-dried tomatoes
- [ ] red wine vinegar
- [ ] dried apricots
- [ ] almonds
- [ ] dried chilli flakes
- [ ] lime juice
- [ ] balsamic vinegar
- [ ] dried rosemary
- [ ] capers
- [ ] lemon juice
- [ ] 160g olives

Staples
- [ ] salt
- [ ] black pepper
- [ ] olive oil
- [ ] extra virgin olive oil
- [ ] canola oil

daily tasks

Sunday

Make the oven-baked omelette. Preheat the oven to 200°C/400°F/Gas Mark 6. Whisk 4 eggs with ⅔ cup (160ml) of milk. Stir in ½ a chopped red capsicum, a handful of coarsely chopped baby spinach, 2 tablespoons of chopped basil and 1 teaspoon of onion powder. Season with black pepper. Pour into a 22 x 16cm approx. greased ovenproof dish. Bake for 30 minutes, until golden and firm. Leave to cool before removing from the dish. Slice into 4 and divide between 2 lunch boxes. Refrigerate.

Monday

Prepare the rolls. Divide the following between 2 large wholegrain rolls: 60g of crumbled goat's cheese, a spoonful of chargrilled capsicum, 1 sliced tomato and a few basil leaves. Season to taste. Cover in plastic wrap then refrigerate until tomorrow.

Tuesday

Make the pasta salad. Cook 100g of dried pasta according to packet instructions. Once cooked, drain then rinse under cold water. Drain thoroughly and place in a bowl. Add the remaining red capsicum, chopped.

Whilst the pasta is cooking, heat 1 tablespoon of olive oil in a frying pan over a medium heat. Add a chopped onion and fry for 5 minutes, until soft. Remove from the heat and add the remaining baby spinach (coarsely chopped) and a 400g can of rinsed and drained lentils. Spoon half the mixture into the cooked pasta, and place the rest in a container. Place the container in the fridge, once it is cool.

Make the dressing. In a food processor blitz up 2 whole sun-dried tomatoes. Then add 1 tablespoon of extra virgin olive oil, ½ tablespoon of red wine vinegar, 1 tablespoon of chopped basil and some seasoning. Mix well. Stir the dressing into the pasta. Divide the pasta salad between 2 lunch boxes, then refrigerate until tomorrow.

Mix 2 handfuls of dried apricots with 2 handfuls of almonds and divide between 2 containers.

Wednesday

Prepare the goat's cheese turnovers. Preheat the oven to 220°C/425°F/Gas Mark 7. Thaw a sheet of puff pastry then cut it into 4 squares. Get the onion and lentil mixture out of the fridge and stir in ½ teaspoon of dried chilli flakes. Add a spoonful of the mixture onto each pastry square. Top with 60g of crumbled goat's cheese. Fold the pastry in half to form a triangle, then press the edges with a fork to seal. Prick the tops with a fork. Place on a baking tray and bake for 20 minutes until golden. Leave to cool than place in your lunch containers. Refrigerate until tomorrow.

Thursday

Prepare the potato, bean and leek pancakes. You may have some in the freezer. If so, thaw 2-3 per person overnight in the fridge. If not, follow the instructions below. Remember to add the ingredients needed to your shopping list.

Heat 1 tablespoon of olive oil in a frying pan over a medium heat. Add a chopped leek and fry for about 6 minutes until soft. Remove from the heat. Make the batter by combining ½ cup (75g) of wholemeal self-raising flour with ½ cup (75g) of self-raising flour and a pinch of salt. Beat together 2 eggs with ¾ cup (180ml) of milk and stir into the flour, mixing well to form a batter. Add the leek, 200g of rinsed and drained butter beans, 400g of canned potatoes (diced) and 1 tablespoon of chopped chives. Heat 2 tablespoons of canola oil in a large frying pan. Add heaped spoonfuls of the batter mix to the pan, flattening down to form pancakes. Cook for 3-4 minutes, turn and cook for another 3 minutes until golden. Drain on paper towel and leave to cool. Put 3 into each lunch box. Pop them into the fridge. You can freeze the rest by placing baking paper between each pancake and pop them into a container then into the freezer.

Prepare the salsa to accompany the pancakes. In a small bowl, mix together 4 seeded and chopped tomatoes, 1 seeded and finely chopped green chilli, 1 clove of crushed garlic, 1 tablespoon of chopped coriander, 2 tablespoons of lime juice and 1 tablespoon of olive oil. Mix well and season to taste with salt and freshly ground black pepper. Put half of the salsa in a container for Saturday. Divide the rest between 2 containers then refrigerate until needed.

To another 2 containers add some dollops of sour cream.

Saturday

Prepare the potato wedges. Preheat the oven to 210°C/410°F/Gas Mark 7. Cut 2 potatoes in half, then cut each half into 4, making 16 wedges in total. Place on a lined baking tray and drizzle with canola oil and season with salt and freshly ground black pepper. Bake in the oven for 25 minutes. Remove from the oven and turn the potatoes. Return to the oven for another 20 minutes, until the wedges are crisp and golden on the outside and tender on the inside.

Serve the wedges with a diced avocado, some sour cream and leftover salsa.

Sunday

Roast the olives and halloumi. Preheat the oven to 200°C/400°F/Gas Mark 6. In a jar or small bowl, mix together 1 tablespoon of olive oil, 1 tablespoon of balsamic vinegar, a clove of crushed garlic and 1 teaspoon each of dried rosemary, chilli flakes and drained capers. Finally, add 3 tablespoons of lemon juice.

Place 1 cup (160g) of your choice of olives and 180g of diced halloumi on a roasting tray. Drizzle the prepared flavourings over the olives and halloumi. Roast in the oven for 25-30 minutes, until the olives begin to wrinkle and the halloumi browns slightly. Spoon into a serving bowl.

In a separate dish place some cherry tomatoes. Finally, slice some Turkish bread into thick strips and serve with the olives, halloumi and tomatoes. You can warm the bread in the oven for 5 minutes.

Spring Week 13

This week we have a modified version of sausage, mash, onion and peas. I've used sweet potato cubes instead of mash and have used the combination in a rice salad and a chickpea salad. Trust me — it works well and tastes great cold!

Monday
Bean, Corn and Capsicum Tart / Banana

Tuesday
Egg and Cannellini Bean Salad / Mango

Wednesday
Brie, Tomato and Rocket Roll / Dried Cranberries and Cashews

Thursday
Sausage, Onion, Potato, Pea and Rice Salad V / Mango

Friday
Chickpea Salad with Sausage, Onion and Potato V / Sultanas and Pecans

Saturday
Savoury Twists with Artichoke Dip

Sunday
Savoury Twists with Baked Brie and Cranberry Sauce

When buying ready-made pastry, make sure it is suitable for vegetarians. Some may contain animal fat. Also, low-fat varieties are available, which are a good option. These are generally made with canola oil rather than butter.

shopping list

Fruit and Vegetables
- [ ] 1 red capsicum
- [ ] 2 tomatoes
- [ ] 2 bananas
- [ ] 1 small bag rocket
- [ ] 1 bag baby spinach
- [ ] 1 large mango
- [ ] 1 large sweet potato (about 600g)
- [ ] 1 onion
- [ ] 1 clove garlic

Fridge
- [ ] 50g mozzarella cheese
- [ ] 100g Cheddar cheese
- [ ] 3 eggs
- [ ] 200g Brie
- [ ] 4 vegetarian sausages
- [ ] 100g Parmesan-style cheese
- [ ] 60ml light thick cream

Freezer
- [ ] 3 sheets puff pastry
- [ ] 30g frozen peas

Bakery
- [ ] 2 wholegrain rolls

Pantry
- [ ] 400g can cannellini beans
- [ ] 420g can corn kernels
- [ ] kalamata olives
- [ ] lemon juice
- [ ] Dijon mustard
- [ ] dried mint flakes
- [ ] dried cranberries
- [ ] cashews
- [ ] 100g brown rice
- [ ] vegetable stock
- [ ] 400g can chickpeas
- [ ] sultanas
- [ ] pecans
- [ ] caraway seeds
- [ ] dried oregano
- [ ] onion powder
- [ ] 275g jar marinated artichoke hearts
- [ ] pine nuts
- [ ] cranberry sauce
- [ ] garlic powder

Staples
- [ ] salt
- [ ] black pepper
- [ ] olive oil
- [ ] extra virgin olive oil
- [ ] canola oil

daily tasks

Sunday

Prepare the bean, corn and capsicum tart. Preheat the oven to 200°C/400°F/Gas Mark 6. Thaw a sheet of puff pastry. In a bowl, combine 1 diced red capsicum, a 400g can of cannellini beans and a 420g can of corn kernels (both rinsed and drained). Place half of the mixture in a container and pop it into the fridge for tomorrow's lunch.

Score a 2cm border around the edge of the pastry with a sharp knife. Spread the bean mixture over the pastry, inside the border. Add 1 sliced tomato and some black pepper. Finally, top with ½ cup (50g) each of grated mozzarella cheese and Cheddar cheese. Bake for 25 minutes until the pastry is golden. Leave to cool, then slice into quarters with a sharp knife. Put 2 pieces into each lunch box, then refrigerate until tomorrow.

Monday

Prepare the egg and cannellini bean salad. Hard boil 2 eggs, drain under cold water and leave to cool. Coarsely chop the egg then add to the capsicum, bean and corn mixture from yesterday. Stir in a handful each of pitted kalamata olives, baby spinach and rocket.

Make the dressing by combining 1 tablespoon of extra virgin olive oil with ½ tablespoon of lemon juice, ½ teaspoon of Dijon mustard and some black pepper. Pour the dressing over the salad and mix well to coat. Divide the salad between 2 lunch boxes then pop them into the fridge until tomorrow.

Prepare the mango. Peel the mango. Slice the flesh away from the stone and cut into chunks. Place half in a container for later in the week and divide the rest between 2 containers. Refrigerate until needed.

Tuesday

Prepare the rolls. Divide the following between 2 wholegrain rolls: 50g of sliced Brie, 1 sliced tomato and a handful of rocket. Season with black pepper and some dried mint flakes. Cover in plastic wrap and refrigerate until tomorrow.

Mix together a handful of dried cranberries with a handful of cashews per person. Divide between 2 containers.

Wednesday

Prepare the sausage, onion, potato, pea and rice salad. Preheat the oven to 200°C/400°F/Gas Mark 6. Peel and cut the sweet potato into bite-size pieces. Place on a roasting tray and drizzle with canola oil. Roast in the oven for 15 minutes. After 15 minutes, stir in 1 sliced onion and 4 vegetarian sausages chopped into bite-size pieces. Continue cooking for another 20 minutes until the sweet potato is tender. Season to taste. Leave to cool. Place half of the mixture into a container and pop it into the fridge.

Meanwhile, cook ½ cup (100g) of brown rice according to packet instructions. You may like to cook the rice in vegetable stock for extra flavour. Once cooked, stir in ¼ cup (30g) of frozen peas. Leave to stand for 3-4 minutes to heat the peas through. Rinse the cooked rice and peas under cold water and drain thoroughly. Place in a bowl. Add the sweet potato, sausages and onions. Divide the salad between 2 lunch boxes and refrigerate until needed.

Divide the remaining mango between 2 containers. Refrigerate until needed.

Thursday

Make up the chickpea salad. Rinse and drain a 400g can of chickpeas. Stir the chickpeas into the remaining sweet potato mixture and add a handful of coarsely chopped baby spinach. Stir in 1 tablespoon of lemon juice. Divide between 2 lunch boxes, then refrigerate.

Mix 2 handfuls of sultanas with 2 handfuls of pecans and divide between 2 containers.

Saturday

Make the savoury twists. Preheat the oven to 220°C/425°F/Gas Mark 7. Thaw 2 sheets of puff pastry. In a small bowl, mix together ½ cup (60g) each of grated Parmesan-style cheese, and grated Cheddar cheese and 1 teaspoon each of caraway seeds, dried oregano, garlic powder and onion powder. Season well with freshly ground black pepper.

Brush beaten egg over 1 sheet of pastry. Sprinkle the cheese mixture onto the pastry, making sure to go to the edges. Place the second sheet of pastry over the mixture, pressing down firmly. You can use a rolling pin for this. Brush the top layer with more of the beaten egg. Cut the pastry into 2cm strips, then cut each strip in half. Taking each end, twist up the pastry and place on 2 lined baking trays. Bake for 15 minutes, until golden and crisp. Let stand for 5 minutes before transferring to a wire rack to cool.

Prepare the accompanying artichoke dip. In a food processor, blend together a 275g jar of drained marinated artichoke hearts, 1 clove of peeled and crushed garlic, 3 tablespoons of lemon juice and 2 tablespoons of pine nuts. Add ¼ cup (60ml) of light thick cream and 2 tablespoons of grated Parmesan-style cheese. Blend until well combined. Add pepper to taste. Serve with the savoury twists, but keep half of the twists for tomorrow's lunch.

Sunday

Bake the Brie to serve with the remaining savoury twists. Preheat the oven to 200°C/400°F/Gas Mark 6. Slice the remaining Brie in half then divide between 2 ramekins. Cover each ramekin with foil and place on a baking tray. Bake for 20 minutes, until soft. Top with some cranberry sauce then enjoy with savoury twists. You can warm the savoury twists in the oven for about 4 minutes.

almonds apricot artichoke avocado
banana bean beetroot blackberries blue cheese
blueberries brie capers capsicum
carrot cashews cheese
cherries cherry tomatoes chickpea corn
couscous cranberry cream crispbread dip egg

summer

lentil lettuce macadamias melon minty mozzarella olive
onion pasta pavlova pea peach pineapple pita plum
potato radish roasted vegetable roll
salad spinach spring onions
strawberries tofu tomato
tostada turnovers vegetable watermelon wrap

Summer Week 1

Welcome to summer! This week I thought I would do what I did in the first week of spring and make lunches using roasted vegetables. The mixture will last four days, just remember to pop the remaining veg back in the fridge each day after using.

Monday
Roasted Vegetable Pasta Salad V / Apricots

Tuesday
Roasted Vegetable Wrap with Cheese and a Spicy Mayonnaise / Strawberries

Wednesday
Roasted Vegetable Turnovers V / Honeydew Melon

Thursday
Roasted Vegetable Frittata / Strawberries

Friday
Mozzarella, Tomato, Avocado and Basil Roll / Apricot, Strawberry and Melon Smoothie

Saturday
Burger with Onion, Beetroot, Pineapple and More V

Sunday
Bagels with Cream Cheese

"The most remarkable thing about my mother is that for thirty years she served the family nothing but leftovers. The original meal has never been found." Calvin Trillin

shopping list

Fruit and Vegetables
- [ ] 2 onions
- [ ] 1 red capsicum
- [ ] 1 zucchini
- [ ] 1 bunch asparagus
- [ ] 1 head broccoli
- [ ] 1 clove garlic
- [ ] 1 bunch basil
- [ ] 4 apricots
- [ ] 1 punnet strawberries
- [ ] 1 honeydew melon
- [ ] 1 avocado
- [ ] 1 tomato
- [ ] 1 lettuce

Fridge
- [ ] mayonnaise
- [ ] 50g Cheddar cheese
- [ ] 4 eggs
- [ ] 100g mozzarella cheese
- [ ] 200g natural yogurt
- [ ] 2 vegetarian burgers
- [ ] small tub cream cheese

Freezer
- [ ] 1 sheet puff pastry

Bakery
- [ ] 2 wholegrain rolls
- [ ] 2 burger rolls
- [ ] 2 bagels (or recipe)

Pantry
- [ ] 400g can cannellini beans
- [ ] 100g dried pasta
- [ ] lemon juice
- [ ] dried oregano
- [ ] smoked paprika
- [ ] onion powder
- [ ] dried chilli flakes
- [ ] 2 wholegrain flour tortillas
- [ ] 225g can sliced pineapple
- [ ] 225g can sliced beetroot
- [ ] gherkins
- [ ] tomato ketchup

Staples
- [ ] salt
- [ ] black pepper
- [ ] olive oil
- [ ] extra virgin olive oil
- [ ] canola oil

daily tasks

Sunday

Prepare the roasted vegetables. Chop 1 onion, 1 red capsicum, 1 zucchini and a bunch of asparagus into bite-size pieces. Cut the broccoli into small florets. Place the vegetables into a roasting tray and drizzle with canola oil. Roast for 40 minutes in an oven preheated to 210°C/410°F/Gas Mark 7. Give the vegetables a turn after 20 minutes. Remove from the oven, then leave to cool. Stir in a 400g can of rinsed and drained cannellini beans. Spoon a quarter of the vegetables into a bowl and put the rest into a container. Put the container in the fridge.

Make up 100g of pasta according to the instructions on the packet. Drain then rinse the pasta under cold water. Add it to the bowl of roasted vegetables.

To make the herb dressing, whisk together 1 tablespoon of extra virgin olive oil, ½ tablespoon of lemon juice, 1 clove of peeled and crushed garlic, 1 tablespoon of chopped basil and ½ teaspoon of dried oregano. Season to taste. Pour the dressing over the pasta salad and mix well to coat. Divide the pasta salad between 2 lunch boxes. Refrigerate until tomorrow.

Monday

Make the roasted vegetable wraps. Begin by making a spicy mayonnaise. Mix together 3 tablespoons of mayonnaise with ½ teaspoon of smoked paprika, ½ teaspoon of onion powder and ½ teaspoon of dried chilli flakes. Spread the mayonnaise over 2 wholegrain flour tortillas. Grate ½ cup (50g) of Cheddar cheese and sprinkle over the mayonnaise. Top with some of the roasted vegetables. Fold in the sides, then roll up. Cut each wrap in half then cover in plastic wrap. Refrigerate until tomorrow. Any remaining flour tortillas can be frozen.

Place some strawberries into 2 containers.

Tuesday

Make the roasted vegetable turnovers. Preheat the oven to 220°C/425°F/Gas Mark 7. Thaw a sheet of puff pastry then cut it into 4 squares. Add a spoonful of the roasted vegetables to each pastry square. Fold the pastry in half to form a triangle, then press the edges with a fork to seal. Prick the tops with a fork.

Place on a baking tray and bake for 20 minutes until golden. Leave to cool than place in your lunch boxes. Refrigerate until tomorrow.

Cut the honeydew melon in half. Scoop out the seeds and use a melon baller if you have one to scoop out rounds of melon from one half. Alternatively, use a sharp knife to cut squares in the melon half, then scoop out using a metal spoon. Divide between 2 containers. Pop them into the fridge with the remaining melon.

Wednesday

Make the roasted vegetable frittata. Beat together 4 eggs. Add ½ teaspoon of smoked paprika, 1 tablespoon of chopped basil and some seasoning. Heat a 24cm frying pan over a medium heat. Add the remaining roasted vegetable mix and stir to warm up slightly. Add the eggs and 50g of cubed mozzarella cheese, then turn the heat down. Let cook for 8-10 minutes.

Preheat the grill. Once the eggs are nearly set, place the pan under the grill to finish cooking the top. Slide the frittata off the pan then leave to cool. Slice into quarters and place 2 quarters into each lunch box. Refrigerate until tomorrow.

Divide some strawberries between 2 containers.

Thursday

Prepare the wholegrain rolls. Divide the following between 2 rolls: 1 mashed avocado (stir in some lemon juice), 50g of sliced mozzarella cheese, 1 sliced tomato and a few basil leaves. Season to taste with salt and pepper. Cover in plastic wrap, then refrigerate until needed.

Make the smoothies. In a blender add 2 apricots, any remaining strawberries and the rest of the melon (chopped). Add a 200g tub of natural yogurt. Blend until smooth. Divide between 2 x 500ml thermos flasks, then refrigerate until tomorrow.

Saturday

Prepare the burgers. Hopefully it is warm enough outside to cook on the barbecue. If so, grill the burgers, 1 sliced onion (drizzled with olive oil) and 2 slices of pineapple on the barbecue. Else do the following:

Cook the burgers according to packet instructions. Fry the onions in 1 tablespoon of olive oil over a medium heat. You can grill the pineapple or leave them as they are.

Put together the burgers. To each burger roll add a burger, some onions, a pineapple ring and some sliced beetroot. Add some gherkins, lettuce and tomato ketchup.

Sunday

Make a batch of bagels, following the recipe on p.222. If you have any in the freezer, thaw at room temperature. If you are using frozen dough, take the dough from the freezer and pop it into an oiled bowl and cover with plastic wrap. Leave for a few hours to thaw. Times will depend on the warmth of your kitchen. Then follow the recipe from point 2 (dividing the dough into 6 not 12).

If you have bought bagels from the shops, warm in the oven, then serve. Enjoy bagels with cream cheese.

Summer Week 2

This week's menu is inspired by a recent trip to New Zealand. Or rather, by some of the foods I ate whilst there. Of course it features sweet potato (known as kumara to Kiwis), beetroot and pavlova.

Monday
Black Bean Burritos / Pineapple Chunks

Tuesday
Polenta Fingers with Black Bean Dip / Peanuts and Sultanas

Wednesday
Sweet Potato Salad with Baby Beetroot, Mushrooms and Chickpeas V / Kiwifruit

Thursday
Summer Pasta Salad V / Pineapple Chunks

Friday
Sweet Potato and Mushroom Fritters with Baby Beetroot and Cherry Tomatoes / Cherries

Saturday
Sausage, Cranberry, Stuffing and Camembert Tostada / Cheat's Pavlova with Strawberries

Sunday
Lemon and Chive Potato Wedges with Aioli / Lettuce, Tomato and Watercress Salad V / Cheat's Pavlova with Strawberries

As a vegetarian it can be a challenge finding something to eat when you are travelling. Fortunately, most restaurants publish their menus on the internet now, so a bit of research beforehand can make your trip that much more enjoyable.

shopping list

Fruit and Vegetables
- [ ] 2 onions
- [ ] 1 green capsicum
- [ ] 1 avocado
- [ ] 1 sweet potato
- [ ] 200g mushrooms
- [ ] 1 bunch basil
- [ ] 1 clove garlic
- [ ] 2 kiwifruit
- [ ] 1 carrot
- [ ] 1 bunch watercress
- [ ] 200g cherry tomatoes
- [ ] 2 handfuls cherries
- [ ] 1 punnet strawberries
- [ ] 2 potatoes

Fridge
- [ ] 50g Cheddar cheese
- [ ] butter
- [ ] 15g Parmesan-style cheese
- [ ] 2 eggs
- [ ] 180ml milk
- [ ] 4 vegetarian sausages
- [ ] 100g Camembert
- [ ] 300ml whipping cream
- [ ] aioli

Pantry
- [ ] 100g brown rice
- [ ] 400g can black beans
- [ ] 4 large flour tortillas
- [ ] 1 jar salsa
- [ ] 440g can pineapple chunks in juice
- [ ] vegetable stock
- [ ] 225g polenta (cornmeal)
- [ ] unsalted peanuts
- [ ] sultanas
- [ ] whole nutmeg
- [ ] 450g can baby beetroot
- [ ] 400g can chickpeas
- [ ] lemon juice
- [ ] Dijon mustard
- [ ] 100g dried pasta
- [ ] 200g can peas and corn kernels
- [ ] 75g wholemeal self-raising flour
- [ ] 75g self-raising flour
- [ ] stuffing mix
- [ ] cranberry sauce
- [ ] 4 meringues
- [ ] dried chives

Staples
- [ ] salt
- [ ] black pepper
- [ ] olive oil
- [ ] extra virgin olive oil
- [ ] canola oil

daily tasks

Sunday

Prepare the burritos. Cook ½ cup (100g) of brown rice according to packet directions. Once cooked, tip into a sieve and run under cold water to cool. Meanwhile, heat 1 tablespoon of olive oil in a frying pan. Add a sliced onion and cook for 4 minutes. Add ½ a chopped green capsicum and cook for another 4 minutes. Remove from the heat and leave to cool. Place in a bowl along with a 400g can of rinsed and drained black beans.

Divide the rice between 2 large flour tortillas. Top with half of the black bean mixture. Put the rest of the bean mixture in a container in the fridge for tomorrow. Add a diced avocado, ½ cup (50g) of grated Cheddar cheese and a good spoonful of salsa. Fold in the sides, roll up, and then cover in plastic wrap. Refrigerate until needed.

Divide ½ a can of pineapple chunks between 2 containers and put the rest in another container for later in the week.

Monday

Cook the polenta fingers. Bring 3⅔ cups (900ml) of vegetable stock to the boil in a medium saucepan. Once boiling, gradually add 1½ cups (225g) of polenta, stirring constantly with a wooden spoon. Reduce the heat and continue stirring until the polenta has thickened and is coming away from the side of the saucepan. Remove from the heat and stir in 1 tablespoon of butter and 2 tablespoons of grated Parmesan-style cheese. Season.

Tip the mixture into a 30 x 20cm oiled baking tin and spread the mixture evenly. Leave to cool then place in the fridge for a few hours to firm up.

Preheat the grill. Remove the polenta from the tin and slice in half. Wrap half in plastic wrap and pop it into the freezer for another time. Slice the remaining polenta into 8 fingers. Brush with olive oil and place on a wire grill tray. Grill for about 6 minutes on each side until golden and crisp. Leave to cool then place in your lunch boxes.

Make the black bean dip. In a food processor, blitz up the remaining beans, capsicum and onion with

the remaining jar of salsa. Divide between 2 containers to serve with the polenta fingers. Refrigerate, along with the polenta.

Mix 2 handfuls of unsalted peanuts with 2 handfuls of sultanas and divide between 2 containers.

Tuesday

Make the sweet potato and baby beet salad. Preheat the oven to 200°C/400°F/Gas Mark 6. Peel and cut the sweet potato into bite-size pieces. Place on a roasting tray and drizzle with canola oil. Roast in the oven for 15 minutes. After 15 minutes, stir in 1 sliced onion and 200g of sliced mushrooms. Cook for another 20 minutes. Season to taste and grate some nutmeg over the vegetables.

Leave to cool, then place half in a container (refrigerate) and half in a bowl. To the bowl add ½ a 450g can of baby beetroot. Put the remaining beetroot in a container and then into the fridge. Add a 400g can of rinsed and drained chickpeas and stir through a handful of basil leaves.

Make the dressing by mixing together 1 tablespoon of extra virgin olive oil, ½ tablespoon of lemon juice, 1 clove of crushed garlic and ½ teaspoon of Dijon mustard. Pour the dressing over the salad. Divide the salad between 2 lunch boxes, then refrigerate until needed.

Cut the 2 kiwifruit in half then wrap them both in plastic wrap. Remember a spoon for scooping out the flesh.

Wednesday

Prepare the summer pasta salad. Cook 100g of dried pasta according to packet instructions. Drain, then rinse under cold water. Drain thoroughly, then place in a bowl. To the pasta add a 200g can of peas and corn kernels (drained), a grated carrot and the remaining green capsicum, diced. Chop up a handful of watercress and add this to the bowl along with 2 tablespoons of chopped basil. Season. Divide the pasta salad between 2 lunch boxes, then refrigerate until needed.

Divide the remaining pineapple chunks between 2 containers, then pop them into the fridge.

Thursday

Prepare the sweet potato fritters. Make the batter by combining ½ cup (75g) of wholemeal self-raising flour with ½ cup (75g) of self-raising flour and a pinch of salt. Beat together 2 eggs with ¾ cup (180ml) of milk and stir into the flour, mixing well to form a batter. Stir in the leftover sweet potato, mushroom and onion mixture.

Heat 2 tablespoons of canola oil in a large frying pan. Add heaped spoonfuls of the batter mix to the pan, flattening down to form fritters. Cook for 3-4 minutes, turn, then cook for another 3 minutes until golden. Drain on paper towel and leave to cool. Put 3 into each lunch box and refrigerate. You can freeze the rest by placing baking paper between each fritter and pop them into a container then into the freezer.

Serve the fritters with the remaining baby beetroot (cut in half if you prefer) and a handful of cherry tomatoes, divided between 2 containers. Refrigerate.

Divide the cherries between 2 containers.

Saturday

Make the tostadas. Begin by making up the stuffing mix according to packet instructions. You may only need half the packet, so adjust the quantities of water as necessary. Once cool enough to handle, roll the stuffing into balls. Heat 1 tablespoon of olive oil in a frying pan. Add 4 vegetarian sausages and cook until browned, turning often. Remove from the heat and chop into bite-size pieces.

Preheat the grill. Take 2 flour tortillas and spread some cranberry sauce over each. Top with the stuffing balls and sausages. Finally, add 100g of sliced Camembert and some black pepper. Pop under the grill and grill for 1-2 minutes, until the cheese starts to melt. Cut into quarters, then serve.

Put together a quick pavlova. Beat 150ml of whipping cream until thick. Spoon the cream over 2 meringues then top with half of the strawberries, hulled and halved. Serve.

Sunday

Make the lemon and chive potato wedges. Preheat the oven to 210°C/410°F/Gas Mark 7. Cut 2 potatoes in half, then each half into quarters, making 16 in total. Pop them into a bowl. Mix together 2 tablespoons of olive oil with 2 tablespoons of lemon juice, 1 teaspoon of dried chives and some salt and pepper. Pour the mixture over the wedges and mix well to coat. Place the wedges on a baking tray. Bake in the oven for 25 minutes. Remove from the oven and turn the potatoes. Return to the oven for another 20 minutes, until the wedges are crisp and golden on the outside and tender on the inside. Serve with aioli.

Make up an accompanying salad by mixing together the remaining watercress and cherry tomatoes with some lettuce. Drizzle with extra virgin olive oil and season to taste.

Make a pavlova with the remaining cream, strawberries and meringues. Whip the cream until thick then spoon the cream over 2 meringues. Top with the remaining strawberries, hulled and halved.

Summer Week 3

This week we're making the most of foods coming into season. We will be using radishes, zucchini, capsicum as well as fresh peaches, watermelon and blueberries. No need for canned fruit at this time of year!

Monday
Beetroot Spread on Crispbread with Cherry Tomatoes / Peaches

Tuesday
Two-Tomato Pasta Salad V / Watermelon

Wednesday
Beetroot Dip with Carrot, Capsicum, Radish and Celery / Hard Boiled Egg / Cashews and Blueberries

Thursday
Tofu, Bean Sprout, Capsicum and Carrot Wrap V / Watermelon

Friday
Tofu and Couscous Salad / Walnuts and Blueberries

Saturday
Zucchini and Blue Cheese Quesadilla / Spinach, Lettuce and Radish Salad V

Sunday
Crumpets with Cheese / Butter / Vegemite / All Three

Feel free to interchange grains and pasta as you see fit. Pasta, couscous, rice, bulghar wheat, quinoa or your favourite can be easily swapped for my menu ideas.

shopping list

Fruit and Vegetables
- [ ] 250g cherry tomatoes
- [ ] 2 peaches
- [ ] 1 small bag baby spinach
- [ ] 1 bunch basil
- [ ] 2 cloves garlic
- [ ] ¼ watermelon
- [ ] 2 carrots
- [ ] 1 celery stick
- [ ] 1 capsicum
- [ ] 1 bunch radishes
- [ ] 1 punnet blueberries
- [ ] 50g bean sprouts
- [ ] 1 bag mixed lettuce
- [ ] 1 bunch spring onions
- [ ] ginger
- [ ] 1 zucchini

Fridge
- [ ] 100g blue cheese
- [ ] 2 eggs
- [ ] 200g marinated tofu
- [ ] 50g Cheddar cheese

Bakery
- [ ] 4 crumpets

Pantry
- [ ] 450g can sliced beetroot
- [ ] 400g can cannellini beans
- [ ] horseradish sauce
- [ ] 8 crispbread
- [ ] 100g dried pasta
- [ ] sun-dried tomatoes
- [ ] capers
- [ ] black olives
- [ ] pine nuts
- [ ] balsamic vinegar
- [ ] cashews
- [ ] 6 wholegrain flour tortillas
- [ ] sweet chilli sauce
- [ ] 100g couscous
- [ ] lime juice
- [ ] soy sauce
- [ ] honey
- [ ] walnuts
- [ ] Vegemite / Marmite

Staples
- [ ] salt
- [ ] black pepper
- [ ] olive oil
- [ ] extra virgin olive oil
- [ ] canola oil

daily tasks

Sunday

Prepare the beetroot spread. Tip a 450g can of drained beetroot into a food processor. Process until the beetroot is thoroughly chopped. Add a 400g can of rinsed and drained cannellini beans, 1 tablespoon of horseradish sauce, 2 tablespoons of blue cheese and a good grind of black pepper. Process until the mixture is smooth. Put half into a container then divide the rest between 2 lunch boxes. Refrigerate until needed.

Add about 4 crispbread to each lunch box and a handful of cherry tomatoes.

Monday

Prepare the two-tomato pasta salad. Cook 100g of pasta according to packet instructions. Drain, then rinse under cold water. Drain thoroughly and place in a bowl. Add the remaining cherry tomatoes, cut in half if you prefer. Add 3 tablespoons of chopped sun-dried tomatoes, a handful each of coarsely chopped baby spinach and basil, ½ tablespoon of rinsed and drained capers and 2 tablespoons of black olives. Toast 1 tablespoon of pine nuts and stir into the rest of the ingredients.

Make a dressing by mixing together 1 tablespoon of extra virgin olive oil, ½ tablespoon of balsamic vinegar, 1 clove of peeled and crushed garlic and some seasoning. Add to the salad. Divide the salad between 2 lunch boxes and pop them into the fridge.

Prepare the watermelon. Cut the melon in half and put half in the fridge for later in the week. Slice the remaining into bite-size pieces, and divide between 2 containers. If you prefer, cut into 2 slices and cover in plastic wrap. Refrigerate.

Tuesday

For the beetroot dip, simply divide the remaining beetroot spread between 2 containers. It can now be used as a dip!

Prepare the vegetables for dipping. Slice 1 carrot, the celery stick and ½ a capsicum into sticks. Keep the remaining capsicum for another day. Divide between 2 containers and add some radishes (roots removed).

Hard boil 2 eggs. Place them into a saucepan of cold water. Turn the heat to high then leave to cook for 20 minutes. Rinse and drain under cold water, then leave to cool. Add to your lunch boxes and refrigerate.

Mix 2 handfuls of cashews with ½ a punnet of blueberries and divide between containers.

Wednesday

Prepare the tofu wraps. Cut the pack of marinated tofu in half. Wrap half in plastic wrap and put it back in the fridge. Dice the tofu and place in a bowl with a handful of bean sprouts, the remaining capsicum (diced), some shredded lettuce and a grated carrot. Mix together than divide between 2 wholegrain flour tortillas. Add a drizzle of sweet chilli sauce. Fold in the sides, roll up and cover in plastic wrap. Refrigerate.

Chop up the remaining watermelon and divide between 2 containers. Or cut into 2 slices if you prefer. Refrigerate until needed.

Thursday

Make the tofu and couscous salad. Place ½ cup (100g) of couscous in a bowl. Stir in ½ cup (125ml) of boiling water and leave to stand for 3 minutes. Fluff it up with a fork. Stir in the remaining tofu (diced), the rest of the bean sprouts, 2 sliced radishes, a handful of coarsely chopped baby spinach and 3 chopped spring onions.

Make the dressing. Mix together 1 tablespoon of canola oil, ½ tablespoon of lime juice, ½ tablespoon of soy sauce, 1 teaspoon of honey, 1 clove of peeled and crushed garlic and 1 teaspoon of grated fresh ginger. Pour the dressing over the salad and mix to coat the ingredients. Divide the salad between 2 lunch boxes and pop them into the fridge.

Mix 2 handfuls of walnuts with the remaining blueberries and divide between 2 containers.

Saturday

Prepare the quesadillas. If you can, cook these on the barbecue. Slice 1 zucchini, coat in some olive oil then cook on the barbecue until soft and starting to brown. Distribute the zucchini over 2 wholegrain flour tortillas. Divide the remaining spring onions (chopped) between the 2 tortillas. Crumble 60g of blue cheese over the 2 tortillas and top each with another tortilla. Press down firmly. You may find it easier to cut them in half before cooking. Place on the barbecue and cook for a minute or 2, turn and cook for another minute. Cut into quarters.

If you are not using the barbecue, heat 1 tablespoon of olive oil in a frying pan. Add the zucchini and cook for 5 minutes until soft. Distribute the zucchini over 2 wholegrain flour tortillas. Divide the remaining spring onions (chopped) between the 2 tortillas. Crumble 60g of blue cheese over the tortillas and top with another tortilla. Press down firmly. You may find it easier to cut them in half before cooking. Heat a clean frying pan or griddle. Spray with olive oil then add the tortillas, cooking one at a time. Cook for 2-3 minutes on each side, until brown. Cut into quarters.

Make the accompanying salad. Simply mix together any remaining baby spinach and radishes (sliced), with the mixed lettuce and some basil leaves. Make a simple dressing by mixing up 1 tablespoon of extra virgin olive oil with ½ tablespoon of balsamic vinegar. Drizzle the dressing over the salad and serve with the quesadillas.

Sunday

Prepare the crumpets. Toast 4 crumpets either under the grill or in a toaster, cooked to your liking. Top with either butter, cheese, Vegemite or a combination of all three.

Summer Week 4

If you live in Australia, it's now the Christmas break. This week's menu reflects the typical lunches I enjoy at this time. In particular, we always like to get some Wensleydale cheese in and use it in salads. Sunday features my favourite picnic lunch — so quick to prepare.

Monday
Wensleydale and Tomato Tart / Macadamias

Tuesday
Cheese and Biscuits with Antipasti / Cherries

Wednesday
Mango Salad with Cannellini Beans and Cranberries V / Almonds

Thursday
Wensleydale Salad / Cherries

Friday
Potato Salad with Cannellini Beans and Spinach V / Strawberries

Saturday
Balsamic Glaze Roasted Vegetable Salad V / Strawberries

Sunday
Baguette, Cheese, Grapes and Muscatels

When making your meals, an easy way to make them more filling is to add a can of beans. You can choose your favourite, depending on what you are cooking, although butter beans and cannellini beans work well in most dishes.

shopping list

Fruit and Vegetables
- [ ] 2 tomatoes
- [ ] 1 bunch parsley
- [ ] 4 handfuls cherries
- [ ] 1 mango
- [ ] 1 bunch mint
- [ ] 1 lettuce
- [ ] 6 baby potatoes
- [ ] 1 bunch spring onions
- [ ] 1 small bag baby spinach
- [ ] 1 punnet strawberries
- [ ] 1 sweet potato
- [ ] 1 red capsicum
- [ ] 1 onion
- [ ] 4 mushrooms
- [ ] 1 small bunch grapes

Fridge
- [ ] 150g Wensleydale cheese
- [ ] 150g Cheddar cheese
- [ ] 125ml orange juice
- [ ] 50g blue cheese

Freezer
- [ ] 1 sheet puff pastry

Bakery
- [ ] 1 baguette

Pantry
- [ ] macadamias
- [ ] biscuits for cheese
- [ ] olives
- [ ] sun-dried tomatoes
- [ ] stuffed Peppadew
- [ ] 60g dried cranberries
- [ ] 400g can cannellini beans
- [ ] pine nuts
- [ ] almonds
- [ ] lemon juice
- [ ] Dijon mustard
- [ ] balsamic vinegar
- [ ] brown sugar
- [ ] muscatels (or dried figs)

Staples
- [ ] salt
- [ ] black pepper
- [ ] olive oil
- [ ] extra virgin olive oil

daily tasks

Sunday

Make the Wensleydale and tomato tart. Thaw a sheet of puff pastry and place it on a baking tray. Score a 2cm border around the edges with a sharp knife. Next, crumble 50g of Wensleydale cheese over the pastry. Slice 2 tomatoes and layer them over the cheese, within the border. Add 2 tablespoons of chopped parsley, season and drizzle with olive oil. Bake in a preheated oven at 200°C/400°F/Gas Mark 6 for 25 minutes until the pastry is golden. Leave to cool, then slice into quarters with a sharp knife. Put 2 pieces into each lunch box, then refrigerate until tomorrow.

Divide 2 handfuls of macadamias between 2 containers.

Monday

Prepare your cheese and biscuits lunch. Slice 50g of Wensleydale cheese and 50g of Cheddar cheese and divide between 2 lunch boxes. To the boxes, add some biscuits for cheese, according to appetite. Place in the fridge.

In 2 separate containers, make up your antipasti mix. To each container add some olives, sun-dried tomatoes and stuffed Peppadew. Refrigerate until tomorrow.

Divide half the cherries between 2 containers.

Tuesday

Prepare the mango salad. Begin by soaking ½ cup (60g) of dried cranberries in ½ cup (125ml) of orange juice. Whilst they are soaking, prepare the mango. Peel, remove the stone then slice into bite-size pieces. Place in a bowl. Rinse and drain a 400g can of cannellini beans. Place half in the bowl and put the remaining in a container in the fridge for another day. To the bowl add 2 tablespoons of toasted pine nuts and 2 tablespoons of chopped mint.

Use a slotted spoon to drain half of the cranberries from the orange juice and stir them into the bowl. The rest of the cranberries can be left in the orange juice (cover in plastic wrap and pop them into the fridge). Layer some lettuce at the bottom of 2 lunch boxes, then divide the mango salad between the 2 boxes. Refrigerate until needed.

Divide 2 handfuls of almonds between 2 containers.

Wednesday

Make up the Wensleydale salad. Crumble 50g of Wensleydale cheese into a bowl. Add the remaining cranberries that were soaking in the orange juice (drain them first). Add 2 tablespoons of toasted pine nuts, a large handful of shredded lettuce and 2 tablespoons of chopped parsley. Divide between 2 lunch boxes. Refrigerate.

Divide the remaining cherries between 2 containers.

Thursday

Prepare the potato salad. Scrub 6 baby potatoes and cut in half. Add to a pan of salted cold water. Bring to the boil, then simmer for about 15 minutes until tender. Drain well. Place in a bowl. To the bowl add the remaining cannellini beans, a bunch of chopped spring onions, a handful of baby spinach and some shredded lettuce.

Make a dressing by mixing together 1 tablespoon of extra virgin olive oil, ½ tablespoon of lemon juice, 1 teaspoon of Dijon mustard and 1 tablespoon each of chopped parsley and mint. Drizzle the dressing over the salad and mix well to coat. Season to taste. Divide the salad between 2 lunch boxes, then refrigerate until needed.

Divide half of the strawberries between 2 containers.

Saturday

Prepare the balsamic glaze roasted vegetable salad. Preheat the oven to 210°C/410°F/Gas Mark 7. Peel and chop a sweet potato into bite-size pieces. Add to a roasting tray along with a chopped red capsicum, a sliced onion and 4 sliced mushrooms.

In a small bowl or jar mix together 2 tablespoons of olive oil, 1 tablespoon of balsamic vinegar and 1 teaspoon of brown sugar. Drizzle the mixture over the vegetables. Roast for 30 minutes, remove from the oven, turn the vegetables and cook for another 15 minutes until they are tender. Serve the vegetables on a bed of lettuce.

Eat up the remaining strawberries.

Sunday

Put together your picnic. Allow 100g of Cheddar cheese and 50g of blue cheese for 2 people. Cut your baguette into slices, on an angle. Add a small bunch of grapes and some muscatels.

Summer Week 5

This week's menu carries on from last week as we continue to enjoy the summer holidays here in Australia. Enjoy some lovely fruit options and make use of the great standby: par-baked rolls.

Monday
Fig and Blue Cheese Salad / Cashews and Apricot

Tuesday
Fruit Salad with Feta Cheese / Macadamias

Wednesday
Marinated Feta, Beans and Olives with Almonds and Grissini / Grapes

Thursday
Pea Pâté Sandwich with Carrot and Tomato / Melon

Friday
Couscous with Cranberry, Celery and Walnuts V / Banana

Saturday
Pea Pâté with Par-Baked Rolls

Sunday
Par-Baked Rolls with Cheese and Garlic Butter

It is easy to make a salad dressing. Use extra virgin olive oil and half the amount of vinegar or lemon or lime juice. You can add spices and herbs according to your preference. Including such dressings in salads not only adds flavour, but also slows down digestion, keeping you fuller for longer.

shopping list

Fruit and Vegetables
- [ ] 1 bag mixed lettuce
- [ ] 2 apricots
- [ ] handful cherries
- [ ] 2 plums
- [ ] 2 nectarines
- [ ] ½ honeydew melon
- [ ] 1 small bunch grapes
- [ ] 1 bunch mint
- [ ] 1 lemon
- [ ] 1 tomato
- [ ] 1 carrot
- [ ] 1 celery stick
- [ ] 2 bananas

Fridge
- [ ] 50g blue cheese
- [ ] 200g feta cheese
- [ ] 75g cream cheese
- [ ] 50g mozzarella cheese
- [ ] garlic butter

Freezer
- [ ] 1 cup (125g) frozen peas

Bakery
- [ ] 4 slices wholegrain bread
- [ ] 4 par-baked rolls

Pantry
- [ ] dried figs
- [ ] 400g can cannellini beans
- [ ] balsamic vinegar
- [ ] cashews
- [ ] macadamias
- [ ] olives
- [ ] sun-dried tomatoes
- [ ] dried thyme
- [ ] dried rosemary
- [ ] dried oregano
- [ ] grissini (breadsticks)
- [ ] almonds
- [ ] whole nutmeg
- [ ] 100g couscous
- [ ] 30g dried cranberries
- [ ] walnuts
- [ ] red wine vinegar

Staples
- [ ] salt
- [ ] black pepper
- [ ] extra virgin olive oil

daily tasks

Sunday

Prepare the fig and blue cheese salad. Place a handful of lettuce into 2 lunch boxes. Chop a handful of dried figs and sprinkle them over the lettuce. Add 50g of crumbled blue cheese. Rinse and drain a 400g can of cannellini beans. Place half in a container and put it in the fridge. Divide the remaining beans between the 2 lunch boxes.

Mix together 1 tablespoon of extra virgin olive oil with ½ tablespoon of balsamic vinegar, then drizzle the dressing over the salad. Pop the lunch boxes into the fridge until tomorrow.

Place some cashews into 2 containers. Don't forget your apricot.

Monday

Prepare the fruit salad. Divide the cherries between 2 lunch boxes (you can remove the stones first if you like). Remove the stones from 2 plums and 2 nectarines, chop into bite-size pieces and add to the cherries.

Slice the honeydew melon in half. Put half back in the fridge. Remove the seeds from the remaining chunk, then cut the flesh into bite-size pieces. Add to the lunch boxes. Next, add a handful of grapes to each lunch box. Dice 80g of feta cheese and add to the fruit. Finally, chop 2 tablespoons of mint and add to the salad. Refrigerate until needed.

Place some macadamias into 2 containers.

Tuesday

Marinate the feta, beans and olives. Chop 120g of feta cheese into bite-size chunks and place in a bowl. Add the remaining cannellini beans and 2 tablespoons of olives. In a small bowl or jar, mix together 3 tablespoons of extra virgin olive oil, 2 tablespoons of chopped sun-dried tomatoes, the grated rind of a lemon and 1 teaspoon each of dried thyme, rosemary and oregano. Add a good grind of black pepper. Pour the dressing over the feta, beans and olives and mix well. Divide between 2 lunch boxes and refrigerate.

In another 2 containers add some grissini and a handful of almonds per person.

Divide the remaining grapes between 2 additional containers.

Wednesday

Make the pea pâté. Bring a saucepan of water to the boil. Add 1 cup (125g) of frozen peas and cook for 3 minutes. Drain then leave to cool. Tip the peas into a food processor and add 1 tablespoon of chopped mint and a good grating of nutmeg. Blend until the peas are nicely mashed. Add 75g of cream cheese and process until the mixture is well combined and smooth. Season to taste.

Spread some of the pâté over 2 slices of wholegrain bread (the rest can be put into a container and refrigerated). Top with a sliced tomato, a grated carrot and some lettuce. Top each with another slice of bread, cut in half then cover in plastic wrap. Refrigerate.

Dice up the remaining honeydew melon and divide between 2 containers. Refrigerate until needed.

Thursday

Prepare the couscous. Place ½ cup (100g) of couscous in a bowl along with ¼ cup (30g) of dried cranberries. Add ½ cup (125ml) of boiling water, stand for 3 minutes then fluff up with a fork. Chop a celery stick and a handful of walnuts. Add to the couscous.

Mix together 1 tablespoon of extra virgin olive oil with ½ tablespoon of red wine vinegar to make a quick dressing. Stir into the couscous. Divide between 2 lunch boxes then refrigerate until needed.

Saturday

Prepare the par-baked rolls. Bake 2 par-baked rolls in the oven, according to packet instructions. Serve with the remaining pea pâté.

Sunday

Make the garlic and cheese rolls. Cut 2 par-baked rolls in half. Spread some garlic butter on them and add a slice of mozzarella cheese. Put the lids back on and place on a baking tray. Bake as normal, according to packet instructions. Serve warm, with a salad if you like.

Summer Week 6

I thought we'd travel the world a bit this week. We have tabbouleh from the Middle East, a Mexican salad and a Japanese omelette. I hope you enjoy these tasties, along with slices, salads, stuffed pitas and rolls.

Monday
Goat's Cheese, Tomato and Olive Roll / Almonds and Blueberries

Tuesday
Capsicum, Zucchini and Carrot Slice / Nectarine

Wednesday
Tabbouleh V / Cashews and Blueberries

Thursday
Mixed Bean and Tofu Pita V / Plum

Friday
Mexican Salad V / Apricot

Saturday
Green Bean and Lentil Salad V / Strawberries and Cream

Sunday
Japanese Omelette (Tamagoyaki) / Strawberries and Cream

Find the time to have an occasional clear out of your fridge and pantry. Make a note of forgotten ingredients so you can include them in later meals. This is how I came to use the shitake mushrooms in the Japanese omelette.

shopping list

Fruit and Vegetables
- ☐ 4 tomatoes
- ☐ 1 small bag rocket
- ☐ 1 punnet blueberries
- ☐ 1 red capsicum
- ☐ 1 bunch spring onions
- ☐ 2 zucchini
- ☐ 1 carrot
- ☐ 2 nectarines
- ☐ 1 onion
- ☐ 3 cloves garlic
- ☐ 1 bunch parsley
- ☐ 1 bunch mint
- ☐ 2 plums
- ☐ 1 bunch coriander
- ☐ 2 apricots
- ☐ 100g green beans
- ☐ 1 small red onion
- ☐ 1 punnet strawberries

Fridge
- ☐ 120g goat's cheese
- ☐ 8 eggs
- ☐ 125ml milk
- ☐ 200g marinated tofu
- ☐ 150ml light cream

Bakery
- ☐ 2 wholegrain rolls
- ☐ 2 pita breads

Pantry
- ☐ black olives
- ☐ almonds
- ☐ 75g wholemeal self-raising flour
- ☐ 75g self-raising flour
- ☐ 100g bulghar wheat
- ☐ ground cumin
- ☐ lemon juice
- ☐ cashews
- ☐ 400g can mixed beans
- ☐ sweet chilli sauce
- ☐ 100g brown rice
- ☐ ground coriander
- ☐ Tabasco sauce
- ☐ 400g can lentils
- ☐ sun-dried tomatoes
- ☐ soy sauce
- ☐ dried shitake mushrooms

Staples
- ☐ salt
- ☐ black pepper
- ☐ olive oil
- ☐ extra virgin olive oil
- ☐ canola oil

daily tasks

Sunday

Make up the rolls. Divide 60g of goat's cheese and 1 sliced tomato between 2 wholegrain rolls. Add a handful of sliced black olives and a handful of rocket. Cover in plastic wrap and refrigerate.

Mix 2 handfuls of blueberries with 2 handfuls of almonds and divide between 2 containers.

Monday

Prepare the capsicum, zucchini and carrot slice. Preheat the oven to 180°C/350°F/Gas Mark 4. Grease and line a 30 x 20cm baking tin. In a large bowl, whisk together 4 eggs and ½ cup (125ml) of milk. Beat in ½ cup (75g) of wholemeal self-raising flour and ½ cup (75g) of regular self-raising flour to make a batter.

Dice ½ a red capsicum and ½ a bunch of spring onions. Grate 1 zucchini and 1 carrot. Add the vegetables to the batter along with 60g of crumbled goat's cheese. Season. Pour into the baking tin and bake for 30 minutes until golden brown and firm.

Leave to cool and remove from the tin. Slice into quarters, then halve each quarter. Place 2 slices into each lunch box and refrigerate. The rest can be frozen by wrapping each slice in plastic wrap then placing into a container or freezer bag, then into the freezer.

Tuesday

Make the tabbouleh. Place ½ cup (100g) of bulghar wheat in a bowl and cover with cold water. Leave to soak for 40 minutes and then drain thoroughly into a sieve.

Meanwhile, heat 1 tablespoon of olive oil in a frying pan over a medium heat. Add 1 peeled and chopped onion and cook for 4 minutes, until pale and soft. Place in a bowl.

To the onions, add 2 seeded and chopped tomatoes, 1 clove of crushed garlic, 4 tablespoons of chopped parsley, 2 tablespoons of chopped mint and 1 teaspoon of ground cumin.

When the bulghar wheat is ready, add it to the bowl along with 3 tablespoons of lemon juice and 1 tablespoon of extra virgin olive oil. Mix well. Season to taste with salt and freshly ground black pepper. Divide the tabbouleh between 2 lunch boxes, then refrigerate until needed.

Mix the remaining blueberries with 2 handfuls of almonds and divide between 2 containers.

Wednesday

Make up the pitas. Rinse and drain a 400g can of mixed beans. Place half in a bowl and put the rest in a container then into the fridge for tomorrow's lunch. To the beans add 100g of marinated tofu and the remaining capsicum half (both cut into bite-size pieces).

Split 2 pita breads then fill with the bean mixture. Add some sweet chilli sauce then cover in plastic wrap. Refrigerate until needed.

Thursday

Make the Mexican bean salad. Cook ½ cup (100g) of brown rice, according to packet instructions. Tip the rice into a sieve and rinse in cold water, to cool. Drain well.

Heat 1 tablespoon of olive oil in a frying pan. Add 1 chopped zucchini and 1 clove of crushed garlic and cook for 6-7 minutes, until the zucchini is soft and starting to brown. Stir in ½ teaspoon each of ground cumin and ground coriander and the remaining can of mixed beans.

Leave to cool slightly then place in a bowl. To the bowl, add 1 chopped tomato, the rice, 2 tablespoons of chopped coriander and a couple of drops of Tabasco sauce. Season to taste. Divide the salad between 2 lunch boxes and refrigerate.

Saturday

Prepare the lentil salad. Preheat the oven to 200°C/400°F/Gas Mark 6. Place 100g of green beans on a baking tray and drizzle with olive oil and season with some salt and black pepper. Roast for 15 minutes, until they start to wrinkle and brown. Place in a bowl.

To the green beans add a 400g can of rinsed and drained lentils. Mix in 2 tablespoons of chopped sun-dried tomatoes and 1 small red onion, finely diced. Then add the remaining tofu (chopped) and 2 tablespoons each of chopped mint and parsley.

Mix together 2 tablespoons of extra virgin olive oil, 1 tablespoon of lemon juice and 1 clove of crushed garlic. Stir into the salad. Serve.

Hull some strawberries and serve with some light cream.

Sunday

Prepare the Japanese omelette. Soak a handful of dried shitake mushrooms in a bowl of warm water for 30 minutes. Drain and finely chop. In a bowl, beat 2 eggs. Stir in the mushrooms, 1 teaspoon of soy sauce and some black pepper. In another bowl, beat 2 more eggs. To this bowl add the remaining spring onions, finely chopped, 1 tablespoon of chopped coriander and some seasoning.

Heat 1 tablespoon of canola oil in a medium frying pan. Add a little of the egg mixture (from any bowl), coating the bottom of the pan. Once the egg is nearly set, roll it up and leave it on the side of the pan. Add some egg mixture from the other bowl, letting it cook until it is nearly set.

Take the first rolled egg and roll it back over the egg, to form a bigger roll. Continue adding the egg mixture, alternating the bowls each time, cooking then rolling. Remove from the pan, leave to cool slightly then slice in half and serve.

Hull the remaining strawberries and serve with some light cream.

Summer Week 7

As well as dipping into the freezer for Monday's lunch, we will be putting together some super salads. Make the most of in-season veg as well as all the lovely fruit varieties available right now.

Monday
Bean and Vegetable Loaf / Blackberries and Raspberries

Tuesday
Risoni Salad with Zucchini, Capsicum and Cherry Tomatoes V / Nectarine and Cashews

Wednesday
Bean, Egg and Potato Salad / Blackberries and Raspberries

Thursday
Artichoke Salad with Beans, Corn and Carrot V / Grapes and Almonds

Friday
Crispbread with Artichoke Spread / Capsicum Sticks / Passion Fruit

Saturday
Avocado and Potato Salad V / Grapes

Sunday
Grilled Veggies and Mozzarella Cheese Roll / Grapes

When buying cans of vegetables and beans, look for varieties that contain no added salt. If these are hard to find don't worry, as rinsing the contents will remove a lot of the salt.

shopping list

Fruit and Vegetables
- [ ] 1 punnet blackberries
- [ ] 1 punnet raspberries
- [ ] 2 red onions
- [ ] 1 zucchini
- [ ] 1 yellow capsicum
- [ ] 250g cherry tomatoes
- [ ] 1 bunch basil
- [ ] 2 cloves garlic
- [ ] 2 nectarines
- [ ] 2 carrots
- [ ] 1 bunch chives
- [ ] 1 small bag mixed lettuce
- [ ] 1 small bag rocket
- [ ] 1 bunch grapes
- [ ] 1 red capsicum
- [ ] 1 avocado
- [ ] 2 passion fruit
- [ ] 1 onion
- [ ] 1 tomato
- [ ] 4 mushrooms

Fridge
- [ ] 2 eggs
- [ ] small tub light cream
- [ ] 15g Parmesan-style cheese
- [ ] 50g mozzarella cheese

Freezer
- [ ] 2 slices bean and vegetable loaf

Bakery
- [ ] 2 large crusty rolls

Pantry
- [ ] 100g risoni (orzo)
- [ ] red wine vinegar
- [ ] dried oregano
- [ ] cashews
- [ ] 800g can potatoes
- [ ] 400g can butter beans
- [ ] white wine vinegar
- [ ] Dijon mustard
- [ ] 400g can artichoke hearts
- [ ] 420g can corn kernels
- [ ] lemon juice
- [ ] almonds
- [ ] pine nuts
- [ ] sun-dried tomatoes
- [ ] 8 crispbread
- [ ] apple cider vinegar

Staples
- [ ] salt
- [ ] black pepper
- [ ] olive oil
- [ ] extra virgin olive oil

daily tasks

Sunday

If you have any bean and vegetable loaf in the freezer, thaw 1 slice per person overnight in the fridge. It will be ready to eat for lunch tomorrow. If you do not have any leftovers, follow the recipe below (remember to add the ingredients to your shopping list):

Begin by preparing the vegetables. Heat 1 tablespoon of olive oil in a frying pan over a medium heat. Add 1 chopped onion and a clove of crushed garlic. Cook for 5 minutes, until soft. Remove from the heat. Stir in a handful of chopped baby spinach and 1 grated carrot. Rinse and drain a 420g can of corn kernels and a 400g can of borlotti beans. Add half the amount from each can and put the rest in a container in the fridge. Season with black pepper.

Preheat the oven to 180°C/350°F/Gas Mark 4. In a large bowl, combine ½ cup (75g) of self-raising flour with ½ cup (75g) of wholemeal self-raising flour and a pinch of salt. Whisk together ⅓ cup (80ml) of canola oil with 5 eggs. Stir into the flour, mixing well to make a batter. Finally, stir in the vegetables. Pour into a greased 23 x 13cm loaf tin and bake in the oven for 45 minutes, until golden and firm.

Leave to cool before removing from the tin. Slice into 6. Allow 1 slice per person for tomorrow's lunch. The rest can be placed in freezer bags and frozen for another day.

Mix together half of the raspberries with the blackberries and divide between 2 containers.

Monday

Prepare the risoni salad. Cook 100g of risoni according to packet instructions. Once cooked, drain then rinse under cold water. Drain thoroughly and place in a bowl. Whilst the risoni is cooking, prepare the vegetables. Heat 1 tablespoon of olive oil in a frying pan. Add a sliced red onion, a sliced zucchini and a diced yellow capsicum. Cook until soft, about 6-7 minutes. Remove from the heat then stir in 125g of cherry tomatoes, sliced in half. Add to the bowl of risoni. Stir in 2 tablespoons of chopped basil.

Make a dressing by mixing together 1 tablespoon of extra virgin olive oil, ½ tablespoon of red wine vinegar, 1 clove of peeled and crushed garlic, 1 teaspoon of dried oregano and some seasoning. Pour the dressing over the salad and mix well to coat. Divide between 2 lunch boxes and refrigerate until needed.

Divide 2 handfuls of cashews between 2 containers. Don't forget your nectarine.

Tuesday

Prepare the bean, egg and potato salad. Hard boil 2 eggs. Leave to cool, then peel, roughly chop and place in a bowl. To the bowl add ½ a can of drained potatoes (chopped) and ½ a can of rinsed and drained butter beans (placing the remaining potatoes and beans into 2 separate containers in the fridge). Add 1 grated carrot and 1 tablespoon of chopped chives.

Make a dressing by mixing together 1 tablespoon of extra virgin olive oil, ½ tablespoon of white wine vinegar and 1 teaspoon of Dijon mustard. Stir the dressing into the salad. Place a handful of lettuce into each lunch box, then top with the salad. Refrigerate until needed.

Mix the remaining blackberries and raspberries together and divide between 2 containers.

Wednesday

Prepare the artichoke salad. Rinse and drain a can of artichoke hearts. Place half in a container in the fridge for another day. Coarsely chop the rest and place in a bowl. To the artichokes add the remaining butter beans and 125g of cherry tomatoes, cut in half. Rinse and drain a 420g can of corn kernels and add half to the bowl and put the remaining in a container in the fridge. Cut a carrot into strips and add to the bowl. Finally, stir in a handful of rocket.

Make a quick dressing by mixing together 1 tablespoon of extra virgin olive oil, ½ tablespoon of lemon juice and 1 tablespoon of chopped basil. Pour the dressing over the salad and stir to coat. Divide the salad between 2 containers then refrigerate until needed.

Mix together a handful of almonds with a handful of grapes per person. Divide between 2 containers.

Thursday

Make the artichoke spread to accompany the crispbread. In a food processor, blitz together the remaining artichokes with 1 crushed garlic clove, 1 tablespoon of lemon juice, 1 tablespoon of pine nuts, 2 tablespoons of light cream, 2 tablespoons of Parmesan-style cheese and 1 tablespoon of chopped sun-dried tomatoes. Season to taste with black pepper. Once it is smooth, divide between 2 containers and refrigerate. Add some crispbread (about 4 per person).

Slice a red capsicum in half. Put half in the fridge and cut the rest into sticks. Divide between 2 lunch boxes and refrigerate.

Don't forget a knife and spoon for your passion fruit.

Saturday

Make the avocado and potato salad. Heat 1 tablespoon of olive oil in a frying pan. Add a chopped red onion and fry for 4 minutes until soft. Remove from the heat and place in a bowl. To the bowl add the remaining potatoes (cut into bite-size pieces) and corn kernels. Chop the remaining red capsicum and add to the bowl. Finally, dice an avocado and stir it gently into the salad.

Make a dressing to accompany the salad by mixing together 1 tablespoon of extra virgin olive oil, ½ tablespoon of apple cider vinegar, 1 teaspoon of Dijon mustard and 1 teaspoon of chopped chives. Pour the dressing over the salad and stir to coat. Season to taste. Serve.

Don't forget a handful of grapes per person.

Sunday

Make up the grilled veggies and mozzarella cheese rolls. Grill the vegetables on a barbecue or griddle. If you have neither, cook them in a frying pan. Slice 1 onion, a tomato and 4 mushrooms. Coat lightly in olive oil and barbecue or griddle for a few minutes until softened. Divide the vegetables between 2 large crusty rolls. Top with some basil leaves and a slice of mozzarella cheese.

Finish up your grapes!

Summer Week 8

Wraps are so versatile and are great for lunches. This week I decided to do a week of wraps, using wholegrain flour tortillas. As usual though, there's something different for the weekend. Let's not go overboard here!

Monday
Brie, Grape and Mint Wrap with Lemon Mayonnaise / Banana

Tuesday
Chargrilled Capsicum, Capers, Spinach and Brie Wrap / Blueberries and Cashews

Wednesday
Tofu, Carrot, Corn and Spring Onion Wrap V / Grapes

Thursday
Tofu, Tomato, Cheese and Olive Wrap / Blueberries and Almonds

Friday
Wrap with Refried Beans, Onion, Tomato, Avocado and Cheese / Apricot and Grapes

Saturday
Refried Bean Turnovers with Avocado, Tomato and Cheese

Sunday
Hot Dogs V

When buying wholegrain flour tortillas, do have a quick look at the label for the fibre content. Look at the amount of fibre per 100g. You will find differences between brands. Go for the brand with the higher fibre content – it will keep you fuller for longer.

shopping list

Fruit and Vegetables
- [ ] 1 small bag mixed lettuce
- [ ] 1 bunch seedless grapes
- [ ] 1 bunch mint
- [ ] 2 bananas
- [ ] 1 small bag baby spinach
- [ ] 1 punnet blueberries
- [ ] 1 carrot
- [ ] 1 bunch spring onions
- [ ] 3 tomatoes
- [ ] 1 avocado
- [ ] 1 bunch coriander
- [ ] 2 apricots
- [ ] 1 onion

Fridge
- [ ] 100g Brie
- [ ] mayonnaise
- [ ] 200g marinated tofu
- [ ] 150g Cheddar cheese
- [ ] 2 vegetarian sausages

Freezer
- [ ] 1 sheet puff pastry

Bakery
- [ ] 2 hot dog rolls

Pantry
- [ ] 10 wholegrain flour tortillas
- [ ] lemon juice
- [ ] chargrilled capsicum
- [ ] capers
- [ ] pine nuts
- [ ] cashews
- [ ] 125g can corn kernels
- [ ] white wine vinegar
- [ ] olives
- [ ] dried oregano
- [ ] almonds
- [ ] 400g can refried beans
- [ ] chilli powder
- [ ] ground cumin
- [ ] lime juice
- [ ] mustard
- [ ] tomato ketchup

Staples
- [ ] salt
- [ ] black pepper
- [ ] olive oil
- [ ] extra virgin olive oil

daily tasks

Sunday

Prepare the Brie and grape wraps. Place some mixed lettuce onto 2 wholegrain tortillas. Slice 50g of Brie and divide it between the 2 tortillas. Take a handful of grapes and slice in half. Add to the tortillas along with 8 coarsely chopped mint leaves.

Make the lemon mayonnaise by mixing 2 tablespoons of mayonnaise with 1 teaspoon of lemon juice in a small bowl. Add some black pepper. Dollop the mayonnaise over the Brie and grapes. Fold in the sides of the tortilla and roll up. Cut in half if desired, then cover in plastic wrap. Refrigerate until needed.

Monday

Prepare the chargrilled capsicum, caper, spinach and Brie wraps. Chop 2 tablespoons of chargrilled capsicum and place in a bowl. Add 2 teaspoons of rinsed and drained capers and a handful of coarsely chopped baby spinach. Stir in 1 tablespoon of toasted pine nuts.

Divide the mixture between 2 wholegrain tortillas. Slice 50g of Brie and add it to the tortillas. Finish with a grind of black pepper. Fold in the sides of the tortilla and roll up. Cut in half if desired, then cover in plastic wrap. Refrigerate until needed.

Divide half a punnet of blueberries between 2 containers and add some cashews to each.

Tuesday

Prepare the tofu, carrot, corn and spring onion wraps. Dice 100g of marinated tofu and place in a bowl. Add 1 grated carrot, a 125g can of rinsed and drained corn kernels, ½ a bunch of chopped spring onions and 2 tablespoons of chopped mint.

Mix together 1 tablespoon of extra virgin olive oil with ½ tablespoon of white wine vinegar and stir into the tofu mixture. Divide between 2 wholegrain tortillas. Fold in the sides of the tortilla and roll up. Cut in half if desired, then cover in plastic wrap. Refrigerate until needed.

Pop some grapes into 2 containers, ready for tomorrow.

Wednesday

Make the tofu, tomato, cheese and olive wraps. Dice 100g of marinated tofu and 1 tomato and place in a bowl. Add ½ cup (50g) of grated Cheddar cheese and 2 tablespoons of olives, sliced in half.

In a small bowl or jar, mix together 1 tablespoon of extra virgin olive oil with ½ tablespoon of lemon juice, ½ teaspoon of dried oregano and some seasoning. Pour the dressing over the ingredients and stir to coat.

Place some mixed lettuce onto 2 wholegrain tortillas and top with the tofu mixture. Fold in the sides of the tortilla and roll up. Cut in half if desired, then cover in plastic wrap. Refrigerate until needed.

Divide the remaining blueberries between 2 containers and add some almonds to each.

Thursday

Prepare the bean wraps. Tip the contents of a 400g can of refried beans into a bowl and use a fork to mash them up slightly. Add ½ a bunch of chopped spring onions, ½ teaspoon of chilli powder, 1 teaspoon of ground cumin and 1 tablespoon of lime juice. Spread half of the mixture between 2 wholegrain tortillas. Pop the remaining refried beans in the fridge (cover the bowl in plastic wrap).

Dice a tomato and divide it between the 2 tortillas. Halve an avocado. Remove the stone and scoop one half from its skin using a spoon. Dice this half and divide between the 2 tortillas. Drizzle some lime or lemon juice over the other half, cover in plastic wrap and place in the fridge. Finally, add ½ cup (50g) of grated Cheddar cheese and 2 tablespoons of chopped coriander. Fold in the sides of the tortilla and roll up. Cut in half if desired, then cover in plastic wrap. Refrigerate until needed.

Place some grapes into 2 containers and add an apricot to each.

Saturday

Make the refried bean turnovers. Thaw a sheet of puff pastry then cut it into 4 squares. Divide the remaining refried bean mixture between the pastry squares. Fold the pastry in half to form a triangle, then press the edges with a fork to seal. Prick the tops. Place on a baking tray and bake in a 220°C/425°F/Gas Mark 7 oven for 20 minutes until golden.

Place 2 turnovers on each plate and top with a diced tomato, the remaining avocado (diced), ½ cup (50g) of grated Cheddar cheese and a few coriander leaves. Finish with a drizzle of lime juice.

Sunday

Prepare the hot dogs. Heat 1 tablespoon of olive oil in a frying pan over a medium heat. Add a sliced onion and 2 vegetarian sausages. Cook until the onions are soft and the sausages are heated through, about 6 minutes.

Slice open the hot dog rolls across the top. Divide the onions between the rolls, then add the sausages. Squeeze some mustard and tomato ketchup over the sausages, according to taste.

Summer Week 9

Raiding my pantry this week I find cans of beetroot and chickpeas waving at me. So I promptly put together a couple of salads. I also thought I'd make use of my packet of savoury yeast flakes to give a flavour boost to the Mediterranean potato shells.

Monday
Chickpea, Olive and Capsicum Salad / Dates and Pecans

Tuesday
Beetroot and Green Bean Salad V / Honeydew Melon

Wednesday
Capsicum, Zucchini and Carrot Slice / Strawberries

Thursday
Corn Fritters with Chilli Sauce and Rocket V / Banana

Friday
Wholegrain Crackers with Goat's Cheese and Chargrilled Capsicum / Strawberry, Melon and Banana Smoothie

Saturday
Baby Spinach and Tomato Roulade

Sunday
Mediterranean Potato Shells V

You can create a vegan sour cream by blending together tofu with some soy milk and lemon juice to achieve a creamy consistency. With this base you can add herbs, spices, mustards etc. to create your own tasty dips.

shopping list

Fruit and Vegetables
- [ ] 1 bunch spring onions
- [ ] 3 tomatoes
- [ ] 1 red capsicum
- [ ] 1 bunch parsley
- [ ] 3 cloves garlic
- [ ] 100g green beans
- [ ] ½ honeydew melon
- [ ] 1 punnet strawberries
- [ ] 1 small bag rocket
- [ ] 3 bananas
- [ ] 2 onions
- [ ] 125g bag baby spinach
- [ ] 2 large potatoes
- [ ] 75g mushrooms

Fridge
- [ ] 160ml soy milk
- [ ] 80g goat's cheese
- [ ] 4 eggs
- [ ] 15g Parmesan-style cheese
- [ ] 100g cream cheese
- [ ] small tub sour cream

Freezer
- [ ] 4 slices capsicum, zucchini and carrot slice

Pantry
- [ ] 400g can chickpeas
- [ ] olives
- [ ] lemon juice
- [ ] honey
- [ ] dates
- [ ] pecans
- [ ] 225g can sliced beetroot
- [ ] red wine vinegar
- [ ] 50g wholemeal self-raising flour
- [ ] 310g can corn kernels
- [ ] ground coriander
- [ ] chilli powder
- [ ] lime juice
- [ ] sweet chilli sauce
- [ ] pine nuts
- [ ] balsamic vinegar
- [ ] wholegrain crackers
- [ ] chargrilled capsicum
- [ ] sesame seeds
- [ ] whole nutmeg
- [ ] savoury yeast flakes
- [ ] dried oregano

Staples
- [ ] salt
- [ ] black pepper
- [ ] olive oil
- [ ] extra virgin olive oil
- [ ] canola oil

daily tasks

Sunday

Prepare the chickpea, olive and capsicum salad. Rinse and drain a 400g can of chickpeas and place half in a bowl. Put the rest in a container in the fridge. To the chickpeas add ½ a bunch of chopped spring onions, a chopped tomato, 2 tablespoons of sliced olives and ½ a diced red capsicum (pop the remaining capsicum in the fridge). Stir in 1 tablespoon of chopped parsley.

Make a dressing by mixing together 1 tablespoon of extra virgin olive oil with ½ tablespoon of lemon juice, a clove of crushed garlic and 1 teaspoon of honey. Pour the dressing over the salad and stir to coat. Divide the salad between 2 lunch boxes, then refrigerate.

Pop some dates and pecans into 2 containers.

Monday

Prepare the beetroot and green bean salad. Drain a 225g can of sliced beetroot and coarsely chop. Place in a bowl with the remaining chickpeas. Slice the green beans into bite-size pieces and add to the bowl along with the remaining red capsicum, diced. Add 1 tablespoon of chopped parsley.

Mix together 1 tablespoon of extra virgin olive oil with ½ tablespoon of red wine vinegar and add it to the salad. Divide between 2 lunch boxes then refrigerate until needed.

Cut the honeydew melon in half. Place half in the fridge then dice the remaining chunk. Divide the chunks between 2 containers and pop them into the fridge.

Tuesday

Remove 4 slices of capsicum, zucchini and carrot slice from the freezer. Pop them into the fridge to thaw overnight. You can place them into your lunch boxes. If you do not have any in the freezer, follow the instructions below. Remember to add the ingredients to your shopping list.

Preheat the oven to 180°C/350°F/Gas Mark 4. Grease and line a 30 x 20cm baking tin. In a large bowl, whisk together 4 eggs and ½ cup (125ml) of milk. Beat in ½ cup

(75g) of wholemeal self-raising flour and ½ cup (75g) of regular self-raising flour to make a batter. Dice ½ a red capsicum and ½ a bunch of spring onions. Grate 1 zucchini and 1 carrot. Add the vegetables to the batter along with 60g of crumbled goat's cheese. Season. Pour into the baking tin and bake for 30 minutes until golden brown and firm. Leave to cool then remove from the tin. Slice into quarters, then halve each quarter. Place 2 slices into each lunch box. The rest can be frozen by wrapping each slice in plastic wrap then placing into a container or freezer bag, then into the freezer.

Divide half a punnet of strawberries between 2 containers.

Wednesday

Prepare the corn fritters. In a bowl add ⅓ cup (50g) of wholemeal self-raising flour, a 310g can of rinsed and drained corn kernels, ½ a bunch of chopped spring onions, 1 teaspoon of ground coriander, ½ teaspoon of chilli powder and 1 tablespoon of lime juice. Add ⅓ cup (80ml) of soy milk and 1 teaspoon of canola oil. Stir well to combine all the ingredients together.

Heat 2 tablespoons of canola oil in a large frying pan over a medium heat. Spoon heaped tablespoons of the batter into the pan. Flatten slightly to form fritters. Fry for 3 minutes, turn and cook for another 1-2 minutes, until browned on both sides. Drain on paper towel and leave to cool. Place 3 into each lunch box, along with some sweet chilli sauce. The rest can be frozen between layers of baking paper in a container or in freezer bags.

Place some rocket into 2 containers, add 1 tablespoon of toasted pine nuts and a drizzle of balsamic vinegar. Pop the rocket into the fridge with the corn fritters.

Thursday

Prepare the crackers and toppings. Place some wholegrain crackers into 2 lunch boxes. Add 40g of goat's cheese to each lunch box and 1 tablespoon of diced chargrilled capsicum. Don't forget to add a knife for spreading the goat's cheese on the crackers. Refrigerate until tomorrow. When you are ready to eat, spread some cheese on the crackers than top with some capsicum.

Make 2 smoothies. In a blender, add the remaining strawberries, melon and a banana. Add ⅓ cup (80ml) of soy milk. Blend until smooth. Divide between 2 x 500ml thermos flasks, then refrigerate until tomorrow.

Saturday

Make the baby spinach and tomato roulade. Preheat the oven to 200°C/400°F/Gas Mark 6. Line a 30 x 23cm shallow tin with baking paper. Sprinkle 1 tablespoon of sesame seeds evenly over the tin. In a jug, beat together 4 eggs, 2 tablespoons of Parmesan-style cheese and a good grind of black pepper. Pour into the prepared tin. Cook in the oven for 10 minutes, until the eggs are set. Leave to cool.

Heat 1 tablespoon of olive oil in a large frying pan over a medium heat. Add a chopped onion and a clove of crushed garlic and fry for 4 minutes, until pale and soft. Add 125g of baby spinach, stirring through until it has wilted, about 2 minutes. Remove from the heat.

Beat together 100g of cream cheese with 2 tablespoons of sour cream. Stir in the onion and spinach mixture and a chopped tomato. Grate some nutmeg over the mixture, then season to taste with salt and freshly ground black pepper.

Turn the cooked egg onto your work surface and remove the baking paper. Trim the edges if necessary. Spread the filling evenly over the egg. Next, carefully roll the egg up, starting from the shorter end. Wrap the roulade in plastic wrap then refrigerate for at least 30 minutes. When you are ready to serve, unwrap the roulade and slice into 2cm thick slices. Arrange on a serving plate. Serve.

Sunday

Make the Mediterranean potato shells. Preheat the oven to 200°C/400°F/Gas Mark 6. Prick 2 large potatoes and bake in the oven for 50 minutes, until tender. Alternatively microwave the pricked potatoes on a high power for 10 minutes. Times will vary according to the power of your oven and size of the potatoes. Let stand until the potatoes are cool enough to handle. Halve the potatoes and using a metal spoon, scoop out the flesh leaving 1cm's worth to form a shell for your filling. Place on a baking tray.

To make the filling, heat 1 tablespoon of olive oil in a frying pan over a medium heat. Add 1 peeled and chopped onion and fry for 4 minutes, until pale and soft. Add a clove of crushed garlic and 75g of coarsely chopped mushrooms and fry for a further 5 minutes, until the mushrooms are soft and golden. Remove from the heat and tip into a bowl.

To the bowl add a chopped tomato, 2 tablespoons of pitted and sliced olives, 2 tablespoons of toasted pine nuts, 1 tablespoon of savoury yeast flakes and ½ teaspoon of dried oregano. Mix together, season to taste with salt and black pepper, then spoon into the prepared potato shells. Bake in the oven for 15 minutes, until heated through. Serve warm.

Summer Week 10

Amongst other goodies, this week sees us playing with lentils and tofu — vegetarian classics! Hopefully demonstrating how versatile and tasty these ingredients are.

Monday
Tomato, Bean and Spring Onion Frittata / Grapes

Tuesday
Bulghar Wheat Salad with Beans, Capsicum and Carrot / Plum

Wednesday
Lentil Cakes with Sweet Chilli Sauce V / Salad of Lettuce and Cherry Tomatoes / Grapes

Thursday
Lentil, Beetroot and Capsicum Salad V / Orange

Friday
Blue Cheese and Sun-Dried Tomato Sandwich / Grapes

Saturday
Tofu Cubes with Agave Syrup V / Salad of Lettuce, Red Onion and Tomato

Sunday
Herby Tofu Roll V

Many different foods can be frozen. Bread, slices, muffins, flour tortillas, cake, soups and much more can freeze successfully. Simply pop the food in a freezer bag or container before freezing, making sure the item has been cooled thoroughly beforehand.

shopping list

Fruit and Vegetables
- [ ] 1 bunch spring onions
- [ ] 1 bunch chives
- [ ] 2 tomatoes
- [ ] 1 bunch grapes
- [ ] 1 red capsicum
- [ ] 1 carrot
- [ ] 2 plums
- [ ] 1 onion
- [ ] 1 clove garlic
- [ ] 60g mushrooms
- [ ] 1 bag mixed lettuce
- [ ] 200g cherry tomatoes
- [ ] 2 oranges
- [ ] 1 red onion

Fridge
- [ ] 4 eggs
- [ ] 100g blue cheese
- [ ] mayonnaise
- [ ] 300g firm tofu

Bakery
- [ ] 5 slices wholegrain bread
- [ ] 2 large wholegrain rolls

Pantry
- [ ] 400g can cannellini beans
- [ ] 100g bulghar wheat
- [ ] pine nuts
- [ ] raisins
- [ ] lemon juice
- [ ] honey
- [ ] 400g can lentils
- [ ] cashews
- [ ] tomato paste
- [ ] ground turmeric
- [ ] ground cumin
- [ ] sweet chilli sauce
- [ ] balsamic vinegar
- [ ] olives
- [ ] 225g can sliced beetroot
- [ ] red wine vinegar
- [ ] sun-dried tomatoes
- [ ] agave syrup
- [ ] dried mixed herbs

Staples
- [ ] salt
- [ ] black pepper
- [ ] olive oil
- [ ] extra virgin olive oil
- [ ] canola oil

daily tasks

Sunday

Cook the frittata. Beat together 4 eggs. Add ½ a bunch of chopped spring onions, 1 tablespoon of chopped chives and some seasoning. Heat 1 tablespoon of olive oil in a 24cm frying pan over a medium heat. Add the eggs and scatter 1 chopped tomato and ½ a 400g can of rinsed and drained cannellini beans evenly over the eggs. Keep the remaining beans in a container in the fridge. Turn the heat down and cook for 8-10 minutes.

Preheat the grill. Once the eggs are nearly set, add 50g of crumbled blue cheese and place the pan under the grill to finish cooking the top. Slide the frittata off the pan then leave to cool. Slice into quarters and place 2 quarters into each lunch box. Refrigerate until tomorrow.

Place some grapes into 2 containers.

Monday

Prepare the bulghar salad. Place ½ cup (100g) of bulghar wheat in a bowl and cover with cold water. Leave to soak for 40 minutes and then drain thoroughly into a sieve. Whilst the bulghar wheat is soaking, prepare the rest of your ingredients. Chop ½ a red capsicum into bite-size pieces (put the remaining in the fridge). Chop the remaining spring onions and grate a carrot. Place the vegetables in a bowl along with the remaining cannellini beans. Add 1 tablespoon of toasted pine nuts and 2 tablespoons of raisins. Stir in the bulghar wheat once it is ready.

Make a dressing by mixing together 1 tablespoon of extra virgin olive oil, ½ tablespoon of lemon juice, 1 teaspoon of honey and some seasoning. Pour the dressing over the salad and stir to coat. Divide between 2 lunch boxes then refrigerate until needed.

Tuesday

Make the lentil cakes. Heat 1 tablespoon of olive oil in a large frying pan over a medium heat. Add a peeled and chopped onion and fry for 4 minutes, until pale and soft. Add 1 crushed garlic clove and 60g of chopped mushrooms and fry for another 4 minutes, until the mushrooms are soft. Remove from the heat.

In a food processor, blitz up 1 slice of wholegrain bread to form crumbs. Add the mushrooms and onions, ½ a 400g can of rinsed and drained lentils (put the rest in a container in the fridge), 1 tablespoon of cashews, ½ a tablespoon of tomato paste and ½ a teaspoon each of ground turmeric and ground cumin. Process until the mixture is smooth like a paste and well combined. Season to taste with salt and freshly ground black pepper.

Heat 2 tablespoons of canola oil in a large frying pan over a medium heat. Add heaped tablespoons of the lentil mixture to the pan and flatten down to form cakes. Fry for 4 minutes, until golden on one side. Turn and fry for another 2 minutes. You will need to do this in batches and you may need to add more oil to the pan.

Drain on paper towel. Once cool, divide between 2 lunch boxes. Add some sweet chilli sauce to each lunch box to serve with the lentil cakes. Refrigerate.

Make an accompanying salad by layering some mixed lettuce at the bottom of 2 containers. Top with 100g of halved cherry tomatoes and 1 tablespoon of chopped chives. Drizzle some balsamic vinegar over the salad. Refrigerate until needed.

Place some grapes into 2 containers.

Wednesday

Prepare the lentil, beetroot and capsicum salad. In a bowl place the remaining lentils. Add the remaining red capsicum (diced) and a handful of olives. Drain a 225g can of sliced beetroot and coarsely chop. Add to the bowl. Stir in 1 tablespoon of toasted pine nuts and 1 tablespoon of chopped chives. Mix together 1 tablespoon of extra virgin olive oil with ½ a tablespoon of red wine vinegar and stir in. Place some lettuce at the bottom of 2 lunch boxes, then top with the salad. Refrigerate until needed.

Thursday

Prepare the blue cheese and sun-dried tomato sandwiches. Spread some mayonnaise over 2 slices of wholegrain bread. Add some lettuce and 2 tablespoons of chopped sun-dried tomatoes. Add 50g of crumbled blue cheese and finish with a few chopped chives. Top with another slice of bread, cut in half then cover in plastic wrap. Pop the sandwiches into the fridge.

Place some grapes into 2 containers.

Saturday

Prepare the tofu cubes with agave syrup. Slice 100g of firm tofu (drained) into 8 even-sized pieces. Season with salt and black pepper. Place ¼ cup (35g) of cashews into a food processor and process until coarsely ground. Place the cashews on a plate and coat each tofu cube with the cashews. Place 4 cubes onto each plate and drizzle with agave syrup.

Make a quick accompanying salad by mixing some lettuce with 100g of halved cherry tomatoes and ½ a chopped red onion (keep the other half for tomorrow). Mix together 1 tablespoon of extra virgin olive oil with ½ a tablespoon of red wine vinegar. Pour the dressing over the salad and serve with the tofu cubes.

Sunday

Cook the herby tofu. Slice 200g of drained tofu. Season both sides of the tofu with salt, pepper and 1 teaspoon of dried mixed herbs. Heat 2 tablespoons of canola oil in a frying pan over a medium heat. Add the tofu and cook both sides until golden and crispy on both sides, about 8-10 minutes in total. Drain on paper towel.

Split 2 wholegrain rolls then add the cooked tofu along with some lettuce, a sliced tomato and some thinly sliced red onion. Add some mayonnaise if you like.

Summer Week 11

Garlic features in many of this week's lunches. Don't be put off though — it's just a clove here or there to enhance the flavours. Of course you may like to have a pack of mints close to hand for after lunch!

Monday
Cumin and Oregano Muffins / Mango

Tuesday
Falafel in Pita with Minty Cream Dip V / Peach

Wednesday
Veggies, Pita Strips and Minty Cream Dip V / Hard Boiled Egg / Blueberries and Cashews

Thursday
Spinach, Tomato and Mozzarella Crepe / Plum

Friday
Vegan Empanadas V / Blueberries and Cashews

Saturday
Vegetable Tostada

Sunday
Lemony Noodles V

It is okay to use ready crushed garlic in a jar. It's handy to have some on standby and saves having to peel cloves and then crush them. However, do check the label on the jar as the amount of garlic in the jar does vary considerably between brands.

shopping list

Fruit and Vegetables
- ☐ 1 mango
- ☐ 3 onions
- ☐ 6 cloves garlic
- ☐ 2 peaches
- ☐ 1 carrot
- ☐ 2 red capsicums
- ☐ 1 punnet blueberries
- ☐ 2 tomatoes
- ☐ 1 small bag baby spinach
- ☐ 2 plums
- ☐ 1 zucchini
- ☐ 80g mushrooms
- ☐ 1 bunch coriander
- ☐ 1 bunch spring onions
- ☐ 1 head broccoli
- ☐ handful snow peas
- ☐ 1 lemon

Fridge
- ☐ 300g firm tofu
- ☐ 350ml soy milk
- ☐ 3 eggs
- ☐ 50g mozzarella cheese
- ☐ 50g Cheddar cheese

Freezer
- ☐ 2 sheets shortcrust pastry

Bakery
- ☐ 4 savoury muffins (or recipe)
- ☐ 4 pita breads

Pantry
- ☐ 400g can chickpeas
- ☐ ground cumin
- ☐ ground coriander
- ☐ dried mint flakes
- ☐ ground turmeric
- ☐ caraway seeds
- ☐ lemon juice
- ☐ 150g wholemeal plain flour
- ☐ agave syrup
- ☐ chilli powder
- ☐ cashews
- ☐ 75g plain flour
- ☐ dried thyme
- ☐ red wine
- ☐ 2 wholegrain flour tortillas
- ☐ sliced jalapeños
- ☐ 1 pack ready-cooked noodles

Staples
- ☐ salt
- ☐ black pepper
- ☐ olive oil
- ☐ canola oil
- ☐ olive oil spray

daily tasks

Sunday

Make the cumin and oregano muffins following the recipe on p.228, or buy your favourite savoury muffins from the bakers. Allow 2 per person. Cover in plastic wrap or place in your lunch boxes. Refrigerate.

Prepare the mango. Peel the mango then cut the flesh from the stone. Dice into bite-size pieces then divide between 2 containers. Refrigerate until needed.

Monday

Begin by making the falafel. To a food processor, add a 400g can of rinsed and drained chickpeas, a peeled and chopped onion and a clove of crushed garlic. Add ½ a teaspoon each of ground cumin, ground coriander, dried mint flakes, ground turmeric and caraway seeds. Then add 1 teaspoon of lemon juice. Process until the mixture is well combined. Finally, add ½ cup (75g) of wholemeal plain flour, blending it thoroughly into the mixture until it all comes together.

Heat 2 tablespoons of canola oil in a large frying pan over a medium heat. Add rounded tablespoons of the mixture to the pan and flatten slightly. Fry for 6-8 minutes, until golden brown all over. Drain on paper towel. Once cold, split open 2 pita breads and add 2-3 falafel to each pita. Put in containers or cover in plastic wrap, then pop them in the fridge. The rest can be frozen by popping in a container and then into the freezer.

Make the minty cream dip to accompany the falafel. In a blender or food processor, blend 150g of firm tofu with 3 tablespoons of soy milk and 1 tablespoon of lemon juice. Add 1 tablespoon of dried mint flakes, a clove of garlic, 1 tablespoon of agave syrup and a pinch of chilli powder and salt. Season to taste with black pepper. Blend until smooth. Place a small amount into 2 containers to serve with the falafel. Place the rest into another container and pop everything into the fridge.

Tuesday

Hard boil 2 eggs, then rinse under cold water to cool. Once cool, pop them into your lunch boxes.

Slice a carrot and a red capsicum into sticks. Divide between 2 lunch boxes. Slice 2 pita breads into thick strips for dipping and add these to your lunch boxes.

Divide the remaining minty cream dip between 2 containers. Pop everything into the fridge.

Divide half a punnet of blueberries between 2 containers. Add a handful of cashews to each.

Wednesday

Prepare the crepes. Combine ½ cup (75g) of plain flour and ½ cup (75g) of wholemeal plain flour in a large bowl with a pinch of salt. Stir in a beaten egg. Gradually add 1¼ cups (300ml) of soy milk, beating to form a smooth batter. Add some water if the batter seems thick. Pour into a jug.

Spray a medium non-stick frying pan with olive oil and heat over a medium heat. Add enough batter to thinly cover the pan. Cook for 2-3 minutes, turn the crepe then cook for another 2 minutes, until lightly browned. Transfer to a plate and leave to cool. Spray the pan again with olive oil before cooking the next crepe. Allow 2 per person. You can freeze the rest. Interleaf with baking paper then place in a freezer bag or container before popping them into the freezer.

Fill your crepes by placing some sliced mozzarella cheese, some slices of tomato, and a handful of baby spinach on a quarter of each crepe. Mix together a clove of crushed garlic with 1 tablespoon of olive oil and ½ tablespoon of lemon juice. Drizzle the dressing over the filling and season to taste. Fold the crepe in half, then half again to form a quarter. Cover in plastic wrap or place in 2 containers. Store in the fridge until tomorrow.

Thursday

Prepare the empanadas. Preheat the oven to 200°C/400°F/Gas Mark 6. Thaw 2 sheets of shortcrust pastry. Whilst thawing, heat 1 tablespoon of olive oil in a frying pan over a medium heat. Add 1 chopped onion and 1 clove of crushed garlic and fry for 5 minutes, until slightly golden. Remove from the heat.

In a small bowl, mash 150g of firm tofu with a fork. Add the onions, ½ teaspoon of dried thyme and a pinch of chilli powder. Mix well to combine and season to taste. Using a 10cm round cookie cutter, cut 4 rounds from each pastry sheet. Re-roll the remaining pastry and cut 4 more rounds to make 12 in total.

Divide the tofu mixture between the pastry rounds. Fold the rounds in half and press the sides together firmly to seal. Brush with soy milk and place on a baking tray. Bake in the oven for 25 minutes, until golden and crisp. Leave to cool then place 3 in each lunch box, then refrigerate. The rest can be frozen.

Divide the remaining blueberries between 2 containers and add a handful of cashews to each.

Saturday

Prepare the tostadas. Heat 1 tablespoon of olive oil in a frying pan. Add 1 chopped onion and cook for 3-4 minutes. Add a sliced zucchini, 80g of sliced mushrooms, a diced red capsicum and a clove of crushed garlic. Cook, stirring for another 5 minutes. Add 2 tablespoons of red wine to the pan and cook for a further 2 minutes.

Preheat the grill. Lay 2 wholegrain flour tortillas on a baking tray. Spoon the filling over the tortillas. Top with a chopped tomato, some chopped coriander leaves, ½ cup (50g) of grated Cheddar cheese and some sliced jalapeño peppers. Pop under the grill for a minute or so until the cheese is melted. Place the tostadas on plates then slice into quarters before serving.

Sunday

Prepare the lemony noodles. Heat 1 tablespoon of canola oil in a large frying pan or wok. Add 1 bunch of chopped spring onions, a head of broccoli chopped into small florets and a handful of snow peas. Stir for a few minutes then add a crushed clove of garlic and a handful of cashews. Add a pack of ready-cooked noodles and the juice of 1 lemon. Continue cooking and stirring until the noodles are heated through. Stir through 2 tablespoons of chopped coriander, then serve immediately.

Summer Week 12

This week's menu includes items I feel we've not had for a while. Couscous, pasta salads and turnovers are all included. Then look forward to the weekend where we have an American inspired sandwich and a tasty sausage wrap.

Monday
Artichoke Salad with Carrot, Capers and Tofu V / Grapes

Tuesday
Broccoli, Tofu and Tomato Couscous V / Peach

Wednesday
Pasta Salad with Artichokes and Broccoli V / Grapes

Thursday
Bean Salad with Avocado, Cheese and Spinach / Watermelon

Friday
Cheese, Onion and Potato Turnovers / Watermelon

Saturday
American Inspired Sub

Sunday
Sausage Wrap with Onion, Tomato, Cheese and Gherkins

Broccoli, like many other vegetables can be eaten raw. Varying how you prepare vegetables offers you a greater number of choices as well as providing you with different nutrients.

shopping list

Fruit and Vegetables
- ☐ 1 carrot
- ☐ 1 small bag mixed lettuce
- ☐ 1 bunch parsley
- ☐ 1 bunch grapes
- ☐ 200g cherry tomatoes
- ☐ 1 head broccoli
- ☐ handful snow peas
- ☐ 2 peaches
- ☐ 1 clove garlic
- ☐ 1 small bag baby spinach
- ☐ 1 avocado
- ☐ 1 chunk watermelon
- ☐ 1 large potato
- ☐ 1 onion
- ☐ 2 tomatoes

Fridge
- ☐ 200g marinated tofu
- ☐ 100g blue cheese
- ☐ 100g Cheddar cheese
- ☐ 4 vegetarian slices
- ☐ mayonnaise
- ☐ 4 vegetarian sausages

Freezer
- ☐ 1 sheet puff pastry

Bakery
- ☐ 2 submarine rolls (or 1 baguette)

Pantry
- ☐ 400g can artichoke hearts
- ☐ capers
- ☐ cashews
- ☐ apple cider vinegar
- ☐ Dijon mustard
- ☐ 100g couscous
- ☐ dried chilli flakes
- ☐ lemon juice
- ☐ 100g dried pasta
- ☐ 400g can butter beans
- ☐ dried sage
- ☐ gherkins
- ☐ mustard
- ☐ 2 wholegrain flour tortillas
- ☐ Tabasco sauce

Staples
- ☐ salt
- ☐ black pepper
- ☐ olive oil
- ☐ extra virgin olive oil

daily tasks

Sunday

Prepare the artichoke salad. Rinse and drain a 400g can of artichoke hearts. Pop half in a container, then into the fridge. Chop the rest then place in a bowl. To the bowl add 100g of marinated tofu (chopped) and a grated carrot. Add 1 tablespoon of capers and 2 tablespoons of cashews. Add some of the mixed lettuce and a tablespoon of chopped parsley. Stir to combine.

Make a dressing by mixing together 1 tablespoon of extra virgin olive oil with ½ tablespoon of apple cider vinegar, ½ teaspoon of Dijon mustard and some seasoning. Pour the dressing over the salad and mix well. Divide between 2 lunch boxes then refrigerate until needed.

Place some grapes into 2 containers.

Monday

Prepare the couscous. Place ½ cup (100g) of couscous in a bowl. Add ½ cup (125ml) of boiling water, stand for 3 minutes and then fluff up with a fork. Chop the remaining 100g of tofu and cut 100g of cherry tomatoes in half. Cut the broccoli head in half (keep half for tomorrow) then cut into small florets. Add to the couscous along with the tofu and tomatoes.

Stir in a handful of snow peas (cut into smaller pieces if you prefer), and 1 tablespoon of chopped parsley. Add ½ teaspoon of dried chilli flakes, or to taste. Mix together 1 tablespoon of extra virgin olive oil with ½ tablespoon of lemon juice. Pour the dressing over the salad and stir to coat. Season to taste. Divide the salad between 2 lunch boxes then refrigerate until needed.

Tuesday

Prepare the pasta salad. Cook 100g of dried pasta according to the instructions on the packet. Drain then rinse the pasta under cold water. Whilst the pasta is cooking, prepare the remaining ingredients. Chop the remaining artichoke hearts and broccoli and place in a bowl. Add 100g of cherry tomatoes, sliced in half. Once the pasta is ready, add it to the bowl.

Make a dressing by mixing together 1 tablespoon of extra virgin olive oil with ½ tablespoon of lemon juice, a clove of crushed garlic and ½ teaspoon of dried chilli flakes. Stir the dressing into the pasta salad. Divide between 2 lunch boxes and refrigerate until needed.

Divide the remaining grapes between 2 containers.

Wednesday

Prepare the bean salad. Rinse and drain a 400g can of butter beans. Place in a bowl. To the bowl add a handful of baby spinach, 50g of crumbled blue cheese and a handful of cashews. Dice the flesh of an avocado and add it to the bowl. Add 1 tablespoon of chopped parsley.

Mix together 1 tablespoon of olive oil and ½ tablespoon of lemon juice and stir it into the salad. Season to taste. Divide the salad between 2 lunch boxes, then refrigerate until needed.

Cut the watermelon chunk in half. Pop half in the fridge for tomorrow. Cut the remaining flesh from the skin and chop into bite-size pieces. Divide between 2 containers, then refrigerate until needed.

Thursday

Bake the cheese, onion and potato turnovers. Thaw a sheet of puff pastry. Peel and chop a large potato into even-sized pieces and place in a microwave-safe container with a drop of water. Cook for 8-10 minutes, until tender. Alternatively, boil the chopped potato in a saucepan until tender, about 15 minutes. Drain, then place in a bowl. Mash the potato.

Heat 1 tablespoon of olive oil in a frying pan. Add ½ a chopped onion (the rest can be kept in the fridge for the weekend) and fry for 4-5 minutes until soft and starting to brown. Add the onions to the potato, along with 50g of crumbled blue cheese and ¼ teaspoon of dried sage. Mix well and season to taste.

Preheat the oven to 220°C/425°F/Gas Mark 7. Cut the pastry into 4 squares. Divide the potato mixture between the pastry squares. Fold the pastry in half to form a triangle, then press the edges with a fork to seal. Prick the tops. Place on a baking tray and bake for 20 minutes, until golden. Leave to cool, before placing 2 in each lunch box. Refrigerate.

Dice up the remaining watermelon and divide between 2 containers. Pop them into the fridge.

Saturday

Prepare your rolls. Slice open 2 submarine rolls and spread on some mayonnaise. Add your chosen vegetarian slices, some slices of cheese and a sliced tomato. Add some lettuce, sliced gherkins and finish with a dollop of your favourite mustard. Cut in half if you like, then serve.

Sunday

Prepare the sausage wraps. Heat 1 tablespoon of olive oil in a frying pan. Cook the remaining chopped onion and 4 vegetarian sausages, cooking until the sausages are heated through. Place 2 sausages on each flour tortilla and divide up the onions. Top the sausages with a chopped tomato, $\frac{1}{2}$ cup (50g) of grated Cheddar cheese, some sliced gherkins and a few drops of Tabasco sauce. Fold in the sides, then roll up the wraps. Serve warm.

Summer Week 13

It's herby week this week! As I was writing the menu I realised herbs were featuring in each lunch. So I decided to continue for the whole week. When you get to Sunday, use whatever herbs you have left over for herby potatoes.

Monday
Herby Bean Spread with Crispbread V / Cherry Tomatoes / Blueberries and Cashews

Tuesday
Herby Bean Wrap with Capsicum, Olives and Tomatoes V / Banana

Wednesday
Herby and Caramelised Onion Couscous V / Blueberries and Cashews

Thursday
Herby Chickpea and Tofu Salad V / Grapes

Friday
Herby Rice Salad V / Chickpeas in Sun-Dried Tomato Puree V / Grapes

Saturday
Herby Tomato Tarts V

Sunday
Herby Potatoes with Corn, Avocado, Tomato and Cheese

"If more of us valued food and cheer and song above hoarded gold, it would be a merrier world."
J.R.R. Tolkien

shopping list

Fruit and Vegetables
- [ ] 1 bunch spring onions
- [ ] 1 bunch parsley
- [ ] 200g cherry tomatoes
- [ ] 1 punnet blueberries
- [ ] 1 red capsicum
- [ ] 1 lettuce
- [ ] 2 bananas
- [ ] 1 onion
- [ ] 1 bunch chives
- [ ] 3 tomatoes
- [ ] 1 bunch grapes
- [ ] 1 bunch thyme
- [ ] 1 bunch oregano
- [ ] 1 bunch basil
- [ ] 2 potatoes
- [ ] 1 avocado

Fridge
- [ ] 200g marinated tofu
- [ ] 50g grated Cheddar cheese

Freezer
- [ ] 1 sheet puff pastry

Pantry
- [ ] 400g can cannellini beans
- [ ] dried sage
- [ ] lemon juice
- [ ] 6-8 crispbread
- [ ] cashews
- [ ] 2 wholegrain flour tortillas
- [ ] olives
- [ ] balsamic vinegar
- [ ] brown sugar
- [ ] 100g couscous
- [ ] 400g can chickpeas
- [ ] 100g brown rice
- [ ] savoury yeast flakes
- [ ] sun-dried tomatoes
- [ ] 125g can corn kernels

Staples
- [ ] salt
- [ ] black pepper
- [ ] olive oil
- [ ] extra virgin olive oil
- [ ] canola oil

daily tasks

Sunday

Prepare the herby bean spread. Rinse and drain a 400g can of cannellini beans and pop them into a food processor. Coarsely chop ½ a bunch of spring onions and add to the processor along with 1 tablespoon of chopped parsley and 1 teaspoon of dried sage. Finally, add 1 tablespoon of lemon juice. Blitz it all up until smooth. Season to taste. Spoon half the mixture in a container for another day, then divide the rest between 2 lunch boxes.

To the lunch boxes add 3-4 crispbread per person and a handful of cherry tomatoes. Refrigerate until needed.

Divide half a punnet of blueberries between 2 containers and add some cashews.

Monday

Make the herby bean wraps. Spread the remaining herby bean spread over 2 wholegrain flour tortillas. Dice ½ a red capsicum and slice a handful of olives. Scatter the capsicum and olives over the bean spread along with a handful of cherry tomatoes (halved or quartered) and some lettuce. Add a few parsley leaves then season to taste. Fold in the sides, roll up then cover in plastic wrap. Refrigerate until needed.

Tuesday

Prepare the herby and caramelised onion couscous. Heat 1 tablespoon of olive oil in a frying pan over a medium heat. Add a peeled and chopped onion then cook until pale and soft, about 4 minutes. Add 1 tablespoon each of balsamic vinegar and brown sugar and mix well into the onions. Cook for another 5 minutes, until the onions are caramelised. Remove from the heat.

Place ½ cup (100g) of couscous in a bowl and stir in ½ cup (125ml) of boiling water. Let it stand for 3 minutes. Fluff up with a fork to separate the grains. Add the onions to the couscous, together with 100g of diced marinated tofu and 1 tablespoon each of chopped parsley and chives. Season to taste. Divide between 2 lunch boxes, then pop them into the fridge.

Divide the remaining blueberries between 2 containers and add some cashews.

Wednesday

Make the herby chickpea and tofu salad. Place the following in a bowl and mix together: 100g of chopped marinated tofu, ½ a 400g can of rinsed and drained chickpeas (put the rest in a container in the fridge), ½ a diced red capsicum, ½ a bunch of chopped spring onions and 1 diced tomato. Stir in 1 tablespoon each of chopped parsley and chives.

Mix together 1 tablespoon of extra virgin olive oil with ½ tablespoon of lemon juice, then stir into the salad. Divide the salad between 2 lunch boxes, then refrigerate until needed.

Divide some grapes between 2 containers.

Thursday

Prepare the herby rice salad. Cook ½ cup (100g) of brown rice, according to packet directions. Once cooked, drain and rinse under cold water. Place in a bowl. Stir in 1 tablespoon each of fresh thyme, parsley and oregano. Add 1 tablespoon each of savoury yeast flakes, lemon juice and extra virgin olive oil. Season to taste. Divide between 2 lunch boxes and refrigerate until needed.

Make the sun-dried tomato puree by blitzing 3 tablespoons of sun-dried tomatoes in a food processor. Season to taste. Place in a bowl and stir in the remaining chickpeas. Divide between 2 containers then refrigerate until needed.

Divide the remaining grapes between 2 containers.

Saturday

Prepare the herby tomato tarts. Preheat the oven to 220°C/425°F/Gas Mark 7. Thaw a sheet of puff pastry. Once thawed, cut the pastry into 9 even-sized squares. Place on a lined baking tray then score around the edge of each, 1cm in.

Sprinkle 1 teaspoon of savoury yeast flakes over the pastry, then top each square with a slice or 2 of tomato. Season with salt and freshly ground black pepper. Bake in the oven for about 18 minutes, until the pastry is golden and puffed.

In a jar or small bowl, mix together 1 tablespoon each of chopped basil, parsley and oregano with 3 tablespoons of extra virgin olive oil. Just before serving, drizzle a small amount of the oil over each tart.

Sunday

Roast the herby potatoes. Preheat the oven to 220°C/425°F/Gas Mark 7. Dice 2 potatoes into 2cm cubes. Place on a roasting tray and season to taste. Drizzle some canola oil over the potatoes and roast for 30 minutes. Remove from the oven, turn the potatoes and add 3-4 tablespoons of chopped herbs. You can use any remaining herbs that you have in the fridge. Return the potatoes to the oven then continue cooking for another 15 minutes until the potatoes are golden and crunchy.

Once the potatoes are ready, divide between 2 plates. Top with a 125g can of rinsed and drained corn kernels, a diced avocado and tomato and ½ cup (50g) of grated Cheddar cheese. You can pop the plates under the grill if you like, to melt the cheese.

aioli **apple** artichoke avocado

baby spinach baguette **banana** **bean**

beetroot blue cheese brie **broccoli** butter bean

caper **capsicum** carrot cashews

cheese **chickpea** chutney coleslaw

couscous cranberries dates dried egg frittata

autumn

kidney bean lentil lettuce **mandarin** muffins

mushrooms mustard **olive** omelette **onion**

pasta **pear** pecans roasted vegetable **rocket**

roll **salad** sandwich **sausage** slice

spinach spring onion sultanas sweet potato

tofu **tomato** wholemeal

Autumn Week 1

I did it for the first week of the other seasons, so I'll do it here too. This week we'll roast a batch of vegetables and create four lunches from them. Hopefully this is an opportunity to showcase seasonal produce.

Monday
Roasted Vegetable and Sausage Wrap V / Banana

Tuesday
Roasted Vegetable Stuffed Pita V / Apple

Wednesday
Roasted Vegetable and Bean Pasta Salad V / Grapes

Thursday
Roasted Vegetable and Bean Frittata / Pear

Friday
Cumin and Oregano Muffins or Something from the Freezer / Grapes

Saturday
Mushroom Pâté and Biscuits

Sunday
Egg and Cheese Rolls

Don't be afraid to try different kitchen gadgets. True, there are some that you may use once and never pick up again, but others may become firm favourites. One of my favourites is my V-slicer. I've had it for years and use it daily to chop vegetables quickly and easily.

shopping list

Fruit and Vegetables
- ☐ 1 large potato
- ☐ ½ head cauliflower
- ☐ 2 onions
- ☐ 1 zucchini
- ☐ 100g cherry tomatoes
- ☐ 2 bananas
- ☐ 2 apples
- ☐ 1 bunch parsley
- ☐ 1 bunch grapes
- ☐ 2 pears
- ☐ 1 clove garlic
- ☐ 150g mushrooms

Fridge
- ☐ 2 vegetarian sausages
- ☐ 6 eggs
- ☐ small tub cream cheese
- ☐ 50g Cheddar cheese
- ☐ mayonnaise

Freezer
- ☐ 4 cumin and oregano muffins

Bakery
- ☐ 2 pita breads
- ☐ 2 wholegrain rolls

Pantry
- ☐ 2 wholegrain flour tortillas
- ☐ Tabasco sauce
- ☐ 100g dried pasta
- ☐ 400g can cannellini beans
- ☐ red wine
- ☐ cashews
- ☐ savoury biscuits for serving with pâté

Staples
- ☐ salt
- ☐ black pepper
- ☐ olive oil
- ☐ canola oil

daily tasks

Sunday

Prepare the roasted vegetables. Chop the potato, cauliflower, 1 onion and the zucchini into bite-size pieces. Add to a roasting tray and drizzle with canola oil. Roast for 30 minutes in a 210°C/410°F/Gas Mark 7 oven. Add 100g of cherry tomatoes and 2 chopped vegetarian sausages and roast for another 20 minutes. Leave to cool.

Spoon some of the vegetables over 2 wholegrain flour tortillas. Roll up then cover in plastic wrap. Pop the remaining vegetables into a container. Place everything into the fridge.

Monday

Prepare the roasted vegetable stuffed pitas. Split 2 pita breads and fill with some of the roasted vegetables. You can add some Tabasco sauce for extra spice. Cover in plastic wrap or place in 2 lunch boxes. Refrigerate until needed.

Tuesday

Prepare the roasted vegetable and bean pasta salad. Cook 100g of pasta according to the instructions on the packet. Drain, then rinse the pasta in cold water. Once drained, place in a bowl. Stir in a good spoonful of the roasted vegetables (remember to keep some for tomorrow). Rinse and drain a 400g can of cannellini beans and add half to the pasta mixture (pop the rest in a container, in the fridge). Finally, stir in 1 tablespoon of chopped parsley. Divide the pasta salad between 2 lunch boxes. Refrigerate until tomorrow.

Place some grapes into 2 containers.

Wednesday

Prepare the roasted vegetable and bean frittata. Beat together 4 eggs and season. Add 1 tablespoon of chopped parsley to the eggs. Heat a 24cm frying pan over a medium heat. Mix together the cannellini beans with the remaining roasted vegetables and add to the pan. Let them warm up slightly. Add the eggs, then turn the heat down. Let cook for 8-10 minutes.

Preheat the grill. Once the eggs are nearly set, place the pan under the grill to finish cooking the top. Slide the frittata off the pan then leave to cool. Slice into quarters and place 2 quarters into each lunch box. Refrigerate until tomorrow.

Thursday

Raid the freezer. Thaw 4 cumin and oregano muffins overnight in the freezer. If you do not have any muffins in the freezer, you can thaw any other item you have frozen on a previous occasion for your lunch. Else you can make a batch of muffins following the recipe on p.228.

Place some grapes into 2 containers.

Saturday

Make the mushroom pâté. Heat 1 tablespoon of olive oil in a frying pan over a medium heat. Add 1 peeled and chopped onion and 1 clove of crushed garlic and cook for 5 minutes, until pale and soft. Add 150g of sliced mushrooms and continue cooking for 3-4 minutes, until the mushrooms are soft. Stir in 1 tablespoon of red wine, letting it cook for 1 minute. Remove from the heat and leave to cool for about 10 minutes.

Tip the mushrooms into a food processor, together with 2 tablespoons of cashews, 1 teaspoon of chopped parsley and seasoning. Blend until the ingredients come together in a smooth consistency. Add 2 tablespoons of cream cheese and blend until combined. Spoon into a serving bowl and serve with your choice of biscuits.

Sunday

Prepare the egg and cheese rolls. Hard boil 2 eggs. Once cooked, rinse under cold water to cool. Peel and place in a bowl. Chop the eggs then add ½ cup (50g) of grated Cheddar cheese and 1 tablespoon of mayonnaise. Mix together and season to taste. Divide the egg mixture between 2 wholegrain rolls. Serve.

Autumn Week 2

It's a rollover week! Yes, I've decided to do a week's worth of rolls. Remember, you can keep the rolls in the freezer and thaw them as needed. Lots of different fillings to enjoy this week.

Monday
Wholemeal Roll Filled with Artichoke Spread, Baby Spinach and Tomato V / Apple

Tuesday
Wholemeal Roll Filled with Cheese, Sun-Dried Tomatoes, Coriander, Chilli Flakes and Artichoke Spread / Banana

Wednesday
Wholemeal Roll Filled with Kidney Bean Spread and Lettuce V / Plum

Thursday
Wholemeal Roll Filled with Sausage and Kidney Bean Spread V / Nectarine

Friday
Wholemeal Roll Filled with Blue Cheese, Tomato, Baby Spinach, Pine Nuts, Spring Onion and Lettuce / Pear

Saturday
Wholemeal Roll Filled with Grilled Mushrooms, Capsicum, Mozzarella and Basil

Sunday
Wholemeal Roll Filled with a Cheese Omelette and Onion Chutney

When buying rolls, do check the ingredients list. Try to get rolls made with wholemeal flour – they are better for you and will keep you fuller for longer. Wholegrain rolls are not necessarily made with wholemeal flour. Ideally you would find a wholegrain roll that is made using wholemeal flour.

shopping list

Fruit and Vegetables
- ☐ 1 small bag baby spinach
- ☐ 3 tomatoes
- ☐ 2 apples
- ☐ 1 bunch coriander
- ☐ 2 bananas
- ☐ 1 bunch spring onions
- ☐ 1 lettuce
- ☐ 2 plums
- ☐ 2 nectarines
- ☐ 2 pears
- ☐ 4 mushrooms
- ☐ 1 bunch basil

Fridge
- ☐ 100g Cheddar cheese
- ☐ 2 vegetarian sausages
- ☐ 50g blue cheese
- ☐ 50g mozzarella cheese
- ☐ 3 eggs

Bakery
- ☐ 14 wholemeal rolls

Pantry
- ☐ 275g jar marinated artichoke hearts
- ☐ sun-dried tomatoes
- ☐ dried chilli flakes
- ☐ 400g can kidney beans
- ☐ Tabasco sauce
- ☐ pine nuts
- ☐ chargrilled capsicum
- ☐ onion chutney

Staples
- ☐ salt
- ☐ black pepper
- ☐ olive oil

daily tasks

Sunday

Prepare the artichoke spread. Drain a 275g jar of marinated artichokes and pop them in a food processor. Process until more or less smooth. Make the rolls. Spread a good dollop of the spread over 2 rolls (put the remaining spread in the fridge). Top with a handful of baby spinach and some tomato slices. Season with some black pepper. Cover in plastic wrap and refrigerate until needed.

Monday

Make up your rolls. Spread the remaining artichoke spread over 2 rolls. Divide 50g of sliced Cheddar cheese between the rolls. Chop 1-2 tablespoons of sun-dried tomatoes and divide between the rolls. Add some chopped coriander and dried chilli flakes. Cover the rolls in plastic wrap, then pop them into the fridge.

Tuesday

Prepare the kidney bean spread. Rinse and drain a 400g can of kidney beans. Pop them into a food processor along with 1 tomato and 3 spring onions. Add 1 tablespoon of chopped coriander and a few drops of Tabasco sauce. Process the ingredients until smooth and well combined.

Divide some of the spread between 2 rolls and top with some lettuce. Cover in plastic wrap and refrigerate until needed. Store the remaining kidney bean spread in a container in the fridge.

Wednesday

Cook 2 vegetarian sausages. Heat 1 tablespoon of olive oil in a frying pan over a medium heat. Add the sausages and turn often, until the sausages are cooked through. Remove from the heat, leave to cool then slice.

Spread the remaining kidney bean spread over 2 rolls. Top with the sliced sausages. Cover in plastic wrap, then refrigerate until needed.

Thursday

Prepare the rolls. Divide 50g of crumbled blue cheese between 2 rolls as well as a sliced tomato. Top with 2 tablespoons of toasted pine nuts, 3 chopped spring onions and some baby spinach. Season with some black pepper. Cover in plastic wrap, then refrigerate until needed.

Saturday

Cook the mushrooms. Heat 1 tablespoon of olive oil in a frying pan over a medium heat. Add 4 sliced mushrooms and cook for about 6 minutes until they are softened and starting to brown. Remove from the heat.

Make up the rolls by adding a tablespoon of chargrilled capsicum to each roll. Divide the mushrooms and 50g of sliced mozzarella cheese between the rolls. Add some lettuce and a few basil leaves, if you like. Serve warm.

Sunday

Make the omelette. Heat 1 tablespoon of olive oil in a 24cm frying pan, over a medium heat. Beat 3 eggs together and add some seasoning. Stir in 2 tablespoons of grated Cheddar cheese. Add to the pan and cook for a few minutes until the eggs are set. Turn the omelette to finish cooking the eggs. Remove from the heat.

Slice the omelette in half and add to the rolls. Top each roll with a dollop of onion chutney. Serve.

Autumn Week 3

It's baking week this week. This is a chance to stock up the freezer with goodies to eat at a later date. This week we have a vegetable slice, a quiche, spring onion cakes and some date and apple muffins.

Monday
Sweet Potato, Zucchini and Broccoli Slice / Peach

Tuesday
Orange and Rocket Couscous V / Pear

Wednesday
Broccoli, Tomato and Mustard Quiche / Grapes

Thursday
Brie, Capsicum, Spinach, Tomato and Olive Wrap / Apple

Friday
Onion, Brie, Tomato and Capsicum Pasta Salad / Grapes

Saturday
Date and Apple Muffins

Sunday
Spring Onion Cakes V

If you have green tomatoes, to speed up their ripening pop them in a paper bag with an apple, then put the bag in a dark warm place. You will soon have red tomatoes.

shopping list

Fruit and Vegetables
- ☐ 1 small sweet potato (about 300g)
- ☐ 1 zucchini
- ☐ 1 onion
- ☐ 1 head broccoli
- ☐ 2 peaches
- ☐ 1 orange
- ☐ 1 small bag rocket
- ☐ 2 pears
- ☐ 250g cherry tomatoes
- ☐ 1 bunch grapes
- ☐ 1 small bag baby spinach
- ☐ 2 apples
- ☐ 1 red onion
- ☐ 1 bunch spring onions

Fridge
- ☐ 6 eggs
- ☐ 125ml milk
- ☐ small tub double cream
- ☐ 100g Brie
- ☐ mayonnaise

Freezer
- ☐ 1 sheet puff pastry

Bakery
- ☐ 4 sweet muffins (or recipe)

Pantry
- ☐ 75g wholemeal self-raising flour
- ☐ 75g self-raising flour
- ☐ whole nutmeg
- ☐ 100g couscous
- ☐ sultanas
- ☐ pine nuts
- ☐ ground cinnamon
- ☐ Dijon mustard
- ☐ 2 wholegrain flour tortillas
- ☐ chargrilled capsicum
- ☐ olives
- ☐ 100g dried pasta
- ☐ 450g plain flour
- ☐ baking powder
- ☐ sweet chilli sauce

Staples
- ☐ salt
- ☐ black pepper
- ☐ olive oil
- ☐ extra virgin olive oil
- ☐ canola oil

daily tasks

Sunday

Make the sweet potato, zucchini and broccoli slice. Preheat the oven to 180°C/350°F/Gas Mark 4. Grease and line a 30 x 20cm baking tin. In a large bowl, whisk together 4 eggs and ½ cup (125ml) of milk. Beat in ½ cup (75g) of wholemeal self-raising flour and ½ cup (75g) of regular self-raising flour.

Peel and grate the sweet potato and chop a zucchini, onion and ½ a head of broccoli. Add to the prepared batter. Stir in some grated nutmeg, then season. Pour the mixture into the baking tin and bake for 30-35 minutes until golden brown and firm. Leave to cool then remove from the tin. Slice into quarters, then halve each quarter. Place 2 slices into each lunch box and refrigerate. The rest can be frozen by wrapping each slice in plastic wrap then placing into a container or freezer bag, then into the freezer.

Monday

Prepare the orange and rocket couscous. Place ½ cup (100g) of couscous in a bowl with 3 tablespoons of sultanas. Stir in ½ cup (125ml) of boiling water then let stand for 3 minutes. Fluff up with a fork. Grate the rind from 1 orange and set aside. Chop the flesh of the orange into bite-size pieces and add to the couscous. Stir in 1 tablespoon of toasted pine nuts and a good handful of rocket.

Mix together 1 tablespoon of extra virgin olive oil with the orange rind and ¼ teaspoon of ground cinnamon. Pour the dressing over the salad and stir carefully to coat. Divide the couscous between 2 lunch boxes then refrigerate until needed.

Tuesday

Make the broccoli, tomato and mustard quiche. Preheat the oven to 200°C/400°F/Gas Mark 6. Thaw a sheet of puff pastry. Line a 20cm tart tin with the pastry. Spread 1 teaspoon of Dijon mustard over the pastry base. Chop the remaining broccoli into small florets then scatter them over the pastry. Cut 100g of cherry tomatoes in half then add them to the tin.

Beat together 3 tablespoons of double cream, 2 eggs, 1 teaspoon of Dijon mustard and some seasoning. Pour into the tart tin and bake for 40 minutes until

golden and puffed. Leave to cool then cut into quarters. Place a quarter (or 2!) in each lunch box, then pop them into the fridge. The other 2 quarters can be frozen by wrapping in plastic wrap then placing in a container in the freezer.

Divide some grapes between 2 containers.

Wednesday

Prepare the wraps. Slice 50g of Brie and divide between 2 wholegrain flour tortillas. Cut 50g of cherry tomatoes in half and add to the tortillas along with some baby spinach, a few chargrilled capsicums and some olives. Add some mayonnaise, then season to taste. Roll up the tortillas, then cover in plastic wrap. Refrigerate.

Thursday

Prepare the pasta salad. Cook 100g of dried pasta according to packet directions. Drain then rinse under cold water to cool completely. Drain well then place in a bowl.

Whilst the pasta is cooking, heat 1 tablespoon of olive oil in a frying pan over a medium heat. Add a sliced red onion and cook until soft, about 6 minutes. Remove from the heat. Once cool, stir the onions into the pasta.

To the pasta add 100g of halved cherry tomatoes and 2 tablespoons of chargrilled capsicum (diced if needed). Finally, chop 50g of Brie and stir it into the pasta. Season to taste then divide between 2 lunch boxes. Refrigerate until needed.

Divide some grapes between 2 containers.

Saturday

Make date and apple muffins according to the recipe (p.229), or buy your favourite muffins from the bakers. Allow 2 per person, then freeze the rest. Pop them into a container or freezer bags, then into the freezer.

Sunday

Make the spring onion cakes. Place 3 cups (450g) of plain flour in a bowl and stir in ¼ teaspoon of baking powder and 1 teaspoon of salt. Add 1¼ cups (300ml) of boiling water and mix well. Once combined, knead the mixture for a few minutes then stand for 30 minutes. After 30 minutes, knead in a bunch of chopped spring onions. Divide the dough into 10 pieces then roll each piece into a ball. Flatten the balls to form cakes about 5mm thick.

Heat 3 tablespoons of canola oil in a large frying pan over a medium-high heat. Add the cakes and cook for 3-4 minutes on each side, until golden brown. Remove from the pan and drain on paper towel. Serve alone or with sweet chilli sauce. Any leftovers can be frozen by popping them into a freezer bag then into the freezer.

Autumn Week 4

This week's menu features chickpeas, lentils and fresh mint. Such simple ingredients resulting in such good lunches. If you cannot get hold of fresh mint for this week's lunches you can use dried mint flakes as they still retain a lot of flavour. Enjoy.

Monday
Falafel with Minty Brown Rice and Cherry Tomatoes V / Diced Pear with Cardamom

Tuesday
Lentil and Tomato Turnovers V / Dried Apricots and Almonds

Wednesday
Goat's Cheese, Lentil and Pasta Salad / Peach

Thursday
Halloumi and Chickpea Salad with Lime and Mint Dressing / Sultanas and Pecans

Friday
Beetroot, Halloumi and Chickpea Salad / Nectarine

Saturday
Goat's Cheese, Beetroot and Rocket Baguette

Sunday
Cheese on Toast

Halloumi cheese can be cooked under a grill or in a frying pan. Brush with olive oil then place under the grill or into the frying pan. Cook until golden, turning as needed.

shopping list

Fruit and Vegetables
- [ ] 1 bunch mint
- [ ] 200g cherry tomatoes
- [ ] 2 pears
- [ ] 1 onion
- [ ] 1 red capsicum
- [ ] 1 small bunch basil
- [ ] 2 peaches
- [ ] 1 small bag baby spinach
- [ ] 1 lime
- [ ] 1 small bag rocket
- [ ] 2 nectarines

Fridge
- [ ] 120g goat's cheese
- [ ] 180g halloumi cheese
- [ ] 80g Cheddar cheese

Freezer
- [ ] 4-6 falafel
- [ ] 1 sheet puff pastry

Bakery
- [ ] 1 baguette

Pantry
- [ ] 100g brown rice
- [ ] lemon juice
- [ ] ground cardamom
- [ ] 400g can lentils
- [ ] sun-dried tomatoes
- [ ] dried chilli flakes
- [ ] dried thyme
- [ ] dried apricots
- [ ] almonds
- [ ] 100g dried pasta
- [ ] pine nuts
- [ ] 400g can chickpeas
- [ ] honey
- [ ] sultanas
- [ ] pecans
- [ ] 450g can baby beetroot

Staples
- [ ] salt
- [ ] black pepper
- [ ] olive oil
- [ ] extra virgin olive oil
- [ ] canola oil

daily tasks

Sunday

Prepare the minty brown rice. Cook ½ cup (100g) of brown rice according to packet instructions. Once cooked, rinse under cold water and drain well. Stir in 2 tablespoons of chopped mint and 100g of halved cherry tomatoes. Stir in ½ tablespoon of extra virgin olive oil and season to taste. Divide the rice between 2 lunch boxes.

Thaw 2-3 falafel per person and add them to the lunch boxes. Pop them into the fridge. If you do not have any falafel in the freezer, follow the instructions below. Remember to add any ingredients you need to your shopping list.

To make falafel: To a food processor, add a 400g can of rinsed and drained chickpeas, a peeled and chopped onion and a clove of crushed garlic. Add ½ a teaspoon each of ground cumin, ground coriander, dried mint flakes, ground turmeric and caraway seeds. Then add 1 teaspoon of lemon juice. Process until the mixture is well combined. Finally, add ½ cup (75g) of wholemeal plain flour, blending it thoroughly into the mixture until it all comes together. Heat 2 tablespoons of canola oil in a large frying pan over a medium heat. Add rounded tablespoons of the mixture to the pan and flatten slightly. Fry for 6-8 minutes, until golden brown all over. Drain on paper towel and leave to cool. Any remaining falafel can be frozen by popping in a container and then into the freezer.

Prepare the pear. Core and dice 2 pears (no need to peel) and divide between 2 containers. Add some lemon juice and top with ¼ teaspoon of ground cardamom. Refrigerate into needed.

Monday

Make the lentil and tomato turnovers. Thaw a sheet of puff pastry. Whilst thawing, heat 1 tablespoon of olive oil in a frying pan. Add a chopped onion and fry for 5-6 minutes until soft and starting to brown. Remove from the heat and stir in a 400g can of rinsed and drained lentils. Season with black pepper.

Preheat the oven to 220°C/425°F/Gas Mark 7. Cut the pastry into 4 squares. Spoon some of the lentil mixture onto each square. The remaining lentils and onions should be placed in a container in the fridge. Chop 2 tablespoons of sun-dried tomatoes and

divide between the pastry squares. Finally, sprinkle some dried chilli flakes and dried thyme over the mixture, according to taste.

Fold each pastry in half to form a triangle, then press the edges with a fork to seal. Prick the tops. Place on a baking tray and bake for 20 minutes, until golden. Leave to cool, before placing 2 in each lunch box. Refrigerate.

Mix 2 handfuls of dried apricots with 2 handfuls of almonds and divide between 2 containers.

Tuesday

Prepare the goat's cheese, lentil and pasta salad. Cook 100g of dried pasta according to packet instructions. Once cooked, drain then rinse under cold water. Drain thoroughly, then place in a bowl. To the pasta add the remaining lentils and onions, ½ a chopped red capsicum and 1 tablespoon of toasted pine nuts. Stir through 60g of crumbled goat's cheese.

Make a lemon and basil dressing. Mix together 1 tablespoon of extra virgin olive oil with ½ tablespoon of lemon juice. Add 1 tablespoon of chopped basil and season to taste. Stir the dressing into the salad. Divide the salad between 2 lunch boxes, then refrigerate until needed.

Wednesday

Prepare the halloumi and chickpea salad. Preheat the grill. Dice a 180g pack of halloumi into cubes and place on a baking tray. Brush the halloumi with olive oil and season with black pepper. Place under the grill and turn often until the cubes are golden. Set aside to cool. Place half of the halloumi cubes in a container in the fridge and pop the rest in a bowl.

Rinse and drain a 400g can of chickpeas and add half to the halloumi. Put the rest in a container in the fridge. Cut 100g of cherry tomatoes in half and add to the bowl. Finally, stir in a handful of shredded baby spinach.

Make the lime and mint dressing. Mix together 1 tablespoon of extra virgin olive oil with the grated rind and juice of 1 lime. Add 1 tablespoon of chopped mint, a teaspoon of honey, then season to taste. Stir the dressing through the salad. Divide the salad between 2 lunch boxes then refrigerate until needed.

Mix 2 handfuls of sultanas with 2 handfuls of pecans. Divide between 2 containers.

Thursday
Prepare the beetroot, halloumi and chickpea salad. Drain a 450g can of baby beetroot. Pop 4 beetroot into a container in the fridge. Cut the rest into quarters and place in a bowl. To the beetroot add the remaining halloumi and chickpeas. Chop the remaining capsicum half and add to the bowl. Finally, add a handful of rocket.

Mix up a lemon and mint dressing. Mix together 1 tablespoon of extra virgin olive oil with ½ tablespoon of lemon juice, 1 tablespoon of chopped mint and a teaspoon of honey. Season to taste. Stir the dressing into the salad. Divide the salad between 2 lunch boxes then pop them into the fridge.

Saturday
Prepare the goat's cheese, beetroot and rocket baguette. Cut 2 pieces of baguette, according to appetite (you will use the rest of the baguette tomorrow). Slice the baby beetroot and add it to the bread along with 60g of goat's cheese and some rocket and basil leaves. Season to taste.

Sunday
Make cheese on toast. Preheat the grill. Slice the remaining baguette into 2cm pieces, on an angle. Pop the slices under the grill to brown one side. Turn the slices then top with 80g of sliced or grated Cheddar cheese or your choice of cheese. Grill until the cheese has melted. Serve immediately.

Autumn Week 5

There's a bit of everything this week, including a sandwich that features shredded halloumi which is cooked until it is golden and crispy. The week ends with comforting potato cakes and jacket potatoes.

Monday
Sweetcorn Dip V and Dippers / Banana

Tuesday
Halloumi, Avocado, Onion and Tomato Sandwich / Grapes

Wednesday
Tofu and Cranberry Puffs V / Pecans and Dates

Thursday
Shredded Omelette in a Wrap with Carrot, Spring Onions, Parsley and Aioli / Grapes

Friday
Cannellini Bean Salad with Olives, Capers, Spring Onions and Cherry Tomatoes V / Apple

Saturday
Herby Potato Cakes with a Tomato and Rocket Salad V

Sunday
Jacket Potato with Cheese and Beans

Savoury yeast flakes are also known as nutritional yeast flakes and are found in health food shops and many supermarkets. They are high in Vitamin B and offer a cheesy flavour to foods, making them great for vegans. They are not the same as yeast extract or brewer's yeast.

shopping list

Fruit and Vegetables
- [ ] 1 clove garlic
- [ ] 2 carrots
- [ ] 1 celery stick
- [ ] 1 red capsicum
- [ ] 2 bananas
- [ ] 1 small red onion
- [ ] 1 tomato
- [ ] 1 avocado
- [ ] 1 bunch grapes
- [ ] 1 bunch spring onions
- [ ] 1 bunch parsley
- [ ] 200g cherry tomatoes
- [ ] 1 small bag rocket
- [ ] 2 apples
- [ ] 5 large potatoes
- [ ] 1 small bunch basil
- [ ] 1 small bunch chives

Fridge
- [ ] small tub vegan cream cheese
- [ ] 180g halloumi cheese
- [ ] 80g firm tofu
- [ ] 50ml soy milk
- [ ] 2 eggs
- [ ] aioli
- [ ] 50g Cheddar cheese

Freezer
- [ ] 1 sheet puff pastry

Bakery
- [ ] 4 slices wholegrain bread

Pantry
- [ ] 310g can corn kernels
- [ ] chilli powder
- [ ] smoked paprika
- [ ] grissini (breadsticks)
- [ ] cranberry sauce
- [ ] savoury yeast flakes
- [ ] garlic powder
- [ ] onion powder
- [ ] pecans
- [ ] dates
- [ ] 2 wholegrain flour tortillas
- [ ] 400g can cannellini beans
- [ ] olives
- [ ] capers
- [ ] lemon juice
- [ ] sun-dried tomatoes
- [ ] 400g can baked beans

Staples
- [ ] salt
- [ ] black pepper
- [ ] olive oil
- [ ] extra virgin olive oil
- [ ] canola oil

daily tasks

Sunday

Prepare the sweetcorn dip. In a food processor blend together a 310g can of rinsed and drained corn kernels, 2 tablespoons of vegan cream cheese, 1 clove of crushed garlic, ¼ teaspoon of chilli powder and ¼ teaspoon of smoked paprika. Season to taste with freshly ground black pepper. Divide the dip between 2 containers. Refrigerate until needed.

Prepare the dippers. Preheat the grill. Cut 90g of halloumi into slices. Brush with olive oil and season with black pepper. Grill on both sides until golden. Once cool, divide between 2 lunch boxes. Chop a carrot, celery stick and red capsicum into sticks suitable for dipping. Add to the lunch boxes along with some grissini. Pop everything into the fridge.

Monday

Prepare the sandwiches. Heat ½ tablespoon of olive oil in a frying pan over a medium heat. Shred 90g of halloumi using a coarse grater. Add to the pan and cook and stir for a few minutes until the cheese starts to brown. Remove from the heat.

Once cool, divide between 2 slices of bread. Add a small chopped red onion and a sliced tomato and avocado. Season with black pepper. Top each with another slice of bread and cut each sandwich in half. Cover in plastic wrap then refrigerate until needed.

Divide some grapes between 2 containers.

Tuesday

Make the tofu and cranberry puffs. Preheat the oven to 200°C/400°F/Gas Mark 6. Thaw 1 sheet of puff pastry. Cut the pastry into 4 even-sized squares. Spoon ½ tablespoon of cranberry sauce into the middle of each square, spreading it evenly. Slice 80g of drained firm tofu. Mix together ½ tablespoon of savoury yeast flakes with ¼ teaspoon each of garlic powder and onion powder. Coat the tofu slices in the mixture. Place the tofu on top of the cranberry sauce. Be sure to leave plenty of room to fold your pastry corners inwards.

Fold the corners of the pastry square into the middle. Brush with soy milk. Place on a baking tray and bake for 20-25 minutes, until crisp and golden.

Leave to cool. Once cool, place 2 in each lunch box then refrigerate until needed.

Mix 2 handfuls of pecans with 2 handfuls of dates. Divide between 2 containers.

Wednesday

Make the shredded omelette. Heat ½ tablespoon of canola oil in a frying pan over a medium heat. Beat 2 eggs and add some seasoning. Add to the pan and cook until set, turning once. Remove from the pan and leave to cool. Once cool, roll the omelette up and slice thinly.

Divide the shredded omelette between 2 wholegrain tortillas. Grate a carrot and add to the tortillas. Chop ½ a bunch of spring onions and 1 tablespoon of fresh parsley. Add to the tortillas. Finally, dollop on some aioli. Roll up the wraps then cover in plastic wrap. Refrigerate until needed.

Divide some grapes between 2 containers.

Thursday

Prepare the cannellini bean salad. Rinse and drain a 400g can of cannellini beans. Place in a bowl. Add 2 tablespoons of olives and ½ tablespoon of rinsed and drained capers. Cut 100g of cherry tomatoes in half and add to the bowl. Chop ½ bunch of spring onions and 1 tablespoon of parsley and add to the salad. Stir in a handful of rocket (keep some for tomorrow).

Mix together 1 tablespoon of extra virgin olive oil with ½ tablespoon of lemon juice and stir into the salad. Season with black pepper. Divide the salad between 2 lunch boxes then refrigerate until needed.

Saturday

Make the herby potato cakes. Peel and cut 3 large potatoes into even-sized pieces and place in a large saucepan of lightly salted water. Bring to the boil, reduce the heat very slightly and simmer until the potatoes are tender. This will take about 20 minutes, but will depend on the size of your potato pieces. Drain.

Place the potatoes in a large bowl, then mash until smooth. Add 2 tablespoons of soy milk and 1 tablespoon each of chopped basil, chives and parsley. Add ½ teaspoon each of onion powder and garlic powder and a good grind of black pepper. Mix thoroughly. Once the potato is cool enough to easily handle, take heaped tablespoons of the potato and roll into balls, then flatten to form cakes.

Heat 2 tablespoons of olive oil in a large frying pan over a medium heat. Add the potato cakes and fry for 4 minutes. Carefully turn them, then fry for another 3 minutes, until golden. Any remaining potato cakes can be frozen by popping them into a freezer bag or container then into the freezer.

Put together the tomato and rocket salad. Slice 100g of cherry tomatoes in half and place in a bowl. Chop 2 tablespoons of sun-dried tomatoes and add to the cherry tomatoes. Add a handful of rocket. Chop some herbs of your choice and add to the salad. Drizzle ½ tablespoon of extra virgin olive oil over the salad. Serve with the potato cakes.

Sunday

Cook the jacket potatoes. Prick 2 large potatoes and microwave for 8-10 minutes until they start to soften. Preheat the oven to 210°C/410°F/Gas Mark 7, pop the potatoes in the oven and bake for 30 minutes until crisp.

Heat a 400g can of baked beans in a saucepan. Whilst heating, grate ½ cup (50g) of Cheddar cheese. Cut open the jacket potatoes then top with the beans and cheese.

Autumn Week 6

It's another pantry raid this week. Spotting some TVP at the back of the cupboard I decided to make up some sausage rolls. Then there's the cans of beans, corn and tomatoes that I've put to good use this week.

Monday
Sausage Rolls V / Grapes

Tuesday
Butter Bean and Crispy Vegetable Salad / Dried Cranberries and Cashews

Wednesday
Tofu, Bean, Capsicum and Tomato Salad V / Grapes

Thursday
Artichoke, Tofu, Tomato and Spinach Frittata / Banana

Friday
Niçoisesque Salad with Brown Rice / Apple

Saturday
All-Day Breakfast

Sunday
Beans on Toast V

It is quite easy to make vegetarian versions of meals that contain meat. As well as the many soy products out there, you can use beans and vegetables. Don't be afraid to get creative and make a so-called classic your own.

shopping list

Fruit and Vegetables
- [ ] 2 onions
- [ ] 1 bunch grapes
- [ ] 1 carrot
- [ ] 1 red capsicum
- [ ] 1 bunch spring onions
- [ ] 200g cherry tomatoes
- [ ] 1 lettuce
- [ ] 1 small bag baby spinach
- [ ] 4 tomatoes
- [ ] 2 bananas
- [ ] 2 apples
- [ ] 6 mushrooms

Fridge
- [ ] 50g Cheddar cheese
- [ ] 200g marinated tofu
- [ ] 8 eggs
- [ ] 2 vegetarian sausages

Freezer
- [ ] 1 sheet puff pastry
- [ ] 2-4 hash browns

Bakery
- [ ] 4 slices wholegrain bread

Pantry
- [ ] 35g textured vegetable protein
- [ ] vegetable stock
- [ ] tomato paste
- [ ] Vegemite / Marmite
- [ ] mixed herbs
- [ ] Tabasco sauce
- [ ] 400g can butter beans
- [ ] 420g can corn kernels
- [ ] lemon juice
- [ ] dried cranberries
- [ ] cashews
- [ ] red wine vinegar
- [ ] Dijon mustard
- [ ] 400g can artichoke hearts
- [ ] 100g brown rice
- [ ] olives
- [ ] capers
- [ ] white wine vinegar
- [ ] 400g can mixed beans
- [ ] 400g can chopped tomatoes
- [ ] barbecue sauce

Staples
- [ ] salt
- [ ] black pepper
- [ ] olive oil
- [ ] extra virgin olive oil

daily tasks

Sunday

Make the sausage rolls. Preheat the oven to 220°C/425°F/Gas Mark 7. Thaw a sheet of puff pastry. Whilst the pastry is thawing, soak ½ cup (35g) of textured vegetable protein in 1 cup (250ml) of vegetable stock. Let soak for 10 minutes then drain.

Heat 1 tablespoon of olive oil in a frying pan over a medium heat. Add a chopped onion and cook and stir for 5 minutes until the onion is pale and soft. Stir in the TVP, ½ tablespoon of tomato paste, ½ tablespoon of Vegemite or Marmite, ½ teaspoon of dried mixed herbs and a few drops of Tabasco sauce. Cook for 3 minutes then remove from the heat. Season well.

Cut the pastry into 3 equal-sized lengths. Add the TVP mixture along the middle of the 3 lengths of pastry. Roll each piece up then cut into 4. Place seam side down on a baking tray then bake for 20 minutes until golden brown and puffed. Leave to cool then place into 2 lunch boxes. Refrigerate until needed. Any leftovers can be frozen by popping them into a freezer bag or container then into the freezer.

Place some grapes into 2 containers.

Monday

Prepare the butter bean and crispy vegetable salad. Rinse and drain a 400g can of butter beans and a 420g can of corn kernels. Place half of each into a bowl and pop the rest into a container for another day. Grate a carrot and add to the bowl. Chop ½ a red capsicum and ½ a bunch of spring onions and place in the bowl. Next, cut 100g of cherry tomatoes in half and add to the salad.

Mix together 1 tablespoon of extra virgin olive oil with ½ tablespoon of lemon juice. Season with black pepper. Stir the dressing into the bowl. Place some lettuce into 2 lunch boxes and top with the butter bean salad. Finally, grate ½ cup (50g) of Cheddar cheese over the salad. Place in the fridge.

Mix 2 handfuls of dried cranberries with 2 handfuls of cashews and divide between 2 containers.

Tuesday

Make the tofu, bean, capsicum and tomato salad. Place the remaining butter beans and corn kernels in a bowl. Add 100g of cherry tomatoes, cut in half, the remaining capsicum half and the remaining ½ bunch of spring onions, both chopped. Slice 100g of marinated tofu into bite-size cubes. Add to the salad along with a handful of baby spinach (save some for tomorrow).

Make a dressing by mixing together 1 tablespoon of extra virgin olive oil with ½ tablespoon of red wine vinegar and ½ teaspoon of Dijon mustard. Stir into the salad. Divide the salad between 2 lunch boxes then refrigerate until needed.

Divide the remaining grapes between 2 containers.

Wednesday

Prepare the artichoke, tofu, tomato and spinach frittata. Rinse and drain a 400g can of artichoke hearts. Place half in a container in the fridge then coarsely chop the rest. Cut the remaining 100g of marinated tofu into pieces. Chop up 1 tomato.

Heat 1 tablespoon of olive oil in a 24cm frying pan over a medium heat. Lightly whisk 4 eggs in a bowl with some seasoning. Stir in the artichokes, tofu, tomato and some baby spinach. Add the mixture to the pan, turn the heat down and cook for 8-10 minutes, until the eggs are nearly set. A few minutes before the end, preheat the grill.

Place the frying pan under the grill to cook the top of the frittata. This will only take about 2 minutes. Slide the frittata off the pan then leave to cool. Slice into quarters and place 2 quarters in each lunch box. Refrigerate.

Thursday

Make the Niçoisesque salad with brown rice. Cook ½ cup (100g) of brown rice according to packet directions. Once cooked, rinse and drain under cold water to cool. Place in a bowl. Hard boil 2 eggs. Leave to cool then peel. Chop 1 tomato and the remaining artichoke hearts. Add the tomato and artichoke hearts to the rice along with 2 tablespoons of olives and ½ tablespoon of rinsed and drained capers.

Make a dressing by mixing together 1 tablespoon of extra virgin olive oil with ½ tablespoon of white wine vinegar. Season to taste. Add to the rice salad. Divide between 2 lunch boxes. Finally, cut the eggs into quarters and place on top of the salad. Refrigerate until needed.

Saturday

Make the all-day breakfast. Cook the hash browns according to packet instructions. It is probably easiest to cook them in the oven as this frees up your hob. Heat 2 large frying pans with 1 tablespoon of olive oil in each. In one pan, fry 2 eggs and 2 vegetarian sausages, until cooked to your liking. Cook 2 halved tomatoes and the mushrooms (sliced or quartered) in the other pan. You can add some chopped herbs if you like. Pop some bread in the toaster to make toast to accompany your breakfast. Serve with your choice of sauce.

Sunday

Make the beans for beans on toast. Heat 1 tablespoon of olive oil in a frying pan over a medium heat. Add 1 chopped onion and fry for 5 minutes until pale and soft. Rinse and drain a 400g can of mixed beans and add to the onion along with a 400g can of chopped tomatoes. Stir in 1 tablespoon of barbecue sauce and season to taste. Cook and stir for 5 minutes.

Make some toast to go with the beans. Place on your plates, then top with the prepared beans. Any leftover beans can be refrigerated once cooled and would go nicely with jacket potatoes.

Autumn Week 7

It's a super quick week this week. All of these lunches require minimal effort. As such we'll be raiding the freezer for any goodies, as well as putting together simple but tasty salads, spreads and rolls.

Monday
Raid the Freezer: Cumin and Oregano Muffins / Apple

Tuesday
Couscous with Olives, Corn, Chickpeas and Rocket V / Banana

Wednesday
Raid the Freezer: Sweet Potato, Zucchini and Broccoli Slice / Grapes

Thursday
Crispbread with Bean Spread V / Seasoned Chickpeas V / Walnuts and Sultanas

Friday
Wholegrain Roll Filled with Bean Spread, Olives, Tomato and Lettuce V / Grapes

Saturday
Grilled Cheese Turkish Rolls

Sunday
Quick Fresh Salad

"If hunger makes you irritable, better eat and be pleasant." Sefer Hasidim

shopping list

Fruit and Vegetables
- ☐ 2 apples
- ☐ 1 small bag rocket
- ☐ 2 bananas
- ☐ 1 bunch grapes
- ☐ 2 tomatoes
- ☐ 1 lettuce

Fridge
- ☐ 100g Cheddar cheese

Freezer
- ☐ 4 cumin and oregano muffins
- ☐ 4 sweet potato, zucchini and broccoli slice

Bakery
- ☐ 2 wholegrain rolls
- ☐ 2 Turkish rolls

Pantry
- ☐ 100g couscous
- ☐ 125g can corn kernels
- ☐ green olives
- ☐ 400g can chickpeas
- ☐ lemon juice
- ☐ ground cumin
- ☐ 400g can butter beans
- ☐ sun-dried tomatoes
- ☐ dried mixed herbs
- ☐ Tabasco sauce
- ☐ 6-8 crispbread
- ☐ dried thyme
- ☐ walnuts
- ☐ sultanas
- ☐ black olives
- ☐ pine nuts
- ☐ red wine vinegar

Staples
- ☐ salt
- ☐ black pepper
- ☐ extra virgin olive oil

daily tasks

Sunday
Raid the freezer for previously made goodies. Keep an eye out for cumin and oregano muffins or perhaps some vegetable loaf. Thaw in the fridge overnight. They will be ready for your lunch tomorrow. You can place them in your lunch boxes. If you cannot find any muffins, you will find the recipe on p.228.

Monday
Prepare the couscous. Place ½ cup (100g) of couscous in a bowl. Stir in ½ cup (125ml) of boiling water then let stand for 3 minutes. Fluff up with a fork. Rinse and drain a 125g can of corn kernels and add to the couscous. Then add 2 tablespoons of green olives and a handful of rocket. Rinse and drain a 400g can of chickpeas. Add half to the couscous and put the rest in a container, in the fridge.

Mix together 1 tablespoon of extra virgin olive oil with ½ tablespoon of lemon juice and ½ teaspoon of ground cumin. Stir the dressing into the couscous. Divide the couscous between 2 lunch boxes then refrigerate until needed.

Tuesday
Raid the freezer. You may find some sweet potato, zucchini and broccoli slice. You can thaw it overnight in the fridge. You can place them in your lunch boxes. If not, and you cannot find anything else, here are the instructions for the slice. Remember to add the ingredients to your shopping list.

Preheat the oven to 180°C/350°F/Gas Mark 4. Grease and line a 30 x 20cm baking tin. In a large bowl, whisk together 4 eggs and ½ cup (125ml) of milk. Beat in ½ cup (75g) of wholemeal self-raising flour and ½ cup (75g) of regular self-raising flour. Peel and grate the sweet potato and chop 1 zucchini, 1 onion and ½ a head of broccoli. Add to the batter. Stir in some grated nutmeg then season. Pour into the baking tin and bake for 30-35 minutes until golden brown and firm. Leave to cool then remove from the tin. Slice into quarters, then halve each quarter. Place 2 slices into each lunch box. The rest can be frozen.

Place some of the grapes into 2 containers.

Wednesday
Prepare the bean spread. Rinse and drain a 400g can of butter beans and pop them into a food processor. Add 1 tablespoon of sun-dried tomatoes, 1 tablespoon of extra virgin olive oil, 1 teaspoon of dried mixed herbs and a few drops of Tabasco sauce. Blitz until smooth. Season to taste with black pepper. Save some of the spread to go on rolls tomorrow. Divide the rest between 2 containers, add some crispbread (3 or 4 per person – depending on appetite), then pop them into the fridge.

Season the remaining chickpeas with some black pepper and a sprinkle of dried thyme. Divide between 2 lunch boxes, then pop them into the fridge.

Mix 2 handfuls of walnuts with 2 handfuls of sultanas. Divide between 2 containers.

Thursday
Prepare the rolls. Split 2 wholegrain rolls and spread with the remaining bean spread. Slice a few black olives and a tomato and add to the rolls. Finish with some lettuce. Cover in plastic wrap then refrigerate until needed.

Divide the remaining grapes between 2 containers.

Saturday

Prepare the grilled cheese Turkish rolls. Preheat the grill. Split 2 rolls and top the base with 50g of sliced Cheddar cheese. Place the lid and the base under the grill and grill until the cheese is melted and the lid is browned. Pop the lids back on, cut in half and then serve.

Sunday

Put together a quick fresh salad. Chop a tomato and place in a bowl. Slice a handful of black olives and add to the tomato. Cube 50g of Cheddar cheese and place in the bowl along with 1 tablespoon of toasted pine nuts and a handful of lettuce and rocket. Mix together 1 tablespoon of extra virgin olive oil with ½ tablespoon of red wine vinegar. Pour the dressing over the salad then stir well. Divide the salad between 2 plates, then serve.

Autumn Week 8

No real theme for this week's lunches. Rather, it just contains items I fancied eating or hadn't had for a while. I had an urge for avocado, artichoke and Brie so they all feature this week, along with other good things.

Monday
Cheese and Onion Oven Omelette / Grapes

Tuesday
Brie, Olive and Chargrilled Capsicum Sandwich / Dried Apricots

Wednesday
Brie, Butter Bean, Artichoke and Capsicum Pasta Salad / Grapes

Thursday
Bulghar Wheat Salad with Beans, Capsicum, Artichoke and Spinach V / Apple

Friday
Brie and Biscuits with Chutney / Cashews and Sultanas

Saturday
Baked Avocado

Sunday
Sausage and Onion Baguette

When cooking pasta, there is no need to add oil to the water to prevent the pasta from sticking. Once the water is boiling, add the pasta then stir with a wooden spoon whilst the water comes back to boil. Once it is boiling again, you can stop stirring and your pasta will not stick.

shopping list

Fruit and Vegetables
- ☐ 2 onions
- ☐ 1 bunch grapes
- ☐ 1 lettuce
- ☐ 1 red capsicum
- ☐ 1 small bag baby spinach
- ☐ 2 apples
- ☐ 2 avocados
- ☐ 2 tomatoes

Fridge
- ☐ 4 eggs
- ☐ 160ml milk
- ☐ 150g Cheddar cheese
- ☐ 200g Brie
- ☐ 2 vegetarian sausages

Bakery
- ☐ 5 slices wholegrain bread
- ☐ 1 baguette

Pantry
- ☐ dried sage
- ☐ chargrilled capsicum
- ☐ olives
- ☐ dried apricots
- ☐ 100g dried pasta
- ☐ 400g can butter beans
- ☐ 400g can artichoke hearts
- ☐ dried chilli flakes
- ☐ dried oregano
- ☐ 100g bulghar wheat
- ☐ sun-dried tomatoes
- ☐ dried rosemary
- ☐ chutney
- ☐ savoury biscuits (for cheese)
- ☐ cashews
- ☐ sultanas
- ☐ lime juice
- ☐ dried thyme

Staples
- ☐ salt
- ☐ black pepper
- ☐ olive oil

daily tasks

Sunday

Make the cheese and onion oven omelette. Preheat the oven to 200°C/400°F/Gas Mark 6. Whisk 4 eggs with ⅔ cup (160ml) of milk. Stir in 1 finely chopped onion, ½ cup (50g) of grated Cheddar cheese and 1 teaspoon of dried sage. Season. Pour the mixture into a 22 x 16cm greased ovenproof dish. Bake for 40 minutes, until golden and firm. Leave to cool before removing the omelette from the dish. Slice into 4 and divide between 2 lunch boxes. Refrigerate.

Place some grapes into 2 containers.

Monday

Prepare the sandwiches. Slice 50g of Brie and divide it between 2 slices of wholegrain bread. Add 2 tablespoons of chargrilled capsicum and 1 tablespoon of sliced olives. Finish with some lettuce. Top with 2 slices of bread, slice each sandwich in half then cover in plastic wrap. Refrigerate until needed.

Don't forget your dried apricots.

Tuesday

Prepare the pasta salad. Cook 100g of dried pasta according to packet directions. Rinse under cold water then drain thoroughly. Place in a bowl. Rinse and drain a 400g can of butter beans and a 400g can of artichoke hearts. Place half of each into a container than pop it into the fridge. Chop up the artichokes then add to the pasta with the butter beans.

Add ½ a chopped red capsicum, ½ teaspoon of chilli flakes and ½ teaspoon of dried oregano. Finally, stir in 50g of cubed Brie. Season to taste. Divide the pasta salad between 2 lunch boxes then pop them into the fridge.

Divide some grapes between 2 containers.

Wednesday

Cook the bulghar wheat. Place ½ cup (100g) of bulghar wheat in a bowl and cover with cold water. Leave to soak for 40 minutes and then drain thoroughly into a sieve. Place in a bowl.

To the bulghar wheat, add the remaining butter beans and artichokes (chopped). Chop the remaining capsicum half and add it to the bowl. Stir in 2 tablespoons of chopped sun-dried tomatoes and some shredded baby spinach. Finally, stir through 1 teaspoon of dried rosemary. Season to taste. Divide between 2 lunch boxes, then refrigerate.

Thursday

Put together the cheese and biscuits. Allow 50g of Brie per person. Add the Brie to your lunch boxes, along with some chutney and biscuits for spreading the cheese and chutney on. Add a handful of grapes. Refrigerate. Don't forget a knife.

Mix 2 handfuls of cashews with 2 handfuls of sultanas. Divide between 2 containers.

Saturday

Bake the avocados. Preheat the oven to 200°C/400°F/Gas Mark 6. Halve 2 avocados and remove the stone. Drizzle with lime juice then place in a baking dish, cut side up. In a food processor blitz up 1 slice of wholegrain bread with 2 tablespoons of cashews. Place in a bowl and stir in 2 chopped tomatoes and 1 teaspoon of dried thyme. Mix well and season. Spoon the mixture over the avocados then top with ½ cup (50g) of grated Cheddar cheese. Bake for 25 minutes. Serve warm.

Sunday

Make the baguette. Heat 1 tablespoon of olive oil in a frying pan over a medium heat. Add 2 vegetarian sausages and 1 sliced onion and cook until the sausages are heated through and the onions are starting to brown. Remove from the heat. Slice the sausages. Cut 2 pieces from the baguette (according to appetite). Cut open and add the sausages and onions. Add some chopped sun-dried tomatoes and some baby spinach. Top with ½ cup (50g) of grated Cheddar cheese. Serve warm.

Autumn Week 9

This week we have lunches where the ingredients are used over two days. So the beans from Monday's lunch are used in the frittata for Tuesday, which itself is used for Wednesday's lunch! We then make up a large tofu salad that will be enough for Thursday and Friday. The weekend sees us putting sweet potato to good use.

Monday
Two-Bean Salad V / Pear

Tuesday
Bean, Capsicum and Tomato Frittata Wrap with Lime Mayonnaise / Apple

Wednesday
Bean, Capsicum and Tomato Frittata in a Roll / Banana

Thursday
Tofu Salad with Broccoli, Carrot and Mushrooms / Passion Fruit

Friday
Tofu Salad with Broccoli, Carrot and Mushrooms / Grapefruit

Saturday
Baked Sweet Potato with Blue Cheese

Sunday
Sweet Potato and Blue Cheese Salad

Remember to sharpen your knives on a regular basis. It will make preparing vegetables so much more enjoyable as you effortlessly slice through those delicate tomatoes and tough-skinned pumpkins.

shopping list

Fruit and Vegetables
- ☐ 2 tomatoes
- ☐ 1 red capsicum
- ☐ 1 red onion
- ☐ 2 pears
- ☐ 2 apples
- ☐ 2 bananas
- ☐ 1 head broccoli
- ☐ 30g bean sprouts
- ☐ 1 bunch spring onions
- ☐ 6 mushrooms
- ☐ 1 carrot
- ☐ 1 clove garlic
- ☐ ginger
- ☐ 2 passion fruit
- ☐ 1 grapefruit
- ☐ 3 small sweet potatoes (about 300g each)
- ☐ 1 small bag baby spinach

Fridge
- ☐ 4 eggs
- ☐ mayonnaise
- ☐ 200g marinated tofu
- ☐ butter
- ☐ 100g blue cheese

Bakery
- ☐ 2 wholegrain rolls

Pantry
- ☐ 400g can kidney beans
- ☐ 400g can cannellini beans
- ☐ 125g can corn kernels
- ☐ lime juice
- ☐ ground cumin
- ☐ smoked paprika
- ☐ garlic powder
- ☐ 2 wholegrain flour tortillas
- ☐ honey
- ☐ whole nutmeg
- ☐ sun-dried tomatoes
- ☐ pine nuts

Staples
- ☐ salt
- ☐ black pepper
- ☐ olive oil
- ☐ extra virgin olive oil

daily tasks

Sunday

Prepare the two-bean salad. Rinse and drain a 400g can of both kidney beans and cannellini beans. Add ½ of each to a bowl and put the rest into a container then into the fridge. To the bowl, add a rinsed and drained 125g can of corn kernels. Dice a tomato and add to the bowl. Chop ½ a red capsicum and ½ a red onion and add to the bowl. Put the remaining capsicum and onion in the fridge.

Make a dressing by mixing together 1 tablespoon of extra virgin olive oil of with ½ tablespoon of lime juice, ½ teaspoon of ground cumin and ½ teaspoon of smoked paprika. Pour the dressing over the salad then stir well to coat. Divide the salad between 2 lunch boxes, then pop them into the fridge.

Monday

Make the frittata. Heat 1 tablespoon of olive oil in a frying pan over a medium heat. Chop the remaining capsicum and red onion and add to the pan along with a chopped tomato and the remaining beans. Beat together 4 eggs with ½ teaspoon of smoked paprika and ½ teaspoon of garlic powder. Add the eggs, turn the heat down and cook for about 8 minutes until nearly set.

Preheat the grill. Once the eggs are nearly set, pop the pan under the grill to finish cooking the top. Slide the frittata off the pan and leave to cool. Cut the frittata in half. Cover one half in plastic wrap, then refrigerate.

Slice the remaining frittata and divide it between 2 wholegrain flour tortillas. Mix together 4 tablespoons of mayonnaise with 2 teaspoons of lime juice, ¼ teaspoon of ground cumin and some black pepper. Spoon half of the mayonnaise over the tortillas and refrigerate the rest. Fold in the sides of the tortillas then roll up, cover in plastic wrap and refrigerate.

Tuesday

Make the frittata rolls. Cut the remaining frittata in half and add them to 2 wholegrain rolls. Top with the remaining mayonnaise. Cover in plastic wrap, then refrigerate until needed.

Wednesday

Prepare the tofu salad. Dice 200g of marinated tofu and place in a bowl. Chop the broccoli into small florets and add to the tofu along with the bean sprouts and a bunch of chopped spring onions. Slice 6 mushrooms and add to the bowl together with a carrot, cut into strips.

Make a dressing by mixing together 2 tablespoons of extra virgin olive oil with 1 tablespoon of lime juice, 1 teaspoon of honey, 1 clove of crushed garlic and 1 teaspoon of grated ginger. Pour the dressing over the salad, then stir well to coat. Place half the salad in a container and divide the rest between 2 lunch boxes. Place all containers into the fridge.

Don't forget a knife and spoon for your passion fruit.

Thursday

Divide the remaining tofu salad between 2 lunch boxes, then place back in the fridge.

Cut the grapefruit in half, sprinkle with sugar if desired then cover each half in plastic wrap. Refrigerate until needed. Don't forget a spoon.

Saturday

Bake 3 sweet potatoes. Preheat the oven to 210°C/410°F/Gas Mark 7. Scrub the sweet potatoes, prick the skins and place on a roasting tray. Brush with olive oil and season with salt and black pepper. Bake for about 1 hour until the sweet potatoes are tender. A knife should be able to go into the flesh with ease. Leave 1 sweet potato to cool, then refrigerate.

Split the 2 remaining sweet potatoes, add a knob of butter, a grating of nutmeg and divide 50g of crumbled blue cheese between the 2 potatoes. Serve.

Sunday

Prepare the sweet potato and blue cheese salad. Dice the sweet potato that was roasted yesterday and place in a bowl. Add the bag of baby spinach, 2 tablespoons of chopped sun-dried tomatoes, 1 tablespoon of toasted pine nuts and 50g of crumbled blue cheese. Season to taste. Serve.

Autumn Week 10

This week's menu includes husband's favourite lunch items. We're on vacation this week, which makes it a great time to cook some favourites.

Monday
Cheese, Onion and Tomato Pastry Scrolls / Kiwifruit

Tuesday
Cheese, Pickled Onion and Tomato Sandwich / Mandarin

Wednesday
Cheese and Coleslaw Baguette / Popcorn and Dried Cranberries

Thursday
Bean and Coleslaw Salad / Apple

Friday
Vegetable Ciabatta Sandwich / Mandarin

Saturday
Potato Wedges with Aioli / Leftover Coleslaw Salad

Sunday
Vegetable Tortilla Pizza

To eat kiwifruit, simply cut it in half then use a teaspoon to scoop out the fruit from each half. No peeling needed and no mess made!

shopping list

Fruit and Vegetables
- ☐ 2 onions
- ☐ 4 tomatoes
- ☐ 2 kiwifruit
- ☐ 1 lettuce
- ☐ 4 mandarins
- ☐ 3 spring onions
- ☐ 1 small bunch parsley
- ☐ 2 apples
- ☐ 3 mushrooms
- ☐ 2 zucchini
- ☐ 1 red capsicum
- ☐ 2 large potatoes

Fridge
- ☐ 200g Cheddar cheese
- ☐ 300g tub coleslaw
- ☐ 120g goat's cheese
- ☐ aioli

Freezer
- ☐ 1 sheet puff pastry

Bakery
- ☐ 4 slices wholegrain bread
- ☐ 1 baguette (or 2 rolls)
- ☐ 1 ciabatta

Pantry
- ☐ pickled onions
- ☐ popcorn kernels
- ☐ dried cranberries
- ☐ 400g can cannellini beans
- ☐ dried rosemary
- ☐ chargrilled capsicum
- ☐ 2 wholegrain flour tortillas

Staples
- ☐ salt
- ☐ black pepper
- ☐ olive oil
- ☐ canola oil

daily tasks

Sunday

Make the pastry scrolls. Thaw a sheet of puff pastry. Preheat the oven to 200°C/400°F/Gas Mark 6. Heat 1 tablespoon of olive oil in a frying pan over a medium heat. Add 1 chopped onion and cook for 4-5 minutes until pale and soft. Remove from the heat.

Chop 1 tomato and grate ½ cup (50g) of Cheddar cheese. Scatter the onion, tomato and cheese evenly over the pastry. Season to taste. Roll up the pastry then slice into 2cm thick pieces. Lay cut side up on a baking tray. Bake for 25-30 minutes, until golden and puffed. Leave to cool before placing in your lunch boxes. Refrigerate until needed.

Don't forget a spoon to scoop the flesh from your kiwifruit.

Monday

Prepare the sandwiches. Divide the following between 2 slices of wholegrain bread: 50g of sliced Cheddar cheese, 2 sliced pickled onions, 1 sliced tomato and a handful of lettuce. Season to taste then top with another slice of bread. Cut each sandwich in half, cover in plastic wrap, then refrigerate.

Tuesday

Prepare your baguettes. Cut 2 pieces from the baguette, according to appetite. Grate ½ cup (50g) of Cheddar cheese and add to the baguettes along with a good dollop of coleslaw. Season to taste. Cover in plastic wrap, then refrigerate.

Pop a small handful of popcorn kernels. Place into 2 containers along with some dried cranberries.

Wednesday

Prepare the coleslaw salad. Tip the remaining coleslaw into a bowl. To the coleslaw add: a 400g can of rinsed and drained cannellini beans, 3 chopped spring onions, ½ cup (50g) of grated Cheddar cheese and 2 tablespoons of chopped parsley. Season to taste. Divide the salad between 2 lunch boxes. If there seems a lot, keep some in a container to go with Saturday's lunch. Refrigerate.

Thursday

Prepare the vegetables. Heat 1 tablespoon of olive oil in a frying pan over a medium heat. Add 3 sliced mushrooms, 1 chopped zucchini and 1 chopped capsicum. Cook until they are softened and starting to brown, about 6 minutes. Remove from the heat, season and leave to cool. Stir in 1 chopped tomato.

Make up the sandwich. Split the ciabatta and top with the prepared vegetables. Crumble 60g of goat's cheese over the vegetables and finish with some chopped parsley. Cut the ciabatta in half, then cover each half in plastic wrap. Refrigerate.

Saturday

Bake the potato wedges. Preheat the oven to 210°C/410°F/Gas Mark 7. Halve 2 potatoes, then cut each half into 4, making 16 wedges in total. Place on a lined baking tray and drizzle with canola oil. Add a sprinkling of dried rosemary and season with some salt and freshly ground black pepper. Bake in the oven for 25 minutes. Remove from the oven and turn the potatoes. Return to the oven for another 20 minutes, until the wedges are crisp and golden on the outside and tender on the inside. Serve with a good dollop of aioli.

Sunday

Make the tortilla pizzas. Preheat the oven to 200°C/400°F/Gas Mark 6. Heat 1 tablespoon of olive oil in a frying pan over a medium heat. Add 1 sliced onion and 1 sliced zucchini and cook for 5-6 minutes until softened. Remove from the heat.

Place 2 flour tortillas on a baking tray and place in the oven for 6 minutes to brown slightly. Remove from the oven then turn the tortillas. Top the tortillas with the onion and zucchini, 1 chopped tomato, 2 tablespoons of chargrilled capsicum and 60g of crumbled goat's cheese. Season. Return to the oven and bake for 8 minutes, until warmed through. Cut each tortilla into quarters, then serve.

Autumn Week 11

After using up many of the items in the freezer, I thought it was time to start stocking up again. As such, this week we will make a broccoli, carrot and feta slice, some polenta fingers and feta, capsicum and olive turnovers. All suitable for freezing.

Monday
Broccoli, Carrot and Feta Slice / Banana

Tuesday
Tomato and Caper Rice / Mandarin

Wednesday
Polenta Fingers with Tomato and Caper Salsa and Capsicum Strips / Apple

Thursday
Feta, Capsicum and Olive Turnovers / Dates and Walnuts

Friday
Sausage, Mashed Avocado and Chutney Roll V / Grapefruit

Saturday
Stir-Fried Noodles

Sunday
Cheese, Mushroom and Tomato Quesadilla

Ever been asked "where do you get your protein from?" Well here's a list to get you started: nuts, beans, textured vegetable protein, tofu, cheese, lentils, peas, yogurt, broccoli, spinach, avocado and soy.

shopping list

Fruit and Vegetables
- [ ] 1 head broccoli
- [ ] 1 small bag baby spinach
- [ ] 2 carrots
- [ ] 2 bananas
- [ ] 250g cherry tomatoes
- [ ] 2 cloves garlic
- [ ] 1 bunch basil
- [ ] 2 mandarins
- [ ] 1 red capsicum
- [ ] 2 apples
- [ ] 1 avocado
- [ ] 1 grapefruit
- [ ] 1 onion
- [ ] 1 bunch choy sum
- [ ] 30g bean sprouts
- [ ] ginger
- [ ] 4 mushrooms
- [ ] 1 tomato

Fridge
- [ ] 4 eggs
- [ ] 125ml milk
- [ ] 200g feta cheese
- [ ] 25g Parmesan-style cheese
- [ ] butter
- [ ] 2 vegetarian sausages
- [ ] 50g mozzarella cheese
- [ ] 50g Cheddar cheese

Freezer
- [ ] 2 sheets puff pastry

Bakery
- [ ] 2 wholegrain rolls

Pantry
- [ ] 75g wholemeal self-raising flour
- [ ] 75g self-raising flour
- [ ] 100g brown rice
- [ ] capers
- [ ] lemon juice
- [ ] pine nuts
- [ ] vegetable stock
- [ ] 225g polenta (cornmeal)
- [ ] olives
- [ ] dried mixed herbs
- [ ] dates
- [ ] walnuts
- [ ] lime juice
- [ ] tomato chutney
- [ ] ready-cooked noodles
- [ ] soy sauce
- [ ] tomato paste
- [ ] sesame oil
- [ ] honey
- [ ] all-purpose seasoning
- [ ] 4 wholegrain flour tortillas

Staples
- [ ] salt
- [ ] black pepper
- [ ] olive oil
- [ ] extra virgin olive oil
- [ ] canola oil
- [ ] olive oil spray

daily tasks

Sunday

Make the broccoli, carrot and feta slice. Preheat the oven to 180°C/350°F/Gas Mark 4. Grease and line a 30 x 20cm baking tin. In a large bowl, whisk together 4 eggs and ½ cup (125ml) of milk. Beat in ½ cup (75g) of wholemeal self-raising flour and ½ cup (75g) of regular self-raising flour to make a batter.

Finely chop the broccoli and ½ cup (25g) of baby spinach. Cube 100g of feta cheese and grate 1 carrot. Stir the vegetables and cheese into the batter. Season. Pour into the baking tin and bake for 30 minutes until golden brown and firm.

Leave to cool and remove from the tin. Slice into quarters, then halve each quarter. Place 2 slices into each lunch box, then into the fridge. The rest can be frozen by wrapping each slice in plastic wrap then placing into a container or freezer bag, then popping into the freezer.

Monday

Prepare the tomato and caper rice. Cook ½ cup (100g) of brown rice according to packet instructions. Once cooked, rinse under cold water and drain thoroughly. Place in a bowl.

Whilst the rice is cooking, heat 1 tablespoon of olive oil in a frying pan over a medium heat. Cut 250g of cherry tomatoes in half then add to the pan along with 1 clove of crushed garlic and 1 tablespoon of rinsed and drained capers. Cook for 5 minutes. Remove from the heat and leave to cool.

Place half of the tomatoes into a container in the fridge and add the rest to the cooked rice. To the tomatoes and rice stir in 1 tablespoon each of lemon juice, grated Parmesan-style cheese, chopped basil and toasted pine nuts. Season to taste. Divide the rice salad between 2 lunch boxes. Refrigerate.

Tuesday

Cook the polenta fingers. Bring 3⅔ cups (900ml) of vegetable stock to the boil in a medium saucepan. Once boiling, gradually add 1½ cups (225g) of polenta, stirring constantly with a wooden spoon. Reduce the heat and continue stirring until the polenta has thickened and is coming away from the side of the saucepan.

Remove from the heat and stir in 1 tablespoon of butter and 2 tablespoons of grated Parmesan-style cheese. Season. Tip the mixture into a 30 x 20cm oiled baking tin and spread the mixture evenly. Leave to cool then place in the fridge for a few hours to firm up.

Preheat the grill. Remove the polenta from the tin and slice in half. Wrap half in plastic wrap and pop it into the freezer for another time. Slice the remaining polenta into 8 fingers. Brush with olive oil and place on a wire grill tray. Grill for about 6 minutes on each side until golden and crisp. Leave to cool then place in your lunch boxes. Refrigerate.

In a food processor place the cherry tomatoes and capers that were cooked yesterday. Add some basil leaves, 1 tablespoon of lemon juice and plenty of black pepper. Process until the mixture resembles a salsa. Divide between 2 containers and refrigerate.

Cut a capsicum in half. Place half back in the fridge then cut the other half into strips. Add these to your lunch boxes.

Wednesday

Make the feta, capsicum and olive turnovers. Preheat the oven to 220°C/425°F/Gas Mark 7. Thaw 2 sheets of puff pastry then cut each sheet into 4 squares.

In a bowl, mix together 100g of cubed feta cheese, 2 tablespoons of chopped olives, ½ a chopped red capsicum and ¼ cup (15g) of chopped baby spinach. Stir in 1 teaspoon of dried mixed herbs. Season to taste. Add a spoonful of the mixture to each pastry square. Fold the pastry in half to form a triangle, then press the edges with a fork to seal. Prick the tops with a fork. Place on a baking tray and bake for 20 minutes until golden. Leave to cool than place 2 in each lunch box. Refrigerate until tomorrow. Freeze the remaining turnovers by placing into a container then into the freezer.

Mix together 2 handfuls of dates with 2 handfuls of walnuts and divide between 2 containers.

Thursday

Prepare the vegetarian sausage and avocado rolls. Heat 1 tablespoon of olive oil in a frying pan over a medium heat. Add 2 vegetarian sausages and cook until they are heated through and browned. Remove from the heat and leave to cool. Slice thickly.

Halve the avocado, remove the stone and scoop the flesh from the skin. Place in a bowl and coarsely mash with 1 tablespoon of lime juice. Spread the avocado over 2 wholegrain rolls. Top with the sliced sausages and a dollop of tomato chutney. Cover the rolls in plastic wrap, then pop them into the fridge.

Halve the grapefruit. If desired, sprinkle with sugar then cover each half in plastic wrap. Refrigerate until needed. Don't forget a spoon.

Saturday

Cook the stir fry. Heat 1 tablespoon of canola oil in a large frying pan or wok. Add 1 sliced carrot and 1 sliced onion and cook for a few minutes until they start to soften. Add 1 clove of peeled and crushed garlic and 1 bunch of shredded choy sum. Cook for a few more minutes before stirring through the packet of ready-cooked noodles and the bean sprouts.

Mix together 1 tablespoon of soy sauce, 1 tablespoon of tomato paste, 1 teaspoon of grated ginger, 1 teaspoon of sesame oil and 1 teaspoon of honey. Add to the wok and stir well to coat the vegetables and noodles. Serve.

Sunday

Make the quesadillas. Heat 1 tablespoon of olive oil in a frying pan over a medium heat. Add 4 sliced mushrooms and a good sprinkle of all-purpose seasoning. Cook until the mushrooms are soft, about 5 minutes. Remove from the heat.

Grate ½ cup (50g) each of mozzarella cheese and Cheddar cheese and mix together. Divide the cheese between 2 wholegrain tortillas. Spoon the mushrooms and 1 chopped tomato over the cheese. Top each with another flour tortilla, pressing down firmly. Heat a clean frying pan over a medium heat and spray with olive oil. Cook 1 quesadilla at a time. Add to the pan and cook for a few minutes until golden, before turning. Remove from the pan and slice into quarters. Serve.

Autumn Week 12

There are a lot of pantry ingredients featuring in this week's menu. Which of course makes for easy to prepare lunches. Remember if you have access to a microwave, you can heat up the salads.

Monday
Apple and Beetroot Rice Salad V / Mandarin

Tuesday
Chickpea and Artichoke Pasta Salad V / Cashews and Dried Cranberries

Wednesday
Beetroot, Goat's Cheese and Chickpea Couscous / Apple

Thursday
Antipasti with Goat's Cheese / Carrot Sticks / Crispbread / Banana

Friday
Tofu, Spinach and Tomato Pastry Rolls V / Chocolate

Saturday
Stir-Fried Vegetables in an Omelette Wrap

Sunday
Halloumi Salad with Red Onion, Tomato and Capers

You can use fresh baby beetroot rather than canned – just buy enough to last for two days. However, cans work just as well and are a real time-saver as you do not need to cook the beetroot first.

shopping list

Fruit and Vegetables
- ☐ 3 apples
- ☐ 2 mandarins
- ☐ 1 carrot
- ☐ 2 bananas
- ☐ 1 small bag baby spinach
- ☐ 1 bunch bok choy
- ☐ 3 spring onions
- ☐ 30g bean sprouts
- ☐ 1 small red onion
- ☐ 1 tomato

Fridge
- ☐ 120g goat's cheese
- ☐ 200g marinated tofu
- ☐ 4 eggs
- ☐ 90g halloumi cheese

Freezer
- ☐ 1 sheet puff pastry

Pantry
- ☐ 100g brown rice
- ☐ 450g can baby beetroot
- ☐ lemon juice
- ☐ walnuts
- ☐ 100g dried pasta
- ☐ 400g can chickpeas
- ☐ 400g can artichoke hearts
- ☐ olives
- ☐ sun-dried tomatoes
- ☐ white wine vinegar
- ☐ cashews
- ☐ dried cranberries
- ☐ 100g couscous
- ☐ chargrilled capsicum
- ☐ 6-8 crispbread
- ☐ 2 chocolate bars
- ☐ sesame oil
- ☐ soy sauce
- ☐ sesame seeds
- ☐ capers

Staples
- ☐ salt
- ☐ black pepper
- ☐ olive oil
- ☐ extra virgin olive oil
- ☐ canola oil

daily tasks

Sunday

Prepare the apple and beetroot salad. Cook ½ cup (100g) of brown rice according to packet directions. Rinse under cold water, drain thoroughly and place in a bowl. Drain a 450g can of baby beetroot. Place half in a container in the fridge. Cut the rest into quarters and add to the rice.

Core and dice 1 apple, drizzle with some lemon juice and add to the bowl. Coarsely chop a handful of walnuts and stir them in. Season to taste. Divide the salad between 2 lunch boxes. Refrigerate until needed.

Monday

Prepare the chickpea and artichoke pasta salad. Cook 100g of dried pasta according to packet instructions. Once cooked, rinse under cold water then drain. Place in a bowl. Rinse and drain a 400g can of chickpeas and a 400g can of artichoke hearts. Reserve half of the chickpeas and artichokes and place them in separate containers in the fridge. Add the remaining chickpeas to the pasta. Coarsely chop the artichokes and add them to the bowl.

Slice 2 tablespoons each of olives and sun-dried tomatoes and stir them in. Mix together 1 tablespoon of extra virgin olive oil with ½ tablespoon of white wine vinegar. Stir the dressing into the salad. Season to taste. Divide between 2 lunch boxes then refrigerate.

Mix 2 handfuls of cashews with 2 handfuls of dried cranberries. Divide between 2 containers.

Tuesday

Prepare the couscous. Place ½ cup (100g) of couscous in a bowl. Stir in ½ cup (125ml) of boiling water then let stand for 3 minutes. Fluff up with a fork.

Dice the remaining baby beetroot and add to the bowl along with the remaining chickpeas. Crumble in 60g of goat's cheese. Finally, stir in 2 tablespoons of toasted cashews. Season to taste then divide between 2 lunch boxes. Refrigerate until needed.

Wednesday

Prepare the antipasti. Divide the following between 2 containers: the remaining artichoke hearts (quartered), a handful of olives and some chargrilled capsicums (diced if needed). Top with 60g of goat's cheese.

Slice 1 carrot into sticks and divide between another 2 containers.

Allow 3-4 crispbread per person and add to the carrots, or place in another 2 containers if you wish. Pop everything into the fridge.

Don't forget a knife for adding the antipasti to your crispbread.

Thursday

Make the tofu, spinach and tomato pastry rolls. Preheat the oven to 220°C/425°F/Gas Mark 7. Thaw a sheet of puff pastry. Slice the pastry into 3 equal lengths. Slice 100g of marinated tofu into 9 long sticks. Place 3 sticks along the length of each piece of pastry, close to one edge. Top with a handful of baby spinach, coarsely chopped. Finally, add 3 tablespoons of chopped sun-dried tomatoes. Season to taste.

Starting from the long end, roll up the pastry. Cut into 4 pieces then place on a baking tray, seal side down. Bake for 20 minutes, until golden and puffed. Leave to cool before dividing between 2 lunch boxes and refrigerating.

Saturday

Make the omelette wraps. Heat 1 tablespoon of canola oil in a medium frying pan. Beat together 4 eggs and add some seasoning. Add half of the eggs to the pan then cook until set. Remove from the pan and keep warm. Cook the remaining egg the same way.

In another pan, heat 1 tablespoon of canola oil. Add 1 bunch of chopped bok choy, 3 chopped spring onions and 100g of chopped marinated tofu. Stir for a few minutes until the bok choy starts to wilt. Stir through the bean sprouts, 1 teaspoon of sesame oil and 1 tablespoon of soy sauce. Finally, sprinkle a few sesame seeds over the vegetables. Divide the vegetables between the 2 omelettes. Roll up the omelettes and serve immediately with extra soy sauce, if desired.

Sunday

Prepare the halloumi salad. Heat 1 tablespoon of olive oil in a frying pan over a medium heat. Slice 90g of halloumi and add to the pan. Cook until golden on both sides, about 5 minutes in total. Remove from the heat, cut into cubes then place in a bowl.

Slice a small red onion and dice a tomato. Add to the halloumi along with 2 tablespoons of olives and 1 tablespoon of rinsed capers. Mix together 1 tablespoon of extra virgin olive oil with ½ tablespoon of lemon juice. Stir the dressing into the salad. Season to taste with black pepper. Divide the salad between 2 plates and serve.

Autumn Week 13

This week we have a few ways with beans, as well as a tasty tart made with cream cheese, spinach and cherry tomatoes. We have a leisurely Saturday lunch and end with a soup on Sunday as we say goodbye to autumn.

Monday
Halloumi and Butter Bean Salad / Mandarin

Tuesday
Cheese, Tomato and Baby Spinach Tart / Grapes

Wednesday
Bean, Cheese and Tomato Wrap with Paprika Mayonnaise / Apple

Thursday
Egg, Bean and Avocado Salad / Grapes

Friday
Cheese and Mustard Sandwich / Mandarin

Saturday
Garlic Pita Bread with Capsicum Dip

Sunday
Lentil and Capsicum Soup with Crusty Roll V

I love condiments. Mustards, horseradish, cranberry and mint sauce. Don't ever believe they are just for meat eaters. Serve them as you fancy: with your roasts, in sandwiches, salads, dips, however you like.

shopping list

Fruit and Vegetables
- [ ] 250g cherry tomatoes
- [ ] 1 bag baby spinach
- [ ] 4 mandarins
- [ ] 2 onions
- [ ] 3 tomatoes
- [ ] 1 bunch grapes
- [ ] 1 bunch spring onions
- [ ] 2 apples
- [ ] 1 avocado
- [ ] 1 lettuce
- [ ] 2 cloves garlic
- [ ] 1 small bunch parsley
- [ ] 1 red capsicum

Fridge
- [ ] 90g halloumi cheese
- [ ] 150g cream cheese
- [ ] 150g Cheddar cheese
- [ ] mayonnaise
- [ ] 2 eggs
- [ ] 60g Parmesan-style cheese

Freezer
- [ ] 1 sheet puff pastry

Bakery
- [ ] 4 slices wholegrain bread
- [ ] 2 pita breads
- [ ] 2 crusty rolls

Pantry
- [ ] 400g can butter beans
- [ ] chargrilled capsicum
- [ ] lemon juice
- [ ] Dijon mustard
- [ ] whole nutmeg
- [ ] 400g can kidney beans
- [ ] 2 wholegrain flour tortillas
- [ ] smoked paprika
- [ ] lime juice
- [ ] dried chilli flakes
- [ ] dried oregano
- [ ] English mustard
- [ ] 400g can chopped tomatoes
- [ ] 400g can lentils
- [ ] vegetable stock

Staples
- [ ] salt
- [ ] black pepper
- [ ] olive oil
- [ ] extra virgin olive oil

daily tasks

Sunday

Prepare the halloumi and butter bean salad. Heat 1 tablespoon of olive oil in a frying pan over a medium heat. Add 90g of sliced halloumi and cook until it is golden on both sides. Remove from the heat, cut into cubes and place in a bowl. Rinse and drain a 400g can of butter beans and add to the halloumi. Add 125g of cherry tomatoes (halved) and a handful of chopped baby spinach. Finally, add 2 tablespoons of chopped chargrilled capsicum.

Make a dressing for the salad by mixing together 1 tablespoon of extra virgin olive oil, ½ tablespoon of lemon juice and ½ teaspoon of Dijon mustard. Stir the dressing into the salad. Season to taste. Divide the salad between 2 lunch boxes then refrigerate until needed.

Monday

Cook the cheese, tomato and baby spinach tart. Preheat the oven to 200°C/400°F/Gas Mark 6. Thaw a sheet of puff pastry. Whilst it is thawing, heat 1 tablespoon of olive oil in a frying pan over a medium heat. Add 1 chopped onion and fry for a few minutes until the onion is pale and soft. Next, stir in 1 cup (50g) of baby spinach and some grated nutmeg. Once the spinach has started to wilt, remove from the heat. Season to taste.

Place the pastry sheet on a lined baking tray. Score 1cm around the border of the pastry. Spread 100g of cream cheese over the pastry, going to the border. Spoon the onion and spinach mixture over the cream cheese. Top with 1 sliced tomato and ½ cup (50g) of grated Cheddar cheese. Bake for 20 minutes until golden and puffed. Leave to cool, slice into quarters then place 2 quarters into each lunch box. Pop them into the fridge.

Divide some grapes between 2 containers.

Tuesday

Make the bean, cheese and tomato wraps. Rinse and drain a 400g can of kidney beans. Place half in a container in the fridge and divide the rest between 2 wholegrain flour tortillas. To the beans add: 1 chopped tomato, ½ a bunch of chopped spring onions and ½ cup (50g) of grated Cheddar cheese.

Mix together 3 tablespoons of mayonnaise with ½ teaspoon of smoked paprika. Divide the mayonnaise between the 2 tortillas. Fold in the sides of each tortilla, roll up, cut in half if desired then cover in plastic wrap. Refrigerate until needed.

Wednesday

Make the egg, bean and avocado salad. Hard boil 2 eggs. Leave to cool, peel then coarsely chop and add to a bowl. Add the remaining kidney beans to the bowl along with 125g of cherry tomatoes (cut in half) and the remaining spring onions, chopped.

Cut an avocado in half, remove the stone and scoop out the flesh. Dice the flesh and add it to the bowl. Stir in 1 tablespoon of lime juice, ½ teaspoon of dried chilli flakes and 1 teaspoon of dried oregano. Season to taste. Divide the salad between 2 lunch boxes, then refrigerate until needed.

Divide the remaining grapes between 2 containers.

Thursday

Make the cheese and mustard sandwiches. Spread some English mustard over 2 slices of bread. Slice 50g of Cheddar cheese and add to the bread. Top with 1 sliced tomato and a handful of lettuce. Season to taste, top with the other 2 slices of bread. Cut each sandwich in half then cover in plastic wrap or place in a lunch box. Refrigerate until needed.

Saturday

Prepare the garlic pita breads. Preheat the oven to 200°C/400°F/Gas Mark 6. Place 2 pita breads on a baking tray and place in the oven for 5 minutes. Meanwhile, in a small bowl, mix together 3 tablespoons of olive oil with 1 clove of peeled and crushed garlic, 1 tablespoon of chopped parsley and ½ cup (60g) of grated Parmesan-style cheese.

Remove the pitas from the oven, turn them over and brush the cheese mixture over each pita bread. Season to taste then return to the oven for 5 minutes. Remove from the oven, slice into strips and place on a serving plate.

Make the capsicum dip. In a food processor blitz together ¼ cup (50g) of chargrilled capsicum with 150g of cream cheese. Season well with plenty of black pepper. Once the mixture is smooth, spoon into a bowl and serve with the pita bread.

Sunday

Cook the lentil and capsicum soup. Heat 1 tablespoon of olive oil in a large saucepan over a medium heat. Add 1 chopped onion and fry for 3-4 minutes until it begins to soften. Add 1 chopped red capsicum and cook for a further 5 minutes.

Add a 400g can of rinsed and drained lentils, a 400g can of chopped tomatoes and 4 cups (1 litre) of vegetable stock. Turn up the heat and bring to the boil. Once it is boiling, turn the heat down and simmer for 10 minutes. Stir through 2 tablespoons of chopped parsley and season to taste. Serve in warm bowls with a buttered crusty roll for each person.

almonds apple artichoke avocado
banana bean brie butter bean
capsicum carrot cashews
cheese cherry tomatoes chickpeas chips chocolate
chutney corn couscous cranberry dates dip
dried apricots dukkah egg feta

winter

mandarin mexican mushroom olive
onion orange pears pecans pineapple
pita polenta potato quinoa refried beans
roasted vegetable rocket roll
salad sandwich sausage slice soup
sourdough spinach stilton sultanas toasted tofu
tomato turnovers wrap

Winter Week 1

It's the start of a new season and once again we begin it by making a batch of roasted vegetables to be used for four days. Don't get too worried about the size of your vegetables; just pick up what you can and to suit your taste.

Monday
Roasted Vegetable and Pearl Barley Salad V / Orange

Tuesday
Roasted Vegetable Wrap V / Banana

Wednesday
Roasted Vegetable and Bean Frittata / Mandarin

Thursday
Roasted Vegetable Soup V / Apple

Friday
Polenta Fingers with Beetroot Dip / Cherry Tomatoes / Grapefruit

Saturday
Cranberry, Coconut and Orange Loaf

Sunday
Baked Eggs and Tomatoes with Avocado on Toast

If you do not have the time to roast the vegetables, you can microwave them instead. Check your microwave manual for notes on cooking different vegetables. You can always fry them in some olive oil once they are cooked to help them resemble roasted vegetables.

shopping list

Fruit and Vegetables
- [ ] 1 carrot
- [ ] 1 onion
- [ ] ½ butternut squash
- [ ] 1 large potato
- [ ] 1 fennel bulb
- [ ] 2 oranges
- [ ] 2 bananas
- [ ] 2 mandarins
- [ ] 2 apples
- [ ] 200g cherry tomatoes
- [ ] 1 grapefruit
- [ ] 1 avocado

Fridge
- [ ] 6 eggs

Freezer
- [ ] polenta

Bakery
- [ ] fruit loaf / sweet muffins (or recipe)
- [ ] 2 slices bread (your choice)

Pantry
- [ ] 100g pearl barley
- [ ] 2 wholegrain flour tortillas
- [ ] vegetable stock
- [ ] 450g can sliced beetroot
- [ ] 400g can butter beans
- [ ] wasabi
- [ ] smoked paprika

Staples
- [ ] salt
- [ ] black pepper
- [ ] olive oil
- [ ] extra virgin olive oil
- [ ] canola oil

daily tasks

Sunday

Prepare the roasted vegetables. Peel the carrot and onion. Peel the butternut squash and scoop out the seeds. Scrub the potato. Remove the core from the fennel. Chop all the vegetables into bite-size pieces and place in a roasting tray. Drizzle with canola oil. Roast for 30 minutes on 210°C/410°F/Gas Mark 7. Remove from the oven, turn the vegetables and roast for another 20 minutes. Leave to cool.

Whilst the vegetables are roasting, cook the pearl barley. Place ½ cup (100g) of pearl barley in a medium saucepan. Cover with plenty of cold water. Bring to the boil, lower the heat then simmer for 30 minutes, until tender. Remove from the heat, drain, then rinse the barley under cold water. Drain well. Add a quarter of the cooked vegetables to the barley and mix well. Put the rest of the vegetables in a container in the fridge. Divide the barley salad between 2 lunch boxes, then refrigerate until needed.

Monday

Make the roasted vegetable wraps. Take 2 wholegrain flour tortillas then spoon some of the roasted vegetables on each. Fold in the sides of the tortilla, then roll up. Cut in half then cover in plastic wrap. Refrigerate until tomorrow.

Tuesday

Make the roasted vegetable frittata. Beat together 4 eggs and season. Heat a 24cm frying pan over a medium heat. Add half of the remaining roasted vegetable mix and stir to warm up slightly. Add the eggs, then turn the heat down. Let cook for 8-10 minutes.

Preheat the grill. Once the eggs are nearly set, place the pan under the grill to finish cooking the top. Slide the frittata off the pan then leave to cool. Slice into quarters and place 2 quarters into each lunch container. Refrigerate until tomorrow.

Wednesday

Prepare the soup. Heat a large saucepan and add the remaining vegetables. Heat for a few minutes. Add 2 cups (500ml) of vegetable stock. Bring to the boil. Reduce the heat and simmer for 15 minutes. Pour the soup into a heat-resistant container and leave to cool. Refrigerate until needed.

If you have access to a microwave, you can divide the soup between 2 containers and reheat tomorrow. Else, reheat the soup tomorrow morning before dividing the soup between 2 thermos flasks.

Don't forget a spoon!

Thaw some polenta overnight in the fridge.

Thursday

This morning: if you are taking your soup in a thermos, remember to heat it in a pan or microwave before dividing the soup between 2 flasks.

Prepare the polenta fingers. If you have any frozen polenta, it should have thawed overnight in the fridge. Preheat the grill and slice the polenta into 8 fingers. Brush with olive oil and place on a wire grill tray. Grill for about 6 minutes on each side until golden and crisp. Leave to cool then place in your lunch boxes. If you do not have any polenta in the freezer, follow the instructions below. Don't forget to add the ingredients to your shopping list.

Bring 3²/₃ cups (900ml) of vegetable stock to the boil in a medium saucepan. Once boiling, gradually add 1¹/₂ cups (225g) of polenta, stirring constantly with a wooden spoon. Reduce the heat and continue stirring until the polenta has thickened and is coming away from the side of the saucepan. Remove from the heat and stir in 1 tablespoon of butter and 2 tablespoons of grated Parmesan-style cheese. Season. Tip the mixture into a 30 x 20cm oiled baking tin and spread the mixture evenly. Leave to cool then place in the fridge for a few hours to firm up.

Preheat the grill. Remove the polenta from the tin and slice in half. Wrap half in plastic wrap and pop it into the freezer for another time. Slice the remaining polenta into 8 fingers. Brush with olive oil and place on a wire grill tray. Grill for about 6 minutes on each side until golden and crisp. Leave to cool then place in your lunch boxes.

Make the beetroot dip. Tip a 450g can of drained beetroot into a food processor along with a 400g can of rinsed and drained butter beans. Add ¹/₂ teaspoon of wasabi and season to taste. Process until the mixture is smooth. Divide the mixture between 2 containers, to serve with the polenta fingers. Refrigerate until needed.

Divide 100g of cherry tomatoes between 2 containers.

Halve the grapefruit. If desired, sprinkle with sugar then cover each half in plastic wrap. Refrigerate until needed. Don't forget a spoon.

Saturday

Bake the cranberry, coconut and orange loaf, following the recipe on p.227. Serve slices with a cup of coffee, tea or hot chocolate. Any leftovers can be frozen. Slice the remaining loaf, pop the slices into a freezer bag, then into the freezer. You can thaw slices as needed at room temperature. If you are not baking the loaf, take a trip to your favourite bakery and choose a sweet loaf ready-made for you.

Sunday

Prepare the baked eggs. Preheat the oven to 200°C/400°F/Gas Mark 6. Lightly oil 2 ramekins. Slice 100g of cherry tomatoes in half and place at the bottom of the ramekins. Crack an egg into each ramekin and season with salt and black pepper. Bake for 15-18 minutes until the egg white is set.

Toast 2 slices of bread. Slice an avocado and divide it between the 2 slices of toast. Top with the baked eggs and tomatoes. Finish with a sprinkle of smoked paprika and a light drizzle of extra virgin olive oil. Serve warm.

Winter Week 2

We've had rolls week and wraps week. This week I thought we'd have sandwiches week! It's an opportunity to try different breads. You may discover a new favourite. Do feel free to seek out different breads to what I've suggested here when you shop.

Monday
Cheese, Pickle and Mustard Pumpernickel Sandwich / Banana

Tuesday
Avocado, Cranberry, Tomato and Spinach Sourdough Sandwich V / Dried Apricots and Almonds

Wednesday
Mexican Tofu Spelt Sandwich V / Mandarin

Thursday
Smoky Tofu and Avocado Turkish Roll V / Dates and Pecans

Friday
Egg Curry and Mango Chutney Rye Sandwich / Orange

Saturday
Vegetarian Slices, Onion and Horseradish Ciabatta Roll

Sunday
Spring Onion, Cheese and Baby Spinach Baguette

Most breads freeze well. Place them in a freezer bag and pop them straight into the freezer. Then you just need to remove the slices as you need them. Thaw at room temperature or in the microwave.

shopping list

Fruit and Vegetables
- [ ] 1 lettuce
- [ ] 2 bananas
- [ ] 2 avocados
- [ ] 2 tomatoes
- [ ] 1 small bag baby spinach
- [ ] 1 small red onion
- [ ] 1 small bunch coriander (optional)
- [ ] 2 mandarins
- [ ] 2 oranges
- [ ] 1 onion
- [ ] 4 spring onions

Fridge
- [ ] mayonnaise
- [ ] 150g vintage Cheddar cheese
- [ ] 300g firm tofu
- [ ] 2 eggs
- [ ] 2 vegetarian slices

Bakery
- [ ] 4 slices pumpernickel bread
- [ ] 4 slices sourdough bread
- [ ] 4 slices spelt bread
- [ ] 2 Turkish rolls
- [ ] 4 slices rye bread
- [ ] 2 ciabatta rolls
- [ ] 1 baguette

Pantry
- [ ] English mustard
- [ ] gherkins
- [ ] lime juice
- [ ] cranberry sauce
- [ ] dried apricots
- [ ] almonds
- [ ] ground cumin
- [ ] ground coriander
- [ ] chilli powder
- [ ] tomato paste
- [ ] 125g can corn kernels
- [ ] savoury yeast flakes
- [ ] soy sauce
- [ ] barbecue sauce
- [ ] liquid smoke
- [ ] dates
- [ ] pecans
- [ ] curry powder
- [ ] mango chutney
- [ ] horseradish sauce

Staples
- [ ] salt
- [ ] black pepper
- [ ] olive oil
- [ ] canola oil

daily tasks

Sunday

Prepare the cheese, pickle and mustard pumpernickel sandwiches. Mix together 2 tablespoons of mayonnaise with ½ teaspoon of English mustard. Spread the mayonnaise over 2 slices of pumpernickel bread. To the bread, add 50g of sliced vintage Cheddar cheese and 3-4 sliced gherkins. Finally, top with some lettuce and seasoning and 2 more slices of bread to make your sandwiches. Cut each sandwich in half, then cover in plastic wrap. Refrigerate until tomorrow.

Monday

Make the avocado, cranberry, tomato and spinach sourdough sandwiches. Cut an avocado in half, remove the stone and scoop the flesh from the skin. Slice the avocado and drizzle with some lime juice. Add the avocado to 2 slices of sourdough bread. Slice a tomato and add to the bread along with a handful of baby spinach. Add some seasoning before topping with some cranberry sauce. Top with 2 more slices of bread to form sandwiches. Cut each sandwich in half then cover in plastic wrap. Pop them into the fridge.

Mix 2 handfuls of dried apricots with 2 handfuls of almonds. Divide between 2 containers.

Tuesday

Prepare the tofu for the Mexican tofu spelt sandwiches. Slice 150g of firm tofu. Wrap the slices in paper towel and top with something heavy (chopping board works well) to drain them. After 15-20 minutes, remove the tofu from the paper towel and place on a plate. In a jar or small bowl, mix together 1 teaspoon each of ground cumin and ground coriander with ½ teaspoon of chilli powder (or to taste), 1 tablespoon of lime juice and 1 tablespoon of tomato paste. Coat the tofu slices with the flavouring and let marinate for as long as possible.

Heat 2 tablespoons of canola oil in a large frying pan over a medium heat. Add the tofu slices then fry for about 8 minutes until the tofu is crispy on both sides. Drain the tofu on paper towel, then leave to cool.

Mix together 1 diced tomato, 1 finely diced small red onion and a 125g can of rinsed and drained corn kernels. Divide the tofu between 2 slices of spelt bread then top with the tomato, onion and corn mixture. Season to taste. Add some coriander leaves if you are using them then top with 2 more slices of bread. Cut the sandwiches in half, then cover in plastic wrap. Refrigerate.

Wednesday

Prepare the smoky tofu. Drain 150g of firm tofu. Crumble the tofu into a bowl. Mix together 1 tablespoon each of savoury yeast flakes, soy sauce and barbecue sauce and 1 teaspoon of liquid smoke. Pour the mixture over the crumbled tofu, mixing well to coat. Leave to stand for as long as possible to marinate.

Heat 1 tablespoon of canola oil in a frying pan. Add the tofu then cook and stir for 8-10 minutes until the tofu has turned crispy. Remove from the heat then leave to cool.

Put together your sandwiches by splitting 2 Turkish rolls. Mash an avocado with some lime juice and seasoning then divide between the 2 rolls. Top with the smoky tofu and a handful of lettuce. Cover the rolls in plastic wrap. Refrigerate until needed.

Mix 2 handfuls of dates with 2 handfuls of pecans. Divide between 2 containers.

Thursday

Prepare the egg curry. Hard boil 2 eggs. Drain under cold water then leave to cool. Peel and mash the eggs with 1 tablespoon of mayonnaise, some seasoning and ½ teaspoon of curry powder (or to taste). Divide the egg between 2 slices of rye bread and top with a dollop of mango chutney. Add 2 more slices of bread. Cut each sandwich in half then cover in plastic wrap. Refrigerate until needed.

Saturday

Prepare the ciabatta rolls. Heat 1 tablespoon of olive oil in a frying pan over a medium heat. Add 1 chopped onion and fry for 5-6 minutes until pale and soft. Remove from the heat. Split 2 warmed ciabatta rolls and spread some horseradish sauce over each. Divide the following between the 2 rolls: 2 vegetarian slices, 50g of sliced Cheddar cheese, the fried onions and a handful of lettuce. Serve warm.

Sunday

Prepare the filling for the baguette. In a bowl mix together 4 chopped spring onions, ½ cup (50g) of grated Cheddar cheese, the remaining baby spinach (shredded) and 2 tablespoons of mayonnaise. Season well.

Cut 2 pieces from the baguette (size according to appetite). Fill the baguettes with the onion and cheese filling. Serve.

Winter Week 3

Confession time. I'm not keen on quinoa, hence its absence until now. So confronting my aversion, I have dedicated this week to quinoa. I'm glad I did – I enjoyed some good food this week. My favourite was the baby kale, quinoa and goat's cheese salad.

Monday
Artichoke, Halloumi, Olive and Quinoa Salad / Mandarin

Tuesday
Quinoa Frittata with Artichoke, Halloumi and Olives / Dates and Cashews

Wednesday
Vegetable and Quinoa Slice with Goat's Cheese / Canned Apricot Halves

Thursday
Baby Kale, Quinoa and Goat's Cheese Salad / Banana

Friday
Lentil, Tomato and Quinoa Salad V / Canned Apricot Halves

Saturday
Lentil, Tomato and Quinoa Turnovers V

Sunday
Quinoa, Lentil, Mushroom and Tomato Soup V

So what makes quinoa so great? Well it's high in fibre and protein and low GI. It's also gluten free and low-fat. It's full of vitamins, minerals and antioxidants.

shopping list

Fruit and Vegetables
- ☐ 1 bunch parsley
- ☐ 2 mandarins
- ☐ 120g baby kale
- ☐ 1 carrot
- ☐ 2 bananas
- ☐ 1 onion
- ☐ 1 clove garlic
- ☐ 2 tomatoes
- ☐ 4 mushrooms

Fridge
- ☐ 180g halloumi cheese
- ☐ 8 eggs
- ☐ 120g goat's cheese
- ☐ 125ml milk

Freezer
- ☐ 1 sheet puff pastry

Pantry
- ☐ 400g quinoa
- ☐ 400g can artichoke hearts
- ☐ sun-dried tomatoes
- ☐ green olives
- ☐ lemon juice
- ☐ dates
- ☐ cashews
- ☐ 75g wholemeal self-raising flour
- ☐ 310g can corn kernels
- ☐ 410g can apricot halves
- ☐ pine nuts
- ☐ dried cranberries
- ☐ white wine vinegar
- ☐ 400g can lentils
- ☐ dried chilli flakes
- ☐ ground cumin
- ☐ dried thyme
- ☐ vegetable stock

Staples
- ☐ salt
- ☐ black pepper
- ☐ olive oil
- ☐ extra virgin olive oil

daily tasks

Sunday

Prepare the quinoa. Rinse 1 cup (130g) of quinoa. Place in a saucepan with 2 cups (500ml) of water. Bring to the boil, reduce the heat then simmer for about 15 minutes until the water is absorbed. Leave to cool.

Meanwhile, cook the halloumi. Heat 1 tablespoon of olive oil in a frying pan over a medium heat. Slice 180g of halloumi and add to the pan. Cook until golden, turning once. Remove from the heat, leave to cool, then cut the slices into bite-size pieces. Place in a bowl with the cooled quinoa. Add a 400g can of rinsed, drained and chopped artichoke hearts. Stir in 3 tablespoons each of chopped sun-dried tomatoes and sliced green olives. Next, stir in 2 tablespoons of chopped parsley. Place just under half of the salad mixture into a container and refrigerate.

Make a dressing for the remaining salad by mixing together 1 tablespoon of extra virgin olive oil with ½ tablespoon of lemon juice. Stir the dressing into the salad then season to taste. Divide the salad between 2 lunch boxes, then refrigerate until needed.

Monday

Make the frittata. Heat 1 tablespoon of olive oil over a medium heat and stir in the remaining quinoa mixture from yesterday. Beat together 4 eggs and add to the pan. Reduce the heat and cook for 8-10 minutes until the egg is nearly set. Preheat the grill.

Once the egg is nearly set, pop the pan under the grill and cook for a couple of minutes to finish cooking the frittata. Slide the frittata off the pan then leave to cool. Slice into quarters and place 2 quarters into each lunch box. Pop them into the fridge.

Mix 2 handfuls of dates with 2 handfuls of cashews and divide between 2 containers.

Tuesday

Bake the vegetable and quinoa slice. Rinse 1 cup (130g) of quinoa. Place in a saucepan with 2 cups (500ml) of water. Bring to the boil, reduce the heat then simmer for about 15 minutes until the water is absorbed. Leave to cool. Place half of the quinoa into a container then refrigerate.

Preheat the oven to 180°C/350°F/Gas Mark 4 and grease and line a 30 x 20cm baking tin. Beat 4 eggs with ½ cup (125ml) of milk in a large bowl. Stir in ½ cup (75g) of wholemeal self-raising flour and the quinoa, to make a batter.

Add a 310g can of rinsed and drained corn kernels, 60g of shredded baby kale, 1 grated carrot and 60g of crumbled goat's cheese. Finally, stir in 2 tablespoons of chopped parsley and some seasoning. Pour the mixture into the prepared tin and bake for about 35 minutes until golden and firm. Leave to cool.

Remove from the tin and slice into 8 pieces. Place 2 slices into each lunch box and refrigerate. The rest can be frozen by wrapping each slice in plastic wrap then placing into a container or freezer bag, then popping into the freezer.

Divide ½ a can of apricot halves between 2 containers. Place the remaining apricots into a container then pop all containers into the fridge.

Wednesday

Prepare the baby kale, quinoa and goat's cheese salad. Place the quinoa cooked yesterday into a bowl. Add 60g of shredded baby kale, 2 tablespoons each of toasted pine nuts and dried cranberries. Stir in 60g of crumbled goat's cheese. Mix together 1 tablespoon of extra virgin olive oil with ½ tablespoon of white wine vinegar. Stir the dressing into the salad, then season to taste. Divide the salad between 2 lunch boxes then refrigerate until needed.

Thursday

Prepare the lentil, tomato and quinoa salad. Rinse 1 cup (130g) of quinoa. Place in a saucepan with 2 cups (500ml) of water. Bring to the boil, reduce the heat then simmer for about 15 minutes until the water is absorbed. Leave to cool.

Meanwhile, heat 1 tablespoon of olive oil in a medium frying pan. Fry 1 chopped onion and 1 clove of peeled and crushed garlic for 5-6 minutes until pale and soft. Remove from the heat. Place in a bowl with the quinoa.

Add a 400g can of rinsed and drained lentils and 2 chopped tomatoes. Stir in 1 teaspoon each of dried chilli flakes, ground cumin and dried thyme. Season to taste. Place half in a container and divide the rest between 2 lunch boxes. Pop everything into the fridge.

Divide the remaining apricot halves between 2 containers.

Saturday

Make the lentil, tomato and quinoa turnovers. Thaw a sheet of puff pastry then cut it into 4 squares. Add a spoonful of the lentil, tomato and quinoa mixture to each pastry square (put the remaining mixture back in the fridge). Fold the pastry in half to form a triangle, then press the edges with a fork to seal. Prick the tops. Place on a baking tray and bake in a 220°C/425°F/Gas Mark 7 oven for 20 minutes until golden. Serve warm.

Sunday

Prepare the quinoa, lentil, mushroom and tomato soup. Heat 1 tablespoon of olive oil in a large saucepan. Add 4 sliced mushrooms and cook for about 6 minutes, until soft. Stir in the remaining lentil and quinoa mixture and cook for 2 minutes. Add 2 cups (500ml) of vegetable stock and bring to the boil. Reduce the heat then simmer for 10 minutes. Stir in 2 tablespoons of chopped parsley. Spoon into warmed bowls, then serve.

Winter Week 4

There's no real theme to this week's menu. Just lots of good flavours and textures and a chance to dip into the freezer! The week ends with cheesy stuffed potatoes — one of my favourite ways with potatoes.

Monday
Broccoli, Carrot and Feta Slice / Dried Apricots and Almonds

Tuesday
Tofu with Crispy Noodles, Savoury Mushrooms and Pineapple V / Banana

Wednesday
Butter Bean Cake with Tofu, Spinach and Carrot Salad V / Pineapple Chunks

Thursday
Stilton and Onion Chutney Roll / Mandarin

Friday
Vegan Tzatziki with Veggies and Crackers V / Hard Boiled Egg / Walnuts and Sultanas

Saturday
Stilton Ploughman's on Pumpernickel

Sunday
Vegan Cheese Stuffed Potatoes V / Cranberry and Pine Nut Salad V

Did you know you can freeze cheese? Simply wrap the cheese block in foil or plastic wrap then place in the freezer. Then simply cut off what you need and thaw at room temperature.

shopping list

Fruit and Vegetables
- ☐ 6 mushrooms
- ☐ 1 lettuce
- ☐ 1 bunch spring onions
- ☐ 2 bananas
- ☐ 2 cloves garlic
- ☐ 1 small bag baby spinach
- ☐ 2 small carrots
- ☐ 1 tomato
- ☐ 2 mandarins
- ☐ 2 Lebanese cucumbers
- ☐ 1 small bunch dill
- ☐ 1 red capsicum
- ☐ 200g cherry tomatoes
- ☐ 1 apple
- ☐ 8 baby potatoes

Fridge
- ☐ 200g marinated tofu
- ☐ 100g Stilton cheese
- ☐ 150g firm tofu
- ☐ 2 eggs
- ☐ 70g vegan cream cheese

Freezer
- ☐ 4 slices broccoli, carrot and feta slice

Bakery
- ☐ 2 wholegrain rolls
- ☐ 4 slices pumpernickel bread

Pantry
- ☐ dried apricots
- ☐ almonds
- ☐ 440g can pineapple chunks in juice
- ☐ crispy fried noodles
- ☐ 400g can butter beans
- ☐ dried mixed herbs
- ☐ dried chilli flakes
- ☐ onion chutney
- ☐ white wine vinegar
- ☐ crackers
- ☐ walnuts
- ☐ sultanas
- ☐ pickled onions
- ☐ dried rosemary
- ☐ dried cranberries
- ☐ pine nuts

Staples
- ☐ salt
- ☐ black pepper
- ☐ olive oil
- ☐ extra virgin olive oil

daily tasks

Sunday

Thaw 4 pieces of broccoli, carrot and feta slice overnight in the fridge. You can place them into your lunch boxes. If you do not have any in the freezer, follow the instructions below. Don't forget to add any ingredients to your shopping list.

Preheat the oven to 180°C/350°F/Gas Mark 4. Grease and line a 30 x 20cm baking tin. In a large bowl, whisk together 4 eggs and ½ cup (125ml) of milk. Beat in ½ cup (75g) of wholemeal self-raising flour and ½ cup (75g) of regular self-raising flour to make a batter. Finely chop the broccoli and ½ cup (25g) of baby spinach. Cube 100g of feta cheese and grate 1 carrot. Stir the vegetables and cheese into the batter. Season. Pour the mixture into the baking tin and bake for 30 minutes until golden brown and firm. Leave to cool and remove from the tin. Slice into quarters, then halve each quarter. Place 2 slices into each lunch box, then into the fridge. The rest can be frozen by wrapping each slice in plastic wrap then placing into a container or freezer bag, then popping them into the freezer.

Mix 2 handfuls of dried apricots with 2 handfuls of almonds. Divide between 2 containers.

Monday

Prepare the tofu salad. Heat 1 tablespoon of olive oil in a frying pan over a medium heat. Add 6 sliced mushrooms and fry until golden, about 6 minutes. Remove from the heat and leave to cool. Place a handful of lettuce at the bottom of 2 lunch boxes.

In a bowl, mix together 100g of sliced marinated tofu with ½ a bunch of chopped spring onions and ½ a can of pineapple chunks (put the remaining pineapple in a container in the fridge). Stir in the cooled mushrooms and divide the mixture between the 2 lunch boxes. Finally, scatter some crispy fried noodles over the mixture (or place in a separate container to keep them crisp). Refrigerate until needed.

Tuesday

Make the butter bean cake. Preheat the oven to 180°C/350°F/Gas Mark 4. Rinse and drain a 400g can of butter beans and place in a food processor. Add ½ a bunch of chopped spring onions, 1 clove of peeled and crushed garlic, 1 tablespoon of olive oil, 1 teaspoon of dried mixed herbs and ½ teaspoon of dried chilli flakes. Season to taste. Process the mixture until it comes together.

Spoon the mixture into a foil-lined 14cm round flan dish and press down firmly. Brush with olive oil. Bake for 30 minutes. Leave to cool in the dish, before removing then slicing and placing in your lunch boxes. Pop them into the fridge.

Make the accompanying salad by mixing together 100g of cubed marinated tofu with a handful of baby spinach and a carrot cut into strips. Drizzle with 1 tablespoon of extra virgin olive oil and season to taste. Divide the salad between 2 containers. Refrigerate until needed.

Divide the remaining pineapple chunks between 2 containers, then pop them back into the fridge.

Wednesday

Split 2 wholegrain rolls and divide 50g of sliced Stilton cheese between them. Add some lettuce, a sliced tomato and a dollop of onion chutney. Cover in plastic wrap, then refrigerate until needed.

Thursday

Make the tzatziki. Peel 2 Lebanese cucumbers, cut into chunks and add to a food processor. Process briefly until the cucumber is coarsely chopped. Place in a bowl. Next, process 150g of crumbled firm tofu with ½ tablespoon of white wine vinegar until smooth. Add the tofu to the cucumber. Stir in 1 tablespoon of chopped dill, 1 clove of peeled and crushed garlic and 1 tablespoon of extra virgin olive oil. Stir well to combine and season to taste with salt and freshly ground black pepper. Divide between 2 containers.

Hard boil 2 eggs, then leave to cool. Place into your lunch boxes along with a handful of cherry tomatoes and crackers. Chop a red capsicum and carrot into sticks and add to the lunch boxes. Refrigerate.

Mix 2 handfuls of walnuts with 2 handfuls of sultanas. Divide between 2 containers.

Saturday

Prepare the Stilton ploughman's. Place 2 slices of pumpernickel bread on each plate. Layer some lettuce on each slice, add a dollop of chutney, some sliced pickled onions and 50g of crumbled Stilton cheese. Slice an apple and add it to each plate. Serve.

Sunday

Bake the stuffed potatoes. Prick 8 scrubbed baby potatoes then place in a large saucepan and cover with water. Bring to the boil and cook for about 20 minutes, until the potatoes are tender. Drain.

Preheat the oven to 200°C/400°F/Gas Mark 6. Once the potatoes are cool enough to handle, use an apple corer to make a hole in each potato, taking care not to go through the bottom. Using a teaspoon, fill each potato with vegan cream cheese.

In a small bowl, mix together the olive oil, rosemary, salt and black pepper. Brush the oil all over the potatoes then place on a baking tray. Bake in the oven for 30 minutes, until the skins are crispy.

Prepare the accompanying salad by mixing together some shredded lettuce with a handful of dried cranberries, 2 tablespoons of toasted pine nuts and the remaining cherry tomatoes sliced in half. Mix together 1 tablespoon of extra virgin olive oil with ½ tablespoon of white wine vinegar, then stir into the salad. Serve with the potatoes.

Winter Week 5

A good mix of lunches this week: pasta salads, wraps and rolls as well as a tasty soup for the weekend. There's also a salad that uses giant couscous (you can use regular if you prefer) as well as chips made using parsnip and swede.

Monday
Halloumi, Tomato and Olive Pasta Salad / Canned Pears with Cardamom

Tuesday
Halloumi and Chickpea Wrap / Canned Pears with Mixed Spice

Wednesday
Chickpeas and Baby Spinach with Giant Couscous (Moghrabieh) V / Banana

Thursday
Avocado, Cheese and Tomato Roll / Cashews and Sultanas

Friday
Sausage and Egg Sandwich / Orange

Saturday
Roast Parsnip and Swede Chips V

Sunday
Sauerkraut, Bean, Potato and Carrot Soup V

"There is no love sincerer than the love of food." George Bernard Shaw

shopping list

Fruit and Vegetables
- ☐ 1 bunch parsley
- ☐ 4 tomatoes
- ☐ 1 lettuce
- ☐ 1 small bag baby spinach
- ☐ 2 bananas
- ☐ 1 avocado
- ☐ 2 oranges
- ☐ 2 parsnips
- ☐ 1 swede
- ☐ 1 potato
- ☐ 1 carrot

Fridge
- ☐ 180g halloumi cheese
- ☐ 50g Cheddar cheese
- ☐ 2 eggs
- ☐ 4 vegetarian sausages
- ☐ aioli

Bakery
- ☐ 2 wholegrain rolls
- ☐ 4 slices wholegrain bread

Pantry
- ☐ 100g dried pasta
- ☐ sun-dried tomatoes
- ☐ olives
- ☐ lemon juice
- ☐ 825g can pears
- ☐ ground cardamom
- ☐ 400g can chickpeas
- ☐ dried mixed herbs
- ☐ smoked paprika
- ☐ 2 wholegrain flour tortillas
- ☐ mixed spice
- ☐ vegetable stock
- ☐ ground cinnamon
- ☐ 100g giant couscous (or regular)
- ☐ sultanas
- ☐ ground cumin
- ☐ cashews
- ☐ English mustard
- ☐ dried rosemary
- ☐ dried sage
- ☐ sea salt flakes
- ☐ 410g can sauerkraut
- ☐ 400g can cannellini beans

Staples
- ☐ salt
- ☐ black pepper
- ☐ olive oil
- ☐ extra virgin olive oil
- ☐ canola oil

daily tasks

Sunday

Prepare the pasta salad. Cook 100g of pasta according to the instructions on the packet. Drain then rinse the pasta in cold water. Once drained, place in a bowl. Heat 1 tablespoon of olive oil in a frying pan over a medium heat. Add 90g of sliced halloumi and cook on both sides until golden, about 4 minutes. Remove from the heat, leave to cool, dice and add to the pasta.

Add 2 tablespoons each of chopped sun-dried tomatoes and olives. Stir in 1 chopped tomato and 2 tablespoons of chopped parsley. Make a quick dressing by mixing together 1 tablespoon of extra virgin olive oil with ½ tablespoon of lemon juice. Stir the dressing into the salad and season to taste. Divide between 2 lunch boxes and refrigerate until needed.

Divide ½ a can of pears between 2 containers. Sprinkle with ground cardamom. Place the rest of the pears in a container. Place all containers in the fridge.

Monday

Prepare the halloumi and chickpea wraps. Heat 1 tablespoon of olive oil in a frying pan over a medium heat. Add 90g of cubed halloumi and ½ a 400g can of rinsed and drained chickpeas (put the remaining in a container in the fridge). Cook until golden. Stir through 1 teaspoon of dried mixed herbs and ¼ teaspoon of smoked paprika. Leave to cool then divide between 2 wholegrain flour tortillas.

Add a dollop of aioli, 1 sliced tomato and some shredded lettuce. Roll up the wraps, cover in plastic wrap then refrigerate until needed.

Divide the remaining pears between 2 containers. Sprinkle with mixed spice then pop them into the fridge.

Tuesday

Prepare the chickpeas and baby spinach with giant couscous. Bring 3 cups (750ml) of vegetable stock to the boil. Sprinkle in ¼ teaspoon of ground cinnamon and add ½ cup (100g) of giant couscous. Bring to the boil, reduce the heat and simmer for 20-25 minutes, until tender. Drain, place in a bowl and leave to cool.

Add the remaining chickpeas, a handful of shredded baby spinach, 1 chopped tomato and a handful of sultanas. Mix 1 tablespoon of extra virgin olive oil with ½ teaspoon of ground cumin. Stir the dressing into the couscous salad. Divide between 2 lunch boxes and refrigerate until needed.

Wednesday

Make the rolls. Slice the flesh of an avocado, squeeze some lemon juice over the avocado and divide it between 2 wholegrain rolls. Add 50g of sliced Cheddar cheese, a sliced tomato and a handful of lettuce. Season to taste. Cover the rolls in plastic wrap and refrigerate until needed.

Mix 2 handfuls of cashews with 2 handfuls of sultanas. Divide between 2 containers.

Thursday

Make the vegetarian sausage and egg sandwiches. Hard boil 2 eggs. Leave to cool, peel and slice. Whilst they are cooking heat 1 tablespoon of olive oil in a frying pan and cook 4 vegetarian sausages until golden. Leave to cool and slice in half lengthwise.

Spread some English mustard over 2 slices of wholegrain bread. Top with the eggs and sausages, season to taste and top with 2 more slices of bread. Cut in half and cover in plastic wrap. Refrigerate until needed.

Saturday

Roast the parsnip and swede. Preheat the oven to 210°C/410°F/Gas Mark 7. Peel the parsnips and swede and slice into thick chips or wedges. Place in a roasting pan, drizzle with canola oil and add some black pepper. Roast for 40 minutes until golden and crisp. Divide the chips between 2 bowls then add a sprinkle of chopped parsley, dried rosemary, dried sage and some sea salt flakes. Serve warm.

Sunday

Make the soup. Heat 1 tablespoon of olive oil in a large saucepan. Add a 410g can of sauerkraut, a peeled potato cut into cubes and a peeled and chopped carrot and cook for 5 minutes. Stir in a 400g can of rinsed and drained cannellini beans.

Next add 2 cups (500ml) of vegetable stock, bring to the boil, reduce the heat and simmer until the carrot and potato are tender, about 15-20 minutes. Stir in 1 tablespoon of chopped parsley. Season to taste then serve in warmed bowls.

Winter Week 6

An easy start this week with a tasty roll. We then have a colourful rice salad followed by a bulghar wheat salad. On Thursday enjoy a quick omelette in a pita then dip into the freezer for some turnovers and polenta for Friday and Saturday. We end with a tasty French onion soup.

Monday
Goat's Cheese, Spinach and Capsicum Roll / Packet Potato Chips and Chocolate Bar

Tuesday
Sweet Potato, Spinach and Tomato Rice Salad V / Orange

Wednesday
Bulghar Wheat Salad with Tomatoes, Spinach and Bocconcini / Apple

Thursday
Pita Filled with a Goat's Cheese and Spring Onion Omelette / Banana

Friday
Feta, Capsicum and Olive Turnovers / Cashews and Dried Apricots

Saturday
Polenta Cubes with Cherry Tomatoes and Bocconcini

Sunday
French Onion Soup

You can microwave grains such as rice and bulghar wheat. You can also microwave pasta. Check your manual for guidance on the water to grain ratio and how long to cook for.

shopping list

Fruit and Vegetables
- [ ] 1 bag baby spinach
- [ ] 1 sweet potato
- [ ] 1 bunch spring onions
- [ ] 2 oranges
- [ ] 2 tomatoes
- [ ] 3 cloves garlic
- [ ] 1 bunch parsley
- [ ] 2 apples
- [ ] 1 lettuce
- [ ] 2 bananas
- [ ] 250g cherry tomatoes
- [ ] 4 onions

Fridge
- [ ] 120g goat's cheese
- [ ] 220g bocconcini cheese
- [ ] 3 eggs
- [ ] mayonnaise
- [ ] 50g Gruyère cheese

Freezer
- [ ] 4 feta, capsicum and olive turnovers
- [ ] polenta

Bakery
- [ ] 2 wholegrain rolls
- [ ] 2 pita breads
- [ ] 2 slices sourdough bread

Pantry
- [ ] chargrilled capsicum
- [ ] 2 small packets potato chips (crisps)
- [ ] 2 small chocolate bars
- [ ] 100g brown rice
- [ ] sun-dried tomatoes
- [ ] red wine vinegar
- [ ] 100g bulghar wheat
- [ ] lemon juice
- [ ] cashews
- [ ] dried apricots
- [ ] brown sugar
- [ ] vegetable stock
- [ ] Vegemite / Marmite

Staples
- [ ] salt
- [ ] black pepper
- [ ] olive oil
- [ ] extra virgin olive oil
- [ ] canola oil

daily tasks

Sunday

Make the rolls. Split 2 wholegrain rolls and divide 60g of goat's cheese between them. Top with some baby spinach and chargrilled capsicum. Season. Cover in plastic wrap and refrigerate until needed.

Monday

Prepare the rice salad. Cook ½ cup (100g) of brown rice according to packet directions. Once cooked, rinse under cold water and drain thoroughly. Place in a bowl. Peel and dice a sweet potato and cook in a saucepan of boiling water until tender, about 15 minutes. Drain, leave to cool then add to the rice.

Chop ½ a bunch of spring onions and 2 tablespoons of sun-dried tomatoes and add to the bowl with a handful of baby spinach. Mix 1 tablespoon of extra virgin olive oil with ½ tablespoon of red wine vinegar and stir it into the salad. Season to taste. Divide the salad between 2 lunch boxes then refrigerate until needed.

Tuesday

Make the bulghar wheat salad. Place ½ cup (100g) of bulghar wheat in a bowl and cover with cold water. Leave to soak for 40 minutes and then drain thoroughly into a sieve. Place in a bowl. Chop 2 tomatoes and add to the bulghar wheat. Add 100g of bocconcini (cut in half or quarters if you like) and a handful of baby spinach.

Mix 1 tablespoon of extra virgin olive oil with ½ tablespoon of lemon juice and 1 clove of crushed garlic. Stir into the salad along with 2 tablespoons of chopped parsley. Season to taste. Divide between 2 lunch boxes and refrigerate until needed.

Wednesday

Make the omelette. Heat ½ tablespoon of canola oil in a frying pan over a medium heat. Beat 3 eggs and add some seasoning. Stir in 60g of crumbled goat's cheese and 2 chopped spring onions. Add to the pan and cook until set, turning once. Remove from the pan and leave to cool.

Once cool, slice into quarters. Split 2 pita breads and add 2 quarters of omelette to each pita along with a handful of shredded lettuce and a small dollop of mayonnaise. Cover in plastic wrap then refrigerate until needed.

Thursday

Thaw 4 feta, capsicum and olive turnovers overnight in the fridge. You can place them in lunch boxes. They will be thawed and ready to eat by tomorrow. If you do not have any, follow the instructions below. Remember to add the ingredients to your shopping list.

Preheat the oven to 220°C/425°F/Gas Mark 7. Thaw 2 sheets of puff pastry then cut each sheet into 4 squares.

In a bowl, mix together 100g of cubed feta cheese, 2 tablespoons of chopped olives, ½ a chopped red capsicum and ¼ cup (15g) of chopped baby spinach. Stir in 1 teaspoon of dried mixed herbs. Season to taste. Add a spoonful of the mixture to each pastry square.

Fold the pastry in half to form a triangle, then press the edges with a fork to seal. Prick the tops with a fork. Place on a baking tray and bake for 20 minutes until golden. Leave to cool than place 2 in each lunch box. Refrigerate until tomorrow. Freeze the remaining turnovers by placing into a container then into the freezer.

Mix 2 handfuls of cashews with 2 handfuls of dried apricots. Divide between 2 containers.

Saturday

Cook the polenta and cherry tomatoes. Thaw some polenta at room temperature for a few hours. If you do not have any in the freezer, follow the instructions below.

Bring 3⅔ cups (900ml) of vegetable stock to the boil in a medium saucepan. Once boiling, gradually add 1½ cups (225g) of polenta, stirring constantly with a wooden spoon. Reduce the heat and continue stirring until the polenta has thickened and is coming away from the side of the saucepan.

Remove from the heat and stir in 1 tablespoon of butter and 2 tablespoons of grated Parmesan-style cheese. Season. Tip the mixture into a 30 x 20cm oiled baking tin and spread the mixture evenly. Leave to cool then place in the fridge for a few hours to firm up.

Remove the polenta from the tin and slice in half. Place half in a freezer bag, then into the freezer. Use the remaining polenta following the instructions below.

Cut the polenta into cubes, brush with olive oil and place on a baking tray. Cut 250g of cherry tomatoes in half and place in another baking dish. Mix 2 tablespoons of olive oil with 1 clove of crushed garlic and some seasoning. Drizzle the oil over the tomatoes. Place the polenta and tomatoes in an oven preheated to 200°C/400°F/Gas Mark 6 and cook for 30 minutes.

Place a handful of shredded lettuce onto 2 plates. Divide the polenta and tomatoes between the plates. Add the remaining tub of bocconcini (cut them in half, if you prefer). Mix 1 tablespoon of extra virgin olive oil with ½ tablespoon of lemon juice and drizzle it over the polenta, tomatoes and cheese. Finish with a sprinkling of chopped parsley and a good grind of black pepper.

Sunday

Make the French onion soup. Heat 1 tablespoon of olive oil in a large saucepan over a medium heat. Add 4 sliced onions and a clove of peeled and crushed garlic. Cook and stir for 5 minutes. Stir in 1 tablespoon of brown sugar, turn the heat down and cook for another 20 minutes, until the onions are caramelised and golden.

Mix 1 tablespoon of Vegemite or Marmite with 4 cups (1 litre) of vegetable stock. Add the stock to the pan, increase the heat and bring to the boil. Once boiling, reduce the heat and simmer for 20 minutes.

Once the soup is nearly ready, toast 2 slices of sourdough bread on one side. Turn the bread and top with 50g of sliced or grated Gruyère cheese and grill until melted. Ladle the soup into warmed bowls then top with the cheesy bread. Serve.

Winter Week 7

This week is all vegan. There are a lot of vegan lunches featured in other weeks, however I thought for this week I'd go all out vegan. I've included tasty fritters and quiches to demonstrate you do not need eggs for these typical egg dishes.

Monday
Mushroom, Onion and Tomato Pita V / Banana

Tuesday
Butter Bean, Cashew and Cranberry Barley Salad V / Orange

Wednesday
Artichoke Fritters with Tomatoes, Rocket and Olives V / Mandarin

Thursday
Crispbread with Cheesy Dip V / Capsicum, Onions and Gherkins / Dates and Pecans

Friday
Chilli and Onion Polenta with Cheesy Dip V / Apple

Saturday
Gorditas Stuffed with Beans and Mushrooms V

Sunday
Caramelised Onion Vegan Quiches V

Herbs are often used as a garnish or flavour enhancer. However, fresh herbs do have health benefits. They contain antioxidants, have anti-inflammatory properties and are a good source of vitamins, iron and fibre.

shopping list

Fruit and Vegetables
- [ ] 3 onions
- [ ] 8 mushrooms
- [ ] 3 tomatoes
- [ ] 1 small bunch parsley
- [ ] 2 bananas
- [ ] 2 oranges
- [ ] 1 clove garlic
- [ ] 1 small bag rocket
- [ ] 2 mandarins
- [ ] 1 red onion
- [ ] 2 apples

Fridge
- [ ] 140ml soy milk
- [ ] 125g vegan cream cheese
- [ ] 100g vegan Cheddar-style cheese
- [ ] 360g firm tofu

Freezer
- [ ] 1 sheet puff pastry

Bakery
- [ ] 2 pita breads

Staples
- [ ] salt
- [ ] black pepper
- [ ] olive oil
- [ ] extra virgin olive oil
- [ ] canola oil

Pantry
- [ ] 100g pearl barley
- [ ] 400g can butter beans
- [ ] cashews
- [ ] dried cranberries
- [ ] lemon juice
- [ ] dried sage
- [ ] 50g self-raising flour
- [ ] 400g can artichoke hearts
- [ ] dried oregano
- [ ] olives
- [ ] dried chives
- [ ] mustard powder
- [ ] 6-8 crispbread
- [ ] chargrilled capsicum
- [ ] cocktail onions
- [ ] gherkins
- [ ] dates
- [ ] pecans
- [ ] vegetable stock
- [ ] 375g polenta (cornmeal)
- [ ] garlic powder
- [ ] chilli powder
- [ ] 150g plain flour
- [ ] baking powder
- [ ] 400g can kidney beans
- [ ] smoked paprika
- [ ] balsamic vinegar
- [ ] brown sugar
- [ ] savoury yeast flakes
- [ ] dried thyme

daily tasks

Sunday

Prepare the pitas. Heat 1 tablespoon of olive oil in a frying pan over a medium heat. Add a peeled and chopped onion and fry for 3 minutes until they start to soften. Add 4 sliced mushrooms and continue cooking until the mushrooms are golden and cooked, about 4 minutes. Remove from the heat and leave to cool. Once cool, divide the filling between 2 split pita breads. Add a sliced tomato and 2 tablespoons of chopped parsley. Cover in plastic wrap, then refrigerate until needed.

Monday

Prepare the barley salad. Place ½ cup (100g) of pearl barley in a medium saucepan. Cover with plenty of cold water. Bring to the boil, lower the heat then simmer for 30 minutes, until tender. Remove from the heat, drain, then rinse the barley under cold water. Drain well and place in a bowl. To the bowl, add a 400g can of rinsed and drained butter beans, a good handful of cashews and 3 tablespoons of dried cranberries.

In a jar or bowl mix together 1 tablespoon of extra virgin olive oil with ½ tablespoon of lemon juice and ½ teaspoon of dried sage. Add to the salad and stir well. Divide between 2 lunch boxes then refrigerate until needed.

Tuesday

Prepare the artichoke fritters. In a bowl, mix together ⅓ cup (50g) of self-raising flour, a drained and chopped can of artichoke hearts, 1 teaspoon of dried oregano, 1 clove of crushed garlic, ⅓ cup (80ml) of soy milk, 1 tablespoon of lemon juice and 1 teaspoon of canola oil. Season well with freshly ground black pepper. Mix to make a batter.

Heat 2 tablespoons of canola oil in a large frying pan over a medium heat. Add heaped tablespoons of the mixture to the pan, pressing down to form fritters. Fry for 3 minutes, until brown. Turn and cook for another 2 minutes. Drain on paper towel. Once cooled, divide between 2 lunch boxes and place them into the fridge. Any leftovers can be frozen.

Mix together 1 chopped tomato with a good handful of rocket and 2 tablespoons of olives. Drizzle some extra virgin olive oil over the salad, divide between 2 containers and then pop them into the fridge.

Wednesday

Make the cheesy dip. Beat together 125g of vegan cream cheese and ½ cup (50g) of grated vegan Cheddar-style cheese. Process ¼ cup (60g) of firm tofu until smooth. Stir the tofu into the cheesy mixture along with 1 teaspoon of dried chives and ½ teaspoon of mustard powder. Season liberally with freshly ground black pepper. Place half of the dip in a container in the fridge and divide the rest between 2 lunch boxes.

In 2 separate containers add 3-4 crispbread per person, some chargrilled capsicum, cocktail onions and gherkins. Refrigerate until needed.

Mix 2 handfuls of dates with 2 handfuls of pecans. Divide between 2 containers.

Thursday

Prepare the chilli and onion polenta. Heat 1 tablespoon of olive oil in a frying pan over a medium heat. Add 1 brown and 1 red onion (both chopped) and fry for 6 minutes, until pale and soft. Remove from the heat.

Bring 3⅔ cups (900ml) of vegetable stock to the boil in a medium non-stick saucepan. Once boiling, gradually add 1½ cups (225g) of polenta, stirring constantly with a wooden spoon. Reduce the heat and continue stirring the polenta until it has thickened. This will take about 10 minutes.

Remove from the heat and add the onions, 2 tablespoons of extra virgin olive oil, 1 teaspoon of garlic powder, ½ teaspoon of chilli powder and a good grind of black pepper, stirring quickly to combine. Pour the mixture into a 30 x 20cm oiled baking tin. Leave to cool, then place in a refrigerator to firm up.

Preheat the grill. Remove the polenta from the tin and using a large, sharp knife cut the polenta into 12 squares. Brush with olive oil. Place on a wire grill tray and grill for about 8 minutes on each side until crispy. Leave to cool, add some squares to 2 lunch boxes and freeze the rest.

Divide the remaining cheesy dip between 2 containers to serve with the polenta. Refrigerate the polenta and dip.

Saturday
Make the gorditas. In a large bowl, mix together 1 cup (150g) of polenta, with 1 cup (150g) of plain flour, 1 teaspoon of baking powder and ½ teaspoon of salt. Add 1 tablespoon of canola oil and 2 cups (500ml) of hot water. Mix together with a wooden spoon, until the mixture comes together. Turn the mixture out onto a floured surface and then divide into 12 even-sized balls. Using floured hands, flatten the balls to make 8cm sized rounds.

Heat a large frying pan over a medium heat. Add the rounds and cook for 3-4 minutes, until they start to brown. Turn and cook for another 2-3 minutes. Remove from the pan. Wipe down the pan and add 4 tablespoons of canola oil. Heat the oil over a medium heat. Return the gorditas to the pan and fry for 3 minutes, until golden. Turn, then fry for another 2 minutes. Drain on paper towel.

To make the filling, heat 1 tablespoon of olive oil in a medium saucepan and fry 4 diced mushrooms for 3-4 minutes. Add a 400g can of rinsed and drained kidney beans and mash slightly. Heat through.

Remove from the heat and stir in 1 chopped tomato, and ½ teaspoon of smoked paprika.

Use a sharp knife to carefully split open the gordita to make a pocket as you would with a pita bread. Fill with spoonfuls of the kidney bean mixture. Serve.

Any leftover gorditas can be frozen.

Sunday
Make the caramelised onion quiches. Thaw 1 sheet of puff pastry. Preheat the oven to 200°C/400°F/Gas Mark 6. Heat 2 tablespoons of olive oil in a frying pan over a low heat. Add 1 peeled and sliced onion and fry for 4 minutes, until pale and soft. Add 1 tablespoon each of balsamic vinegar and brown sugar and cook, stirring for another 10 minutes, until caramelised. Remove from the heat.

Process 300g of firm tofu with ¼ cup (60ml) of soy milk, until smooth. Mix in 2 tablespoons of savoury yeast flakes, 1 teaspoon of dried thyme, a pinch of salt and a good grind of black pepper.

Cut the pastry sheet into 9 equal squares or rounds, then line the holes of a muffin tin with the pastry. Spoon the onions over the pastry. Top with the tofu mixture. Place in the oven and bake for 30 minutes until risen and golden. Leave to stand for 10 minutes before removing the quiches from the muffin tin. Serve warm or cold.

Winter Week 8

The goal of this week's lunches is to have super-quick-to-prepare meals, but still with plenty of variety. Hopefully you will have some quinoa slice or another tasty in the freezer!

Monday
Vegetable and Quinoa Slice with Goat's Cheese / Orange

Tuesday
Corn, Cheese and Rocket Wrap with Aioli / Banana

Wednesday
Bean, Rocket and Artichoke Couscous V / Mandarin

Thursday
Tomato, Feta, Olive and Rocket Roll / Dates and Pecans

Friday
Bean and Artichoke Salad with Capsicum, Feta and Almonds / Banana

Saturday
Nachos with Refried Beans, Salsa, Guacamole and Cheese

Sunday
Blue Cheese and Onion English Muffin

Remember to label foods when you freeze them, so you know what is in the container or bag. Also note the date when it was frozen. I use a label maker, but a marker pen will work just as well.

shopping list

Fruit and Vegetables
- ☐ 2 oranges
- ☐ 1 small bag rocket
- ☐ 4 bananas
- ☐ 1 small bunch parsley
- ☐ 2 mandarins
- ☐ 1 tomato
- ☐ 1 red capsicum
- ☐ 1 onion

Fridge
- ☐ 100g Cheddar cheese
- ☐ aioli
- ☐ 100g feta cheese
- ☐ tub guacamole
- ☐ 50g blue cheese

Freezer
- ☐ 4 slices vegetable and quinoa slice

Bakery
- ☐ 2 wholegrain rolls
- ☐ 2 English muffins

Pantry
- ☐ 125g can corn kernels
- ☐ sun-dried tomatoes
- ☐ smoked paprika
- ☐ 2 wholegrain flour tortillas
- ☐ 100g couscous
- ☐ 400g can cannellini beans
- ☐ 400g can artichoke hearts
- ☐ lime juice
- ☐ olives
- ☐ dates
- ☐ pecans
- ☐ almonds
- ☐ lemon juice
- ☐ 400g can refried beans
- ☐ 175g pack corn chips
- ☐ 300g jar salsa
- ☐ sliced jalapeños (optional)

Staples
- ☐ salt
- ☐ black pepper
- ☐ olive oil
- ☐ extra virgin olive oil

daily tasks

Sunday

Thaw 4 slices of vegetable and quinoa slice overnight in the fridge. You can place them in your lunch boxes, ready for the morning. If you have none in the freezer, you can make some, following the instructions below. Remember to add the ingredients to your shopping list.

Rinse 1 cup (130g) of quinoa. Place in a saucepan with 2 cups (500ml) of water. Bring to the boil, reduce the heat then simmer for about 15 minutes until the water is absorbed. Leave to cool. Place half of the quinoa in a container in the fridge (use it in a salad).

Preheat the oven to 180°C/350°F/Gas Mark 4 and grease and line a 30 x 20cm baking tin. Beat 4 eggs with ½ cup (125ml) of milk in a large bowl. Stir in ½ cup (75g) of wholemeal self-raising flour and the quinoa, to make a batter. Add a 310g can of rinsed and drained corn kernels, 60g of shredded baby kale, 1 grated carrot and 60g of crumbled goat's cheese. Finally, stir in 2 tablespoons of chopped parsley and some seasoning.

Pour the mixture into the prepared tin and bake for about 35 minutes until golden and firm. Leave to cool. Remove from the tin and slice into 8 pieces. Place 2 slices into each lunch box. The rest can be frozen by wrapping each slice in plastic wrap then into a container or freezer bag, then into the freezer.

Monday

Prepare the mixture for the wraps. Rinse and drain a 125g can of corn kernels and place in a bowl. To the corn, add ½ cup (50g) of grated Cheddar cheese, 2 tablespoons of chopped sun-dried tomatoes, and a handful of shredded rocket. Stir in 2 tablespoons of aioli and ½ teaspoon of smoked paprika. Season to taste. Divide the mixture between 2 flour tortillas. Fold in the sides, roll up and cover in plastic wrap. Refrigerate until needed.

Tuesday

Make the couscous. Place ½ cup (100g) of couscous in a bowl and stir in ½ cup (125ml) of boiling water. Let stand for 3 minutes. Fluff up with a fork. Rinse and drain a 400g can of cannellini beans. Place half in the bowl and the rest in a container in the fridge. Drain a 400g can of artichoke hearts. Place half in a container in the fridge, chop the rest and add to the couscous.

Next, add 2 tablespoons of chopped sun-dried tomatoes and a handful of rocket. In a jar or bowl mix together 1 tablespoon of extra virgin olive oil with ½ tablespoon of lime juice and 1 tablespoon of chopped parsley. Stir the dressing into the salad, divide between 2 lunch boxes then refrigerate until needed.

Wednesday

Prepare the rolls. Slice 1 tomato and 50g of feta cheese. Divide between 2 wholegrain rolls. Add a few sliced olives and some rocket. Season to taste. Cover in plastic wrap, then refrigerate until needed.

Mix 2 handfuls of dates with 2 handfuls of pecans. Divide between 2 containers.

Thursday

Prepare the bean and artichoke salad. Place the remaining cannellini beans and artichoke hearts (chopped) in a bowl. Add 50g of cubed feta cheese and 1 chopped red capsicum. Stir in a handful of almonds and 2 tablespoons of chopped parsley.

Make a quick dressing by mixing together 1 tablespoon of extra virgin olive oil with ½ tablespoon of lemon juice and stir into the salad. Divide the salad between 2 lunch boxes, then refrigerate until needed.

Saturday

Make the nachos. Heat a can of refried beans in a small saucepan or microwave. Preheat the grill. Divide 175g bag of corn chips between 2 ovenproof bowls. Top with the refried beans, salsa and ½ cup (50g) of grated Cheddar cheese. Add some jalapeños if you are using them. Pop the bowls under the grill for a minute or so, to melt the cheese. Serve warm, with the guacamole.

Sunday

Make the cheese and onion muffins. Heat 1 tablespoon of olive oil in a frying pan over a medium heat. Add a peeled and sliced onion and cook for 5 minutes until golden. Remove from the heat. Preheat the grill. Split 2 English muffins and lightly toast them. Divide the onions between the 4 pieces of muffin and add 50g of crumbled blue cheese. Pop them back under the grill and cook until the cheese has melted. Serve warm.

Winter Week 9

This week's menu is inspired by a menu I came across whilst browsing the internet for US-based restaurants. Not surprising then that you'll see my version of mac-n-cheese as well as succotash and tacos.

Monday
Mac-N-Cheese / Mandarin

Tuesday
Sausage and Kale Couscous with Orange Dressing / Banana

Wednesday
Spicy Crumbed Tofu Roll / Dried Apple and Pear

Thursday
Succotash V / Almonds and Raisins

Friday
Cheese Salad Roll / Dates and Cashews

Saturday
Black Bean and Corn Tacos

Sunday
Sweet Potato Fries with Ranch Dressing

When using nutmeg, grate from a whole nutmeg rather than using ground. The flavour is far superior. You can use nutmeg on vegetables as well as in sweet dishes. It goes really well with spinach but try adding it to mash for added flavour.

shopping list

Fruit and Vegetables
- [ ] 1 small carrot
- [ ] 1 small head broccoli
- [ ] 2 mandarins
- [ ] 1 small bunch kale
- [ ] 1 orange
- [ ] 2 bananas
- [ ] 1 lettuce
- [ ] 3 tomatoes
- [ ] 1 red onion
- [ ] 1 green capsicum
- [ ] 1 avocado
- [ ] 1 small bunch coriander
- [ ] 1 sweet potato

Fridge
- [ ] 150g Cheddar cheese
- [ ] 15g Parmesan-style cheese
- [ ] 2 vegetarian sausages
- [ ] 180g firm tofu
- [ ] 50ml milk

Bakery
- [ ] 2 slices white bread
- [ ] 4 wholegrain rolls

Pantry
- [ ] 100g dried macaroni
- [ ] 100g couscous
- [ ] dried cranberries
- [ ] pine nuts
- [ ] honey
- [ ] garlic powder
- [ ] onion powder
- [ ] smoked paprika
- [ ] dried oregano
- [ ] dried sage
- [ ] chilli powder
- [ ] ranch dressing
- [ ] dried apples
- [ ] dried pears
- [ ] 400g can black beans
- [ ] 420g can corn kernels
- [ ] jar salsa
- [ ] lime juice
- [ ] sliced jalapeños (optional)
- [ ] almonds
- [ ] raisins
- [ ] gherkins
- [ ] dates
- [ ] cashews
- [ ] 4 taco shells
- [ ] whole nutmeg

Staples
- [ ] salt
- [ ] black pepper
- [ ] olive oil
- [ ] extra virgin olive oil
- [ ] canola oil

daily tasks

Sunday

Prepare the mac-n-cheese. Cook 100g of dried macaroni according to the instructions on the packet. A few minutes before the pasta has finished cooking add a cubed carrot and the broccoli, cut into small florets. Drain then rinse the macaroni and vegetables in cold water. Once drained, place in a bowl. Stir in ½ cup (50g) of grated Cheddar cheese, 2 tablespoons of grated Parmesan-style cheese and plenty of black pepper. Divide the macaroni between 2 lunch boxes, then refrigerate until needed.

Monday

Prepare the sausage and kale couscous. Heat 1 tablespoon of olive oil in a frying pan over a medium heat. Add 2 vegetarian sausages and cook until heated through. Remove from the heat, leave to cool then slice into chunks.

Make the couscous. Place ½ cup (100g) of couscous in a bowl and stir in ½ cup (125ml) of boiling water. Let stand for 3 minutes, then fluff up with a fork. Add the sausages to the couscous. Shred a small bunch of kale and add to the bowl along with 2 tablespoons of dried cranberries and 1 tablespoon of toasted pine nuts.

Make a dressing by mixing together the juice of 1 orange with 2 tablespoons of extra virgin olive oil, 1 tablespoon of honey and season to taste. Stir the dressing into the couscous. Divide the couscous between 2 lunch boxes, then refrigerate until needed.

Tuesday

Prepare the tofu. Slice 180g of drained firm tofu into thick slices. In a bowl mix together ½ cup of fresh white bread crumbs (process 2 slices of white bread), with ½ teaspoon each of garlic powder, onion powder, smoked paprika, oregano and sage. Add ¼ teaspoon of chilli powder and some black pepper. Dip the tofu into some milk then coat with the bread crumb mixture. Heat 2 tablespoons of canola oil in a frying pan over a medium heat and add the prepared tofu. Cook on each side until golden, about 6 minutes in total. Drain on paper towel and leave to cool.

Split 2 wholegrain rolls and add some shredded lettuce, 1 sliced tomato and ½ a sliced red onion (pop the rest in the fridge). Top with the crumbed tofu and a small dollop of ranch dressing. Cover in plastic wrap and refrigerate until needed.

Mix 2 handfuls of dried apples with 2 handfuls of dried pears. Divide between 2 containers.

Wednesday

Prepare the succotash. Rinse and drain a 400g can of black beans and a 420g can of corn kernels. Place half of the beans and corn in a container and pop them into the fridge and put the rest in a bowl. Dice ½ a green capsicum (put the rest in the fridge) and 1 tomato and add to the beans and corn. Stir in a diced avocado and ½ a jar of salsa. Stir in 2 tablespoons of lime juice and a handful of chopped coriander. Finish with some jalapeños if you are using them. Divide the succotash between 2 lunch boxes then refrigerate until needed.

Mix 2 handfuls of almonds with 2 handfuls of raisins and divide between 2 containers.

Thursday

Prepare the cheese salad rolls. Split 2 wholegrain rolls. Add some lettuce, a sliced tomato and the remaining red onion, sliced. Slice or grate 50g of Cheddar cheese and add to the rolls. Top with some sliced gherkins, jalapeños, if desired and a dollop of ranch dressing. Cover in plastic wrap then refrigerate until needed.

Mix 2 handfuls of dates with 2 handfuls of cashews. Divide between 2 containers.

Saturday

Prepare the tacos. Fill 4 taco shells with the following: some shredded lettuce; the remaining black beans, corn kernels, diced green capsicum and salsa; ½ cup (50g) of grated Cheddar cheese and a handful of chopped coriander. Finish with a squeeze of lime juice. Serve 2 per person.

Sunday

Roast the sweet potato fries. Preheat the oven to 210°C/410°F/Gas Mark 7. Peel a sweet potato and cut into chips or wedges. Place in a roasting pan and drizzle with canola oil. Roast for 20 minutes, turn the chips and roast for another 20 minutes until tender and starting to caramelise. Season with salt and black pepper and a grating of nutmeg. Serve with some ranch dressing, for dipping.

Winter Week 10

I'm taking a trip to the US soon so thought I'd come up with some more US-inspired lunches. My research shows the US do some impressive salads and I offer some of these here – without the meat of course.

Monday
Bean and Tomato Stuffed Wontons / Fruit Salad

Tuesday
Bean Cobb Salad / Banana

Wednesday
Mexican Rice Salad / Fruit Salad

Thursday
Potatoes, Olives and Butter Bean Hummus with Crispbread V / Cumquats or Mandarin

Friday
Golden Gnocchi with Blue Cheese, Spinach and Cherry Tomatoes / Walnuts and Dates

Saturday
Salt and Pepper Potato Rounds with Romesco Sauce and Aioli

Sunday
Cheese, Onion and Tomato Stuffed Croissant

When preparing vegetables for cooking, try to cut them into even-sized pieces. It ensures they will cook at the same time and you won't end up with any that are under or over cooked.

shopping list

Fruit and Vegetables
- [ ] 4 tomatoes
- [ ] 1 small bunch coriander
- [ ] 250g cherry tomatoes
- [ ] 1 avocado
- [ ] 1 lettuce
- [ ] 2 bananas
- [ ] 4 potatoes
- [ ] 2 cloves garlic
- [ ] 1 small bag rocket
- [ ] 4 cumquats or 2 mandarins
- [ ] 1 small bag baby spinach
- [ ] 1 red capsicum
- [ ] 1 onion

Fridge
- [ ] 25ml milk
- [ ] 2 eggs
- [ ] 100g blue cheese
- [ ] 4 slices vegetarian bacon
- [ ] 100g smoked cheese
- [ ] aioli

Bakery
- [ ] 2 large croissants

Pantry
- [ ] 400g can black beans
- [ ] chilli powder
- [ ] 12 wonton wrappers
- [ ] 400g can fruit salad in juice
- [ ] 400g can butter beans
- [ ] black olives
- [ ] balsamic vinegar
- [ ] 100g brown rice
- [ ] chargrilled capsicum
- [ ] lime juice
- [ ] dried chilli flakes
- [ ] dried mixed herbs
- [ ] unhulled tahini
- [ ] lemon juice
- [ ] 6-8 crispbread
- [ ] 250g gnocchi
- [ ] pine nuts
- [ ] walnuts
- [ ] dates
- [ ] almonds
- [ ] red wine vinegar
- [ ] smoked paprika

Staples
- [ ] salt
- [ ] black pepper
- [ ] olive oil
- [ ] extra virgin olive oil
- [ ] canola oil

daily tasks

Sunday

Prepare the bean and tomato wontons. Preheat the oven to 200°C/400°F/Gas Mark 6. Rinse and drain a 400g can of black beans. Place half in a container in the fridge and put the rest in a bowl. To the bowl, add 1 chopped tomato, 1 tablespoon of chopped coriander and a pinch of chilli powder. Season to taste.

Lay out 12 wonton wrappers. Divide the filling between the wrappers. Brush the edges with water, fold and seal. Place on a baking tray and brush the tops with milk. Bake for 20 minutes, until golden and crispy. Leave to cool then divide them between 2 lunch boxes. Refrigerate until needed.

Divide ½ a can of fruit salad between 2 containers and place the rest in another container. Pop them all in the fridge.

Monday

Prepare the bean Cobb salad. Hard boil 2 eggs. Leave to cool, peel, coarsely chop and place in a bowl. To the eggs, add ½ a can of rinsed and drained butter beans (put the rest in a container in the fridge), 2 tablespoons of black olives, sliced in half, and 50g of crumbled blue cheese.

Cook 4 slices of vegetarian bacon according to packet directions, leave to cool, chop, then add to the bowl. Next add 125g of halved cherry tomatoes and a diced avocado (drizzled with lime juice). Mix 1 tablespoon of extra virgin olive oil with ½ tablespoon of balsamic vinegar. Stir the dressing into the salad. Season to taste.

Place a layer of shredded lettuce on the bottom of 2 lunch boxes and top with the salad. Refrigerate until needed.

Tuesday

Make the Mexican rice salad. Cook ½ cup (100g) of brown rice according to packet directions. Once cooked, rinse under cold water and drain thoroughly. Place in a bowl. To the bowl, add the remaining black beans, 50g of cubed smoked cheese, 2 tablespoons of chopped chargrilled capsicum and 1 chopped tomato. Add 2 tablespoons of chopped

coriander, 1 tablespoon of lime juice and a pinch of dried chilli flakes. Season to taste.

Place a layer of shredded lettuce on the bottom of 2 lunch boxes and top with the rice salad. Refrigerate until needed.

Divide the remaining fruit salad between 2 containers then place in the fridge.

Wednesday

Prepare the potato. Prick an unpeeled potato and microwave until tender. Once tender, leave to cool and cut into cubes. Drizzle 1 tablespoon of extra virgin olive oil over the potato cubes and sprinkle with 1 teaspoon of mixed herbs. Season to taste. Divide between 2 containers.

Make the hummus by blitzing the following in a food processor: the remaining butter beans, 1 clove of garlic, 1 tablespoon each of tahini, extra virgin olive oil, lemon juice and water. Season to taste then divide between 2 containers.

Finely chop 4 tablespoons of black olives and divide between another 2 containers. To your lunch boxes add a handful of rocket and 3-4 crispbread per person. Pop everything into the fridge.

Thursday

Prepare the gnocchi. Heat 2 tablespoons of olive oil in a frying pan over a medium heat. Add 250g of gnocchi and fry until golden. Remove from the heat, drain on paper towel and leave to cool. Place in a bowl and add 50g of crumbled blue cheese, a handful of baby spinach, 125g of halved cherry tomatoes and 1 tablespoon of toasted pine nuts. Season to taste.

Place a handful of shredded lettuce on the bottom of 2 lunch boxes. Top with the gnocchi and place in the fridge.

Mix 2 handfuls of walnuts with 2 handfuls of dates and divide between 2 containers.

Saturday

Make the romesco sauce. Preheat the grill. On a grill pan place 1 red capsicum sliced into quarters (skin side up), 1 whole tomato and 1 unpeeled clove of garlic. Grill until the skins are blackened – turn the tomato and garlic as needed. Leave to cool, remove the skin and place the capsicum, tomato and garlic in a food processor. Add ¼ cup (35g) of toasted almonds, 1 tablespoon of extra virgin olive oil, ½ tablespoon of red wine vinegar and ¼ teaspoon of smoked paprika. Process until the mixture is thick and smooth. Season to taste.

Prepare the salt and pepper potato rounds. Preheat the oven to 210°C/410°F/Gas Mark 7. Slice 3 potatoes into rounds about 1.5cm thick. Place in a roasting pan, drizzle with canola oil and season well with salt and freshly ground black pepper. Roast for 20 minutes, turn the potatoes then roast for another 20 minutes until they are golden and tender. Add more seasoning if you wish.

Serve the potato rounds with aioli and the romesco sauce.

Sunday

Prepare the cheese, onion and tomato stuffed croissants. Heat 1 tablespoon of olive oil in a frying pan over a medium heat. Add a sliced onion and cook until golden, about 5 minutes.

Warm the croissants in the oven for 5 minutes on 180°C/350°F/Gas Mark 4. Cut in half and add the onion, 1 sliced tomato and 50g of sliced smoked cheese. Season to taste, top with the lids and serve warm. You can melt the cheese under the grill, if you like.

Winter Week 11

This week's lunches includes items that I would have expected to have included by now but haven't. In particular the veggie BLT, breakfast burrito and the toasted Brie and caramelised onion on sourdough.

Monday
BLT Sandwich / Banana

Tuesday
Herbed Tofu, Cheese, Caper and Tomato Stuffed Flatbread / Dried Apples and Pears

Wednesday
Breakfast Burrito / Pecans and Dates

Thursday
Mexican Tofu Salad with Refried Beans / Orange

Friday
Brie, Chargrilled Capsicum and Salad Roll / Peanuts and Sultanas

Saturday
Pita Topped with Egg, Refried Beans, Capsicum, Tomato and More

Sunday
Toasted Brie and Caramelised Red Onion on Sourdough with Side Salad

You can easily toast raw nuts yourself. Simply add them to a dry frying pan over a medium heat and toss frequently until the nuts turn brown. Keep an eye on them as they will go from brown to black very quickly.

shopping list

Fruit and Vegetables
- [ ] 1 lettuce
- [ ] 2 bananas
- [ ] 6 tomatoes
- [ ] 2 red onions
- [ ] 1 small bunch coriander
- [ ] 1 avocado
- [ ] 2 oranges

Fridge
- [ ] 4 slices vegetarian bacon
- [ ] mayonnaise
- [ ] 300g firm tofu
- [ ] 150g Cheddar cheese
- [ ] 4 eggs
- [ ] small tub sour cream
- [ ] 100g Brie

Freezer
- [ ] 2 hash browns

Bakery
- [ ] 4 slices wholegrain bread
- [ ] 2 flatbreads
- [ ] 2 wholegrain rolls
- [ ] 2 pita breads
- [ ] 2 slices sourdough bread

Pantry
- [ ] sun-dried tomatoes
- [ ] dried mixed herbs
- [ ] capers
- [ ] dried apples
- [ ] dried pears
- [ ] 2 wholegrain flour tortillas
- [ ] pecans
- [ ] dates
- [ ] lime juice
- [ ] ground cumin
- [ ] ground coriander
- [ ] 400g can refried beans
- [ ] ranch dressing
- [ ] chargrilled capsicum
- [ ] peanuts
- [ ] sultanas
- [ ] sliced jalapeños (optional)
- [ ] brown sugar
- [ ] balsamic vinegar

Staples
- [ ] salt
- [ ] black pepper
- [ ] olive oil

daily tasks

Sunday

Make the BLT. Cook 4 slices of vegetarian bacon according to packet directions. Leave to cool. Top 2 slices of wholegrain bread with some lettuce, the vegetarian bacon and 2 tablespoons of chopped sun-dried tomatoes. Add a dollop of mayonnaise, then season to taste. Top with 2 more slices of bread, cut each sandwich in half then cover in plastic wrap. Refrigerate until needed.

Monday

Prepare the filling for the flatbread. Drain 150g of firm tofu and cut into bite-size pieces. Heat 1 tablespoon of olive oil in a frying pan over a medium heat. Add the tofu and cook until golden on both sides, about 6 minutes. Sprinkle 1 teaspoon of dried mixed herbs over the tofu. Remove from the heat and leave to cool.

Divide the tofu between 2 flatbreads. Add ½ cup (50g) of grated Cheddar cheese, 1 tablespoon of rinsed and drained capers, 1 chopped tomato and ½ a chopped red onion. Finish with a dollop of mayonnaise. Roll up the flatbreads, cover in plastic wrap and refrigerate until needed.

Mix 2 handfuls of dried apple with 2 handfuls of dried pear. Divide between 2 containers.

Tuesday

Prepare the breakfast burrito. Heat 1 tablespoon of olive oil in a frying pan over a medium heat. Beat together 2 eggs with some seasoning then add to the pan. Cook until set, remove from the heat, leave to cool then cut into strips.

Meanwhile, cook 2 hash browns according to packet instructions. Leave to cool then cut into bite-size pieces. Divide the omelette and hash browns between 2 flour tortillas. Add ½ cup (50g) of grated Cheddar cheese and 1 chopped tomato. Finish with a dollop of sour cream. Roll up the tortillas, cover in plastic wrap and refrigerate until needed.

Mix 2 handfuls of pecans with 2 handfuls of dates. Divide between 2 containers.

Wednesday

Prepare the Mexican tofu salad. Drain 150g of firm tofu and cut into bite-size pieces. Place on a plate and drizzle 2 tablespoons of lime juice over the tofu. Leave to stand for 20 minutes. Heat 1 tablespoon of olive oil in a frying pan over a medium heat. Add the tofu and cook until golden on both sides, about 6 minutes.

Mix together 1 teaspoon each of ground cumin and ground coriander and 1 tablespoon of fresh coriander. Add the mixture to the tofu, stirring well to coat. Remove from the heat and leave to cool.

Layer some lettuce at the bottom of 2 lunch boxes. Top with ½ a can of refried beans (put the rest in a container in the fridge). Add the tofu, a diced avocado (drizzled with lime juice), a diced tomato and ½ a chopped red onion. Finish with some ranch dressing. Refrigerate until needed.

Thursday

Make the rolls. Split 2 wholegrain rolls and add 50g of sliced Brie. Add 2 tablespoons of chopped chargrilled capsicum, 1 chopped tomato and some shredded lettuce. Finish with a dollop of ranch dressing. Cover in plastic wrap then refrigerate until needed.

Mix 2 handfuls of peanuts with 2 handfuls of sultanas. Divide between 2 containers.

Saturday

Prepare the pitas. Warm 2 pita breads in the oven. Heat the remaining refried beans in a small saucepan. Heat 2 tablespoons of olive oil in a frying pan over a medium heat. Fry 2 eggs according to your liking. Place the pitas onto 2 plates and top with the refried beans, some chopped chargrilled capsicum and a chopped tomato. Top with the eggs and finish with some grated Cheddar cheese, chopped coriander and a dollop of sour cream. Add some jalapeños if you like. Serve immediately.

Sunday

Cook the caramelised onion for the toasty. Heat 1 tablespoon of olive oil in a frying pan over a medium heat. Add a sliced red onion and cook for a few minutes until soft. Add 1 tablespoon each of brown sugar and balsamic vinegar. Cook for another 5 minutes, until the onion is caramelised. Preheat the grill. Grill 2 slices of sourdough. Top the toasted bread with the red onion and 50g of sliced Brie. Grill until the cheese has melted. Serve with a side salad of lettuce, tomato, chargrilled capsicum and some ranch dressing.

Winter Week 12

This week is dukkah week! Dukkah is an Egyptian dish and is a mix of toasted nuts, seeds and spices. Traditionally served with bread and olive oil (see Saturday) it can be used many other ways – as you shall see!

Monday
Dukkah Encrusted Goat's Cheese in a Roll with Rocket and Tomato / Mandarin

Tuesday
Butter Bean Salad with Artichokes, Goat's Cheese, Sun-Dried Tomato and Dukkah / Banana

Wednesday
Egg Dukkah Sandwich / Dried Apricots and Cashews

Thursday
Halloumi and Tomato Wrap with Dukkah Infused Avocado / Pecans and Dates

Friday
Broccoli, Capsicum and Halloumi Pasta Salad with Dukkah / Banana

Saturday
Dukkah with Sourdough, Extra Virgin Olive Oil, Olives and Cheese

Sunday
Dukkah Coated Chickpeas with Antipasti and Toasted Pita Bites V

"Acorns were good till bread was found." Francis Bacon

shopping list

Fruit and Vegetables
- ☐ 1 small bag rocket
- ☐ 3 tomatoes
- ☐ 2 mandarins
- ☐ 4 bananas
- ☐ 1 avocado
- ☐ 1 head broccoli
- ☐ 1 red capsicum

Fridge
- ☐ 120g goat's cheese
- ☐ 2 eggs
- ☐ mayonnaise
- ☐ 180g halloumi cheese
- ☐ 50g blue cheese
- ☐ 50g strong Cheddar cheese

Bakery
- ☐ 2 wholegrain rolls
- ☐ 4 slices wholegrain bread
- ☐ 1 sourdough bread
- ☐ 2 pita breads

Pantry
- ☐ 50g dukkah (or recipe)
- ☐ 400g can butter beans
- ☐ 400g can artichoke hearts
- ☐ sun-dried tomatoes
- ☐ dried apricots
- ☐ cashews
- ☐ lime juice
- ☐ 2 wholegrain flour tortillas
- ☐ pecans
- ☐ dates
- ☐ 100g dried pasta
- ☐ olives
- ☐ 400g can chickpeas
- ☐ tub antipasti

Staples
- ☐ salt
- ☐ black pepper
- ☐ olive oil
- ☐ extra virgin olive oil

daily tasks

Sunday

Prepare the goat's cheese encrusted with dukkah. Make the dukkah according to the recipe on p.230, unless you are using store-bought.

Slice 60g of goat's cheese and press into 1-2 teaspoons of dukkah. Add the goat's cheese to 2 wholegrain rolls along with some rocket and a sliced tomato. Cover in plastic wrap, then refrigerate until needed.

Monday

Make the butter bean salad. Rinse and drain a 400g can of butter beans and place in a bowl. Rinse, drain and chop a 400g can of artichokes and add to the bowl. Add 60g of crumbled goat's cheese and 2 tablespoons of chopped sun-dried tomatoes. Stir through 1 tablespoon of dukkah. Divide between 2 lunch boxes, then refrigerate until needed.

Tuesday

Prepare the egg dukkah sandwiches. Hard boil 2 eggs. Cool, peel and place in a bowl. Mash the egg and add 1 tablespoon of dukkah and 2 tablespoons of mayonnaise. Divide the egg between 2 slices of wholegrain bread. Top with 2 more slices and cut each sandwich in half. Cover in plastic wrap, then refrigerate until needed.

Mix 2 handfuls of dried apricots with 2 handfuls of cashews. Divide between 2 containers.

Wednesday

Make the halloumi, avocado and tomato wraps. Heat 1 tablespoon of olive oil in a frying pan over a medium heat. Add 90g of sliced halloumi and cook until golden on both sides. Remove from the heat and leave to cool. Mash an avocado and stir in 1 tablespoon of lime juice and 1 tablespoon of dukkah. Spread the avocado over 2 wholegrain flour tortillas. Top with the halloumi, some rocket and a sliced tomato. Roll up the tortillas and cut in half if you like. Cover in plastic wrap and refrigerate until needed.

Mix 2 handfuls of pecans with 2 handfuls of dates and divide between 2 containers.

Thursday

Make the pasta salad. Cook 100g of pasta according to the instructions on the packet. A few minutes before the pasta has finished cooking add the broccoli, cut into small florets. Drain, rinse in cold water and place in a bowl.

Meanwhile, heat 1 tablespoon of olive oil in a frying pan over a medium heat. Add 90g of sliced halloumi and cook until golden on both sides. Remove from the heat, leave to cool then cut into bite-size pieces. Add the halloumi to the broccoli and pasta. Dice a red capsicum and tomato and add to the bowl. Finally, stir through 2 tablespoons of dukkah and 1 tablespoon of extra virgin olive oil. Divide the pasta salad between 2 lunch boxes and refrigerate until needed.

Saturday

Prepare the platters. On 2 large plates place some slices or chunks of sourdough bread (you can warm the bread if you wish). Add some slices of Cheddar cheese and blue cheese. In 3 separate dishes per person place some dukkah, extra virgin olive oil and olives. Place on the plates and serve.

Sunday

Make the dukkah coated chickpeas. Rinse and drain a 400g can of chickpeas. Heat 1 tablespoon of olive oil in a small saucepan. Add the chickpeas and warm gently for a few minutes. Stir in 1 tablespoon of dukkah, letting it coat the chickpeas. Place the chickpeas in a bowl.

Brush 2 pita breads with olive oil and heat in a 200°C/400°F/Gas Mark 6 oven for 10 minutes until toasted. Cut the pita bread into strips or bite-size pieces and place in another bowl. Serve the chickpeas and pita bites with a bowl of antipasti.

Winter Week 13

It's our last week! Hopefully we're ending with a varied week of lunches. I popped my head in the freezer and retrieved some polenta. We also have wraps, salads, turnovers and a fried egg sandwich. Oh yes, enjoy your Friday chips and chocolate treat.

Monday
Goat's Cheese, Rocket and Caramelised Onion Wrap / Dried Cranberries and Almonds

Tuesday
Artichoke, Zucchini, Olive and Tomato Couscous Salad V / Banana

Wednesday
Zucchini, Goat's Cheese and Capsicum Turnovers / Orange

Thursday
Artichoke Puree V / Polenta Fingers / Capsicum Strips / Hard Boiled Egg / Mandarin

Friday
Halloumi and Lentil Salad with Tomato, Spinach and Onion / Chocolate and Chips

Saturday
Fried Egg Sandwich with Cheese, Avocado and Chutney

Sunday
Beer Battered Halloumi Roll with Tomato Chutney

Some vegetables go floppy very quickly even when stored in the fridge. Keep vegetable such as zucchini and carrot crisp by placing in a container of water. They will last much longer.

shopping list

Fruit and Vegetables
- ☐ 1 onion
- ☐ 1 small bag rocket
- ☐ 2 zucchini
- ☐ 2 tomatoes
- ☐ 2 bananas
- ☐ 1 red capsicum
- ☐ 2 oranges
- ☐ 1 clove garlic
- ☐ 2 mandarins
- ☐ 1 small red onion
- ☐ 1 small bag baby spinach
- ☐ 1 avocado

Fridge
- ☐ 120g goat's cheese
- ☐ 15g Parmesan-style cheese
- ☐ 4 eggs
- ☐ 180g halloumi cheese
- ☐ 50g Cheddar cheese
- ☐ mayonnaise

Freezer
- ☐ 1 sheet puff pastry
- ☐ polenta

Bakery
- ☐ 4 slices wholegrain bread
- ☐ 2 large rolls

Pantry
- ☐ brown sugar
- ☐ balsamic vinegar
- ☐ 2 wholegrain flour tortillas
- ☐ dried cranberries
- ☐ almonds
- ☐ 100g couscous
- ☐ olives
- ☐ 400g can artichoke hearts
- ☐ pine nuts
- ☐ lemon juice
- ☐ 400g can lentils
- ☐ red wine vinegar
- ☐ 2 small packets potato chips (crisps)
- ☐ 2 small chocolate bars
- ☐ tomato chutney
- ☐ 150g plain flour
- ☐ 200ml beer

Staples
- ☐ salt
- ☐ black pepper
- ☐ olive oil
- ☐ extra virgin olive oil
- ☐ canola oil

daily tasks

Sunday

Prepare the wraps. Heat 1 tablespoon of olive oil in a frying pan over a medium heat. Add a sliced onion and cook until pale, about 4 minutes. Stir in 1 tablespoon each of brown sugar and balsamic vinegar. Cook for 5 or 6 minutes, until the onions are caramelised. Remove from the heat and leave to cool.

Layer some rocket over 2 flour tortillas. Add 60g of crumbled goat's cheese and the caramelised onion. Season to taste, roll up and cover in plastic wrap. Refrigerate until needed.

Mix 2 handfuls of dried cranberries with 2 handfuls of almonds. Divide between 2 containers.

Monday

Prepare the couscous salad. Heat 1 tablespoon of olive oil in a frying pan over a medium heat. Add a diced zucchini and fry for 5 minutes until soft and golden. Remove from the heat and leave to cool. Place ½ cup (100g) of couscous in a bowl and stir in ½ cup (125ml) of boiling water. Let stand for 3 minutes. Fluff up with a fork.

Rinse and drain a 400g can of artichoke hearts. Place half in a container in the fridge, chop the rest and stir them into the couscous. Add 2 tablespoons of olives and a chopped tomato. Finally, stir in the zucchini and 1 tablespoon of toasted pine nuts. Divide between 2 lunch boxes then refrigerate until needed.

Tuesday

Make the turnovers. Preheat the oven to 220°C/425°F/Gas Mark 7. Thaw a sheet of puff pastry and cut into 4 squares. Heat 1 tablespoon of olive oil in a frying pan. Add a diced zucchini and ½ a red capsicum (put the remaining capsicum in the fridge) and cook for 5 minutes until soft. Place in a bowl. Add 60g of crumbled goat's cheese and 2 tablespoons of grated Parmesan-style cheese. Season well.

Divide the filling between the 4 pastry squares. Fold the pastry in half to form a triangle, then press the edges with a fork to seal. Prick the tops. Bake for 20 minutes, until golden and puffed. Leave to cool

before placing 2 in each lunch box. Refrigerate until needed.

Thaw some polenta in the fridge overnight.

Wednesday

Prepare the polenta. Preheat the grill. Slice the thawed polenta into 8 fingers. Brush with olive oil, place on a grill tray then grill until golden on both sides, about 10-12 minutes in total. Remove from the heat and leave to cool before dividing between 2 lunch boxes and refrigerating. If you do not have any polenta in the freezer, follow the instructions below, remembering to add the ingredients to your shopping list.

Bring 3⅔ cups (900ml) of vegetable stock to the boil in a medium saucepan. Once boiling, gradually add 1½ cups (225g) of polenta, stirring constantly with a wooden spoon. Reduce the heat and continue stirring until the polenta has thickened and is coming away from the side of the saucepan. Remove from the heat and stir in 1 tablespoon of butter and 2 tablespoons of grated Parmesan-style cheese. Season.

Tip the mixture into a 30 x 20cm oiled baking tin and spread the mixture evenly. Leave to cool then place in the fridge for a few hours to firm up.

Preheat the grill. Remove the polenta from the tin and slice in half. Wrap half in plastic wrap and pop it into the freezer for another time. Slice the remaining polenta into 8 fingers. Brush with olive oil and place on a wire grill tray. Grill for about 6 minutes on each side until golden and crisp. Leave to cool then place in your lunch boxes.

Hard boil 2 eggs. Leave to cool and add to your lunch boxes. Slice the remaining capsicum half into strips and add to the lunch boxes.

Make the artichoke puree. Place the remaining artichoke hearts in a food processor along with 1 tablespoon of lemon juice, a clove of peeled and crushed garlic and plenty of black pepper. Process until smooth then divide between 2 containers.

Remember to place everything into the fridge.

Thursday

Make the halloumi and lentil salad. Heat 1 tablespoon of olive oil in a frying pan over a medium heat. Add 90g of halloumi sliced into bite-size pieces and fry until golden on both sides, about 6 minutes in total. Remove from the heat then leave to cool.

Rinse and drain a 400g can of lentils and place in a bowl. Add 1 chopped tomato and a diced small red onion. Stir in a handful of spinach and the cooked halloumi. Make a quick dressing by mixing together 1 tablespoon of extra virgin olive oil with ½ tablespoon of red wine vinegar. Add the dressing to the salad, season to taste, then divide the salad between 2 lunch boxes. Refrigerate until needed.

Saturday

Prepare the fried egg sandwiches. Mash an avocado and spread it on 2 slices of wholegrain bread. Top with 50g of sliced Cheddar cheese. Heat 2 tablespoons of canola oil or olive oil in a frying pan over a medium heat. Fry 2 eggs according to your preference. Add the eggs to the sandwiches then finish with some tomato chutney and mayonnaise. Season to taste, top with 2 more slices of bread. Cut the sandwiches in half then serve immediately.

Make sure your beer is in the fridge to make tomorrow's batter.

Sunday

Make the beer battered halloumi. Place 1 cup (150g) of plain flour in a bowl with some seasoning. Stir in 200ml of chilled beer. Mix well until you have a smooth batter. Heat 3 tablespoons of canola oil in a frying pan over a medium heat. Slice 90g of halloumi into 6. Dip the slices into the batter then add them to the frying pan. Cook on both sides, until they are crispy and golden. Drain on paper towel.

Split 2 rolls then add some rocket, the battered halloumi and a dollop of tomato chutney. Serve warm.

bagels cheese and herb damper

cheese and onion muffins

cheese and onion scones

cinnamon and sultana fruit loaf

recipes

cumin and oregano muffins

date and apple muffins dukkah

orange and sultana scones

with orange cream

Bagels

3 cups (450g) plain flour

1 tablespoon salt

1 tablespoon (15ml) instant dried yeast

2 tablespoons caster sugar

½ cup (125ml) water

1 cup (250ml) milk

1 egg yolk, beaten

1 teaspoon water

1 tablespoon poppy seeds

2 teaspoons salt flakes

1) In a mixer with a dough hook, combine the flour, salt, yeast and caster sugar. Mix in the water and milk. Process to form a firm dough. Remove from the mixer than knead to achieve a smooth elastic dough. The dough should bounce back when pressed. Place in a greased bowl, then leave to stand in a warm place for 1 hour.

2) Turn the dough onto a floured surface then use a sharp knife to divide it into 12 pieces. Form each piece into a ball then make a hole by pushing your finger into the centre. You may need to let the dough rest for a few seconds then come back to get a sufficiently large hole. Place on a lined baking tray, cover with a tea towel, then leave to stand for 30 minutes.

Preheat the oven to 210°C/410°F/Gas Mark 7

3) Now the fun part. Bring a large saucepan of water to the boil. Drop a bagel into the water, let it poach for 1 minute, turn then cook for another minute. Remove with a slotted spoon, then place back on the baking tray. Mix together the egg yolk and teaspoon of water. Brush the glaze over the bagels. Combine the poppy seeds and salt flakes then sprinkle the mix over the bagels. Bake for 20 minutes until golden brown. Place on a wire rack to cool.

Makes 12

Note: You can freeze the dough and the bagels. I like to freeze half the dough. I place the dough in a freezer bag then pop it into the freezer. On the morning it is needed, I place the frozen dough into a greased bowl covered in plastic wrap. Leave it to stand for a few hours. If you only use half a batch, remember to use less salt and poppy seeds.

Cheese and Herb Damper

3 cups (450g) self-raising flour

pinch salt

½ cup (50g) grated Cheddar cheese

100g mozzarella cheese, cubed

2 teaspoons dried mixed herbs

20g unsalted butter, melted

1¼ cups (310ml) milk

melted butter for glazing

Preheat the oven to 220°C/425°F/Gas Mark 7

1) Combine the flour and salt in a large bowl. Stir in the Cheddar, mozzarella and mixed herbs.

2) Add the melted butter and milk and stir with a metal spoon or knife to form a dough.

3) Tip out onto your work surface and shape into a 20cm round. Place onto a greased baking tray. Mark out 8 wedges with a sharp knife. Brush with melted butter. Bake for 20 minutes until golden brown and cooked. Serve warm or cold with butter, margarine or cream cheese.

Makes 8 wedges

Note: Leftover damper can be frozen. You can freeze individual wedges or the whole thing. Cover in plastic wrap then foil.

Cheese and Onion Muffins

1 tablespoon olive oil

1 onion, peeled and chopped

3 cups (450g) self-raising flour

pinch salt

40g unsalted butter, melted

2 eggs, beaten

1⅔ cups (400ml) milk

1 teaspoon Dijon mustard

1 cup (100g) strong Cheddar cheese, grated

1 tablespoon chopped chives

Preheat the oven to 190°C/375°F/Gas Mark 5

1) Heat the olive oil in a frying pan over a medium heat. Add the onion and fry for 5 minutes, until soft. Remove from the heat.

2) Combine the flour and salt in a large bowl.

3) In a jug beat together the butter, eggs, milk and mustard. Add to the flour and stir to combine. Then stir in the onion, cheese and chives. Spoon the mixture into the holes of a greased 12-hole muffin tray. Bake for 25-30 minutes until golden and firm to touch. Stand for 10 minutes before transferring to a wire rack to cool. Serve warm or cold.

Makes 12

Note: Leftover muffins can be frozen. Pop them into a container or freezer bags.

Cheese and Onion Scones

1½ cups (225g) self-raising flour

½ teaspoon salt

½ teaspoon bicarbonate of soda

1½ teaspoons cream of tartar

50g cold unsalted butter, diced

⅔ cup (160ml) milk

1 cup (100g) strong Cheddar cheese, grated

½ bunch spring onions, chopped

1 egg, beaten

Preheat the oven to 220°C/425°F/Gas Mark 7

1) Sift the flour, salt, bicarbonate of soda and cream of tartar into a large bowl. Rub in the butter to form crumbs. You can always do this in a food processor.

2) Stir in the milk, three quarters of the cheese and spring onions, to form a dough.

3) Tip the dough onto a floured surface and give it a quick knead. Roll out the dough to about 2-3cm thick. Cut out scones using a 7cm cutter. Re-roll as needed to use up all the dough.

4) Place on a lined baking tray, close together. Brush the tops with the beaten egg. Scatter with the remaining Cheddar. Bake for 12 minutes until golden and cooked. Serve warm.

Makes 8

Note: You can freeze leftover scones by placing in a container or wrapping in plastic wrap then foil. Thaw as needed.

Cinnamon and Sultana Fruit Loaf

250ml water

1 tablespoon unsalted butter or margarine, melted

1½ teaspoons salt

2 tablespoons brown sugar

2 teaspoons ground cinnamon

1 tablespoon milk powder

1 teaspoon bread improver

2 cups (300g) plain flour

1 cup (150g) wholemeal plain flour

2 teaspoons instant dried yeast

½ cup (80g) sultanas

1) Place all the ingredients (apart from the sultanas) into an electric mixer with a dough hook. Mix until a dough forms, then add the sultanas. Mix in well. To test readiness, the dough should spring back when pressed.

2) Put the dough into a greased bowl, cover with a clean tea towel and stand in a warm place for an hour.

3) Give the dough a punch to knock it back, then place in a greased loaf pan (size approx. 23 x 13cm). Cover with a tea towel then let it stand for another 30 minutes.

Preheat the oven to 190°C/375°F/Gas Mark 5

4) Place the loaf pan in the oven and bake for 35-40 minutes, until golden brown. Check the loaf is ready by removing from the pan and tapping its bottom. It should sound hollow. Leave to cool slightly before turning out onto a wire rack to cool completely.

Makes a 750g (1.6lb) loaf

Note: The easiest way to make this loaf is to use a bread maker. Add ingredients according to the instructions for your bread maker. Add the sultanas towards the end of mixing (or to your fruit dispenser). Use the sweet setting for a 750g loaf. You can freeze the loaf whole or in slices which you can remove from the freezer as needed.

Cranberry, Coconut and Orange Loaf

2 oranges

1 cup (120g) dried cranberries

2 cups (300g) self-raising flour

½ teaspoon salt

½ cup (100g) light brown sugar

100-150ml milk

100g unsalted butter, melted

2 eggs, beaten

½ cup (40g) desiccated coconut

Preheat the oven to 180°C/350°F/Gas Mark 4. Grease and line a 23 x 13cm loaf tin.

1) Juice 1 orange into a small bowl and stir in the dried cranberries. Leave to soak until needed.

2) In a large bowl, mix together the flour, salt, brown sugar and the grated rind of 1 orange.

3) Juice the 2nd orange and place in a jug. Add enough milk to get to the 200ml mark. Beat in the butter and eggs. Fold the wet ingredients into the dry, being careful not to over mix. Stir in the cranberries along with the juice they were soaked in and the coconut. Spoon the mixture into the prepared loaf tin and bake for 45-50 minutes. A skewer inserted into the loaf should come out clean. Leave to stand for 10 minutes, before removing from the tin and cooling on a wire rack. Slice and enjoy.

Makes a 750g (1.6lb) loaf

Cumin and Oregano Muffins

1⅔ cups (250g) self-raising flour

1⅔ cups (250g) wholemeal self-raising flour

pinch salt

2 teaspoons cumin seeds

2 teaspoons dried oregano

40g unsalted butter, melted

2 eggs, beaten

1⅔ cups (400ml) milk

¼ cup (25g) strong Cheddar cheese, grated

Preheat the oven to 190°C/375°F/Gas Mark 5

1) Combine the flours and salt in a large bowl. Stir in the cumin seeds and oregano.

2) In a jug beat together the butter, eggs and milk. Add to the flour and stir to combine. Stir in the cheese. Spoon the mixture into the holes of a greased 12-hole muffin tray. Bake for 25-30 minutes until golden and firm to touch. Stand for 10 minutes before transferring to a wire rack to cool. Serve warm or cold.

Makes 12

Note: Leftover muffins can be frozen. Pop them into a container or freezer bags.

Date and Apple Muffins

1⅓ cups (200g) self-raising flour

½ cup (100g) light brown sugar

pinch salt

½ teaspoon ground cinnamon

½ teaspoon ground allspice

whole nutmeg

60g unsalted butter

¼ cup (60ml) honey

1 egg, beaten

½ cup (125ml) milk

2 apples, peeled, cored and diced

1 cup (120g) pitted dates, chopped

Preheat the oven to 180°C/350°F/Gas Mark 4

1) Combine the flour, sugar, salt, cinnamon and allspice in a large bowl. Stir in some grated nutmeg.

2) Melt the butter and honey in a small saucepan. In a jug, beat together the eggs and milk, then add the butter and honey. Add to the flour and stir to combine. Fold in the apples and dates. Spoon the mixture into the holes of a greased 12-hole muffin tray. Bake for 25-30 minutes until golden and firm to touch. Stand for 10 minutes before transferring to a wire rack to cool. Serve warm or cold.

Makes 12

Note: Leftover muffins can be frozen. Pop them into a container or freezer bags.

Dukkah

½ cup (75g) blanched almonds

¼ cup (35g) sesame seeds

1 tablespoon cumin seeds

½ tablespoon coriander seeds

½ teaspoon sea salt flakes

½ teaspoon ground black pepper

½ teaspoon dried oregano

½ teaspoon dried thyme

1) Heat a frying pan over a medium heat. Add the almonds and cook, stirring for 4-5 minutes until toasted. Tip them into a bowl, then add the sesame, cumin and coriander seeds to the frying pan. Toast the seeds for 2-3 minutes, until fragrant, stirring all the time. Leave to cool then place in a food processor along with the almonds. Process until coarsely chopped.

2) Add the sea salt, black pepper, oregano and thyme. Process briefly to combine the ingredients. Store the dukkah in a jar or container.

Makes 1 cup

Orange and Sultana Scones with Orange Cream

1½ cups (225g) self-raising flour

½ teaspoon salt

½ teaspoon bicarbonate of soda

1½ teaspoons cream of tartar

50g cold unsalted butter, diced

⅔ cup (160ml) milk

½ cup (85g) sultanas

finely grated zest of 1 orange

extra milk, for brushing

1 tablespoon Demerara sugar

For the orange cream:

125g cream cheese, softened

juice of 1 orange

2 teaspoons caster sugar

Preheat the oven to 220°C/425°F/Gas Mark 7

1) Sift the flour, salt, bicarbonate of soda and cream of tartar into a large bowl. Rub in the butter to form crumbs. You can always do this in a food processor. Stir in the milk, sultanas and orange zest, to form a dough. Tip the dough onto a floured surface and give it a quick knead. Roll out the dough to about 2-3cm thick. Cut out scones using a 7cm cutter. Re-roll as needed to use up all the dough.

2) Place the scones on a lined baking tray, close together. Brush the tops with milk then finish with a sprinkle of Demerara sugar. Bake for 12-14 minutes until golden and cooked. Serve warm with orange cream.

3) To make the orange cream, beat the cream cheese with the orange juice and caster sugar in a small bowl. Spoon into a serving bowl.

Makes 8 scones and ½ cup of orange cream

Index of Meals

A

All-Day Breakfast, 134
American Inspired Sub, 104
Antipasti with Goat's Cheese, 158
Apple and Beetroot Rice Salad, 158
Apricot, Strawberry and Melon Smoothie, 60
Artichoke Fritters with Tomatoes, Rocket and Olives, 192
Artichoke Puree, 216
Artichoke Salad with Beans, Corn and Carrot, 84
Artichoke Salad with Carrot, Capers and Tofu, 104
Artichoke, Halloumi, Olive and Quinoa Salad, 176
Artichoke, Tofu, Tomato and Spinach Frittata, 134
Artichoke, Zucchini, Olive and Tomato Couscous Salad, 216
Asparagus, Tomato and Bean Frittata, 34
Avocado and Potato Salad, 84
Avocado, Cheese and Tomato Roll, 184
Avocado, Cranberry, Tomato and Spinach Sourdough Sandwich, 172

B

Baby Kale, Quinoa and Goat's Cheese Salad, 176
Baby Spinach and Tomato Roulade, 92
Bagels, 10, 60, **222**
Baguette Slices with Blue Cheese Spread, Grapes and Muscatels, 42
Baguette with Hummus, Chargrilled Capsicum, Bocconcini and Tomato, 6
Baguette with Smoked Cheese and Sun-Dried Tomatoes, 18
Baguette, Cheese, Grapes and Muscatels, 72
Baked Avocado, 142
Baked Bean, Onion, Capsicum and Goat's Cheese Tostada, 22
Baked Eggs and Tomatoes with Avocado on Toast, 168
Baked Mushroom and Tomato Slice, 14, 42
Baked Sweet Potato with Blue Cheese, 146
Balsamic Glaze Roasted Vegetable Salad, 72
Banana, Honey and Vanilla Smoothie, 34
Banderillas, 14
Bean and Artichoke Salad with Capsicum, Feta and Almonds, 196
Bean and Coleslaw Salad, 150
Bean and Mushroom Wrap, 30
Bean and Potato Salad, 26

Bean and Tomato Stuffed Wontons, 204
Bean and Vegetable Loaf, 46, 84
Bean Cobb Salad, 204
Bean Salad with Avocado, Cheese and Spinach, 104
Bean Salad with Couscous, 18
Bean Wrap with Avocado, Spinach and Tomato, 10
Bean, Capsicum and Tomato Frittata in a Roll, 146
Bean, Capsicum and Tomato Frittata Wrap with Lime Mayonnaise, 146
Bean, Cheese and Tomato Wrap with Paprika Mayonnaise, 162
Bean, Corn and Capsicum Tart, 54
Bean, Egg and Potato Salad, 84
Bean, Potato and Onion Frittata, 42
Bean, Rocket and Artichoke Couscous, 196
Beans on Toast, 134
Beer Battered Halloumi Roll with Tomato Chutney, 216
Beetroot and Green Bean Salad, 92
Beetroot Dip with Carrot, Capsicum, Radish and Celery, 68
Beetroot Spread on Crispbread with Cherry Tomatoes, 68
Beetroot, Goat's Cheese and Chickpea Couscous, 158
Beetroot, Halloumi and Chickpea Salad, 126
Black Bean and Corn Tacos, 200
Black Bean Burritos, 64
BLT Sandwich, 208
Blue Cheese and Onion English Muffin, 196
Blue Cheese and Sun-Dried Tomato Quiche, 42
Blue Cheese and Sun-Dried Tomato Sandwich, 96
Borlotti Bean Wrap with Avocado, Corn and Tomato, 46
Breakfast Burrito, 208
Brie and Biscuits with Chutney, 142
Brie, Butter Bean, Artichoke and Capsicum Pasta Salad, 142
Brie, Capsicum, Spinach, Tomato and Olive Wrap, 122
Brie, Chargrilled Capsicum and Salad Roll, 208
Brie, Grape and Mint Wrap with Lemon Mayonnaise, 88
Brie, Olive and Chargrilled Capsicum Sandwich, 142
Brie, Tomato and Rocket Roll, 54
Broccoli and Capsicum Slice, 10, 22
Broccoli, Capsicum and Halloumi Pasta Salad with Dukkah, 212
Broccoli, Carrot and Feta Slice, 154, 180
Broccoli, Tofu and Tomato Couscous, 104
Broccoli, Tomato and Mustard Quiche, 122
Bruschetta with Basil, Tomato and Bocconcini, 6

Bulghar Wheat Salad with Beans, Capsicum and Carrot, 96

Bulghar Wheat Salad with Beans, Capsicum, Artichoke and Spinach, 142

Bulghar Wheat Salad with Tomatoes, Spinach and Bocconcini, 188

Burger with Fried Onions, Pickles, Mustard, Sauce, Cheese and Lettuce, 22

Burger with Onion, Beetroot, Pineapple and More, 60

Butter Bean and Crispy Vegetable Salad, 134

Butter Bean Cake, 180

Butter Bean Hummus, 204

Butter Bean Salad with Artichokes, Goat's Cheese, Sun-Dried Tomato and Dukkah, 212

Butter Bean, Cashew and Cranberry Barley Salad, 192

C

Cannellini Bean Salad with Capsicum, Olives, Tomatoes and Spring Onions, 18

Cannellini Bean Salad with Olives, Capers, Spring Onions and Cherry Tomatoes, 130

Cannellini Dip and Goodies to Dip with, 22

Capsicum, Zucchini and Carrot Slice, 80, 92

Caramelised Onion Vegan Quiches, 192

Chargrilled Capsicum, Capers, Spinach and Brie Wrap, 88

Cheat's Pavlova with Strawberries, 64

Cheese and Biscuits with Antipasti, 72

Cheese and Coleslaw Baguette, 150

Cheese and Herb Damper, 14, 34, **223**

Cheese and Mustard Sandwich, 162

Cheese and Onion Muffins, 26, 42, **224**

Cheese and Onion Oven Omelette, 142

Cheese and Onion Scones, 10, **225**

Cheese and Pickled Onion Toasted Sandwich, 38

Cheese on Toast, 126

Cheese Salad Roll, 200

Cheese, Coleslaw, Avocado and Watercress Sandwich, 34

Cheese, Mushroom and Tomato Quesadilla, 154

Cheese, Onion and Potato Turnovers, 104

Cheese, Onion and Tomato Pastry Scrolls, 150

Cheese, Onion and Tomato Stuffed Croissant, 204

Cheese, Pickle and Mustard Pumpernickel Sandwich, 172

Cheese, Pickled Onion and Tomato Sandwich, 150

Cheese, Tomato and Baby Spinach Tart, 162

Cheese, Tomato and Spinach Sandwich with Aioli, 10

Chickpea and Artichoke Pasta Salad, 158

Chickpea Salad with Sausage, Onion and Potato, 54

Chickpea, Olive and Capsicum Salad, 92

Chickpeas and Baby Spinach with Giant Couscous, 184

Chickpeas in Sun-Dried Tomato Puree, 108

Chilli and Onion Polenta with Cheesy Dip, 192

Cinnamon and Sultana Fruit Loaf, 10, **226**

Club Sandwich with Mozzarella and Smoked Cheese, 30

Cold Rolls with Sweet Chilli Sauce, 38

Corn Fritters with Chilli Sauce and Rocket, 92

Corn, Cheese and Rocket Wrap with Aioli, 196

Couscous with Cranberry, Celery and Walnuts, 76

Couscous with Halloumi, Cherry Tomatoes, Capsicum and Chickpeas, 30

Couscous with Olives, Corn, Chickpeas and Rocket, 138

Cranberry and Pine Nut Salad, 180

Cranberry Flapjacks, 34

Cranberry, Coconut and Orange Loaf, 168, **227**

Crepes with Camembert, Pine Nuts, Tomato and Rocket, 30

Crispbread with Artichoke Spread, 84

Crispbread with Bean Spread, 138

Crispbread with Cheesy Dip, 192

Crispbread with Hummus, 6

Crispbread with Kidney Bean Spread, 38

Crumpets, 68

Cumin and Oregano Muffins, 100, 114, 138, **228**

D

Date and Apple Muffins, 122, **229**

Dukkah, **230**

Dukkah Coated Chickpeas, 212

Dukkah Encrusted Goat's Cheese in a Roll with Rocket and Tomato, 212

Dukkah with Sourdough, Extra Virgin Olive Oil, Olives and Cheese, 212

E

Egg and Butter Bean Salad with Asparagus, Olives, Tomatoes and Watercress, 34

Egg and Cannellini Bean Salad, 54

Egg and Cheese Rolls, 114

Egg Curry and Mango Chutney Rye Sandwich, 172

Egg Dukkah Sandwich, 212

Egg Salad Roll, 22

Egg, Bean and Avocado Salad, 162

English Muffin with Fried Egg, Vegetarian Bacon and Tomato Ketchup, 18

F

Falafel in Pita with Minty Cream Dip, 100
Falafel with Minty Brown Rice and Cherry Tomatoes, 126
Feta, Capsicum and Olive Turnovers, 154, 188
Feta, Capsicum, Onion and Tomato Wrap, 46
Fig and Blue Cheese Salad, 76
French Onion Soup, 188
Fried Egg Sandwich with Cheese, Avocado and Chutney, 216
Frittata Salad with Olives, Capsicum, Baby Spinach and Sun-Dried Tomatoes, 42
Fruit Salad with Feta Cheese, 76
Fruity Couscous Salad with Red Onion and Capsicum, 46

G

Garlic Pita Bread with Capsicum Dip, 162
Goat's Cheese Turnovers with Onion, Spinach and Lentils, 50
Goat's Cheese, Beetroot and Rocket Baguette, 126
Goat's Cheese, Lentil and Pasta Salad, 126
Goat's Cheese, Rocket and Caramelised Onion Wrap, 216
Goat's Cheese, Spinach and Capsicum Roll, 188
Goat's Cheese, Tomato and Olive Roll, 80
Golden Gnocchi with Blue Cheese, Spinach and Cherry Tomatoes, 204
Gorditas Stuffed with Beans and Mushrooms, 192
Green Bean and Lentil Salad, 80
Grilled Cheese Turkish Rolls, 138
Grilled Veggies and Mozzarella Cheese Roll, 84

H

Halloumi and Butter Bean Salad, 162
Halloumi and Chickpea Salad with Lime and Mint Dressing, 126
Halloumi and Chickpea Wrap, 184
Halloumi and Lentil Salad with Tomato, Spinach and Onion, 216
Halloumi and Tomato Wrap with Dukkah Infused Avocado, 212
Halloumi Salad with Red Onion, Tomato and Capers, 158
Halloumi, Avocado, Onion and Tomato Sandwich, 130
Halloumi, Tomato and Olive Pasta Salad, 184
Herbed Tofu, Cheese, Caper and Tomato Stuffed Flatbread, 208
Herby and Caramelised Onion Couscous, 108

Herby Bean Spread with Crispbread, 108
Herby Bean Wrap with Capsicum, Olives and Tomatoes, 108
Herby Chickpea and Tofu Salad, 108
Herby Potato Cakes with a Tomato and Rocket Salad, 130
Herby Potatoes with Corn, Avocado, Tomato and Cheese, 108
Herby Rice Salad, 108
Herby Tofu Roll, 96
Herby Tomato Tarts, 108
Hot Dogs, 88

J

Jacket Potato with Cheese and Beans, 130
Japanese Omelette, 80

K

Kidney Bean Salad with Spinach, Broccoli, Carrot and More, 10

L

Lemon and Chive Potato Wedges with Aioli, 64
Lemony Noodles, 100
Lentil and Capsicum Soup with Crusty Roll, 162
Lentil and Rice Salad with Broccoli, Carrot and Pine Nuts, 14
Lentil and Tomato Turnovers, 126
Lentil Cakes with Sweet Chilli Sauce, 96
Lentil Spread with Crispbread, 14
Lentil, Beetroot and Capsicum Salad, 96
Lentil, Tomato and Quinoa Salad, 176
Lentil, Tomato and Quinoa Turnovers, 176
Lettuce, Tomato and Watercress Salad, 64

M

Mac-N-Cheese, 200
Mango Salad with Cannellini Beans and Cranberries, 72
Marinated Feta, Beans and Olives with Almonds and Grissini, 76
Mediterranean Potato Shells, 92
Mexican Ponchos, 26
Mexican Rice Salad, 204
Mexican Salad, 80
Mexican Tofu Salad with Refried Beans, 208
Mexican Tofu Spelt Sandwich, 172

Mix of Olives, Chargrilled Capsicum, Sun-Dried Tomatoes and Baby Spinach, 26
Mixed Bean and Tofu Pita, 80
Mozzarella, Tomato, Avocado and Basil Roll, 60
Mushroom and Onion Quesadilla, 14
Mushroom Pâté, 114
Mushroom, Bean and Zucchini Chimichanga, 38
Mushroom, Onion and Tomato Pita, 192
Mushroom, Spinach and Tomato Turnovers, 34

N

Nachos with Refried Beans, Salsa, Guacamole and Cheese, 196
Niçoisesque Salad with Brown Rice, 134

O

Onion, Brie, Tomato and Capsicum Pasta Salad, 122
Orange and Rocket Couscous, 122
Orange and Sultana Scones with Orange Cream, 46, **231**
Oven-Baked Omelette with Spinach, Capsicum and Basil, 50

P

Papaya Salad with Brown Rice, Tofu, Bean Sprouts and Asparagus, 26
Par-Baked Rolls with Cheese and Garlic Butter, 76
Pasta Frittata, 18
Pasta Salad with Artichokes and Broccoli, 104
Pasta Salad with Goat's Cheese, Artichoke Hearts, Red Onion, Peas and Rocket, 18
Pasta Salad with Halloumi, Cherry Tomatoes, Capsicum and Chickpeas, 30
Pasta Salad with Onion, Spinach, Lentils and Capsicum with a Sun-Dried Tomato Dressing, 50
Pea Pâté Sandwich with Carrot and Tomato, 76
Pea Pâté with Par-Baked Rolls, 76
Pita Bread Stuffed with Omelette, Broccoli and Cherry Tomatoes, 38
Pita Dippers with Tahini Dip, Carrot and Button Mushrooms, 42
Pita Filled with a Goat's Cheese and Spring Onion Omelette, 188
Pita Topped with Egg, Refried Beans, Capsicum, Tomato and More, 208
Pizza Tart, 22
Ploughman's Lunch, 46

Polenta Cubes with Cherry Tomatoes and Bocconcini, 188
Polenta Fingers, 26, 216
Polenta Fingers with Beetroot Dip, 168
Polenta Fingers with Black Bean Dip, 64
Polenta Fingers with Tomato and Caper Salsa and Capsicum Strips, 154
Polenta Wedges with Feta and Parsley, 26
Potato Salad with Cannellini Beans and Spinach, 72
Potato Wedges with Aioli, 150
Potato Wedges with Salsa, Avocado and Sour Cream, 50
Potato, Bean and Leek Pancakes with Salsa and Sour Cream, 50
Potato, Bean and Leek Pancakes with Sour Cream, 26
Potatoes, Olives and Butter Bean Hummus with Crispbread, 204

Q

Quick Fresh Salad, 138
Quinoa Frittata with Artichoke, Halloumi and Olives, 176
Quinoa, Lentil, Mushroom and Tomato Soup, 176

R

Refried Bean Turnovers with Avocado, Tomato and Cheese, 88
Risoni Salad with Zucchini, Capsicum and Cherry Tomatoes, 84
Roast Parsnip and Swede Chips, 184
Roasted Beetroot with Couscous, Spinach, Goat's Cheese, Dates and Pecans, 34
Roasted Olives and Halloumi with Cherry Tomatoes and Turkish Bread, 50
Roasted Vegetable and Bean Frittata, 114, 168
Roasted Vegetable and Bean Pasta Salad, 114
Roasted Vegetable and Bean Wrap, 6
Roasted Vegetable and Pearl Barley Salad, 168
Roasted Vegetable and Sausage Wrap, 114
Roasted Vegetable Frittata, 6, 60
Roasted Vegetable Pasta Salad, 6, 60
Roasted Vegetable Soup, 168
Roasted Vegetable Stuffed Pita, 114
Roasted Vegetable Turnovers, 6, 60
Roasted Vegetable Wrap, 168
Roasted Vegetable Wrap with Cheese and a Spicy Mayonnaise, 60

S

Salad of Lettuce and Cherry Tomatoes, 96
Salad of Lettuce, Red Onion and Tomato, 96
Salt and Pepper Potato Rounds with Romesco Sauce and Aioli, 204
Sauerkraut, Bean, Potato and Carrot Soup, 184
Sausage and Egg Sandwich, 184
Sausage and Kale Couscous with Orange Dressing, 200
Sausage and Onion Baguette, 142
Sausage and Onion Pita, 14
Sausage Rolls, 134
Sausage Rolls with Mozzarella, 30
Sausage Wrap with Onion, Tomato, Cheese and Gherkins, 104
Sausage, Apple and Avocado Salad with Plenty More Goodies, 38
Sausage, Apple and Tomato Salad, 14
Sausage, Cranberry, Stuffing and Camembert Tostada, 64
Sausage, Mashed Avocado and Chutney Roll, 154
Sausage, Onion, Potato, Pea and Rice Salad, 54
Savoury Twists with Artichoke Dip, 54
Savoury Twists with Baked Brie and Cranberry Sauce, 54
Seasoned Chickpeas, 138
Shredded Omelette in a Wrap with Carrot, Spring Onions, Parsley and Aioli, 130
Smoky Tofu and Avocado Turkish Roll, 172
Spicy Crumbed Tofu Roll, 200
Spinach, Corn and Goat's Cheese Turnovers, 18
Spinach, Lettuce and Radish Salad, 68
Spinach, Tomato and Mozzarella Crepe, 100
Spring Onion Cakes, 122
Spring Onion, Cheese and Baby Spinach Baguette, 172
Stilton and Onion Chutney Roll, 180
Stilton Ploughman's on Pumpernickel, 180
Stir-Fried Noodles, 154
Stir-Fried Vegetables in an Omelette Wrap, 158
Strawberry, Melon and Banana Smoothie, 92
Succotash, 200
Summer Pasta Salad, 64
Sweet Potato and Blue Cheese Salad, 146
Sweet Potato and Mushroom Fritters With Baby Beetroot and Cherry Tomatoes, 64
Sweet Potato Fries with Ranch Dressing, 200
Sweet Potato Salad with Baby Beetroot, Mushrooms and Chickpeas, 64
Sweet Potato, Spinach and Tomato Rice Salad, 188
Sweet Potato, Zucchini and Broccoli Slice, 122, 138
Sweetcorn Dip and Dippers, 130

T

Tabbouleh, 80
Tamagoyaki, 80
Tempeh Sticks and Carrots with Barbecue Sauce, 46
Toasted Brie and Caramelised Red Onion on Sourdough, 208
Toasted Pita Bites, 212
Toasted Turkish SOCA Rolls, 34
Tofu and Couscous Salad, 68
Tofu and Cranberry Puffs, 130
Tofu Cubes with Agave Syrup, 96
Tofu Salad with a Ginger and Lime Dressing, 38
Tofu Salad with a Sweet and Sour Dressing, 14
Tofu Salad with Broccoli, Carrot and Mushrooms, 146
Tofu with Crispy Noodles, Savoury Mushrooms and Pineapple, 180
Tofu, Bean Sprout, Capsicum and Carrot Wrap, 68
Tofu, Bean, Capsicum and Tomato Salad, 134
Tofu, Capsicum and Tomato Wrap with Sweet Chilli Sauce, 22
Tofu, Capsicum, Asparagus and Spinach Salad, 26
Tofu, Carrot, Corn and Spring Onion Wrap, 88
Tofu, Spinach and Carrot Salad, 180
Tofu, Spinach and Tomato Pastry Rolls, 158
Tofu, Tomato, Cheese and Olive Wrap, 88
Tomato and Caper Rice, 154
Tomato, Bean and Spring Onion Frittata, 96
Tomato, Feta, Olive and Rocket Roll, 196
Two-Bean Salad, 146
Two-Tomato Pasta Salad, 68

V

Vegan Cheese Stuffed Potatoes, 180
Vegan Empanadas, 100
Vegan Tzatziki with Veggies and Crackers, 180
Vegetable and Quinoa Slice with Goat's Cheese, 176, 196
Vegetable Ciabatta Sandwich, 150
Vegetable Tortilla Pizza, 150
Vegetable Tostada, 100
Vegetarian Slices, Onion and Horseradish Ciabatta Roll, 172
Veggies, Pita Strips and Minty Cream Dip, 100

W

Watercress and Lettuce Salad, 42
Wensleydale and Tomato Tart, 72
Wensleydale Salad, 72

Wholegrain Crackers with Goat's Cheese and
    Chargrilled Capsicum, 92
Wholegrain Roll Filled with Bean Spread, Olives,
    Tomato and Lettuce, 138
Wholegrain Roll Filled with Goat's Cheese, Basil,
    Chargrilled Capsicum and Tomato, 50
Wholemeal Roll Filled with a Cheese Omelette and
    Onion Chutney, 118
Wholemeal Roll Filled with Artichoke Spread, Baby
    Spinach and Tomato, 118
Wholemeal Roll Filled with Blue Cheese, Tomato, Baby
    Spinach, Pine Nuts, Spring Onion and Lettuce, 118
Wholemeal Roll Filled with Camembert, Rocket and
    Cranberry Sauce, 30

Wholemeal Roll Filled with Cheese, Sun-Dried
    Tomatoes, Coriander, Chilli Flakes and Artichoke
    Spread, 118
Wholemeal Roll Filled with Grilled Mushrooms,
    Capsicum, Mozzarella and Basil, 118
Wholemeal Roll Filled with Kidney Bean Spread and
    Lettuce, 118
Wholemeal Roll Filled with Sausage and Kidney Bean
    Spread, 118
Wrap with Refried Beans, Onion, Tomato, Avocado and
    Cheese, 88

Z

Zucchini and Blue Cheese Quesadilla, 68
Zucchini, Goat's Cheese and Capsicum Turnovers, 216

43143894R00138

Made in the USA
Middletown, DE
01 May 2017